Tropical Synagogues

Portico Paperbacks

TROP*i*CAL SY*n*AGOGUES

SHORT STORIES BY

Jewish–Latin American Writers

EDITED AND WITH AN INTRODUCTION BY

ILAN STAVANS

HM

HOLMES & MEIER

New York / London

First paperback edition published in the United States of America 1997 by
Holmes & Meier
160 Broadway
New York, NY 10038

Book design by Miriam Schaer

This book has been printed
on acid-free paper.

Library of Congress Cataloging-in-Publication Data

Tropical synagogues . short stories / by Jewish Latin American writers
 ; edited with an introduction by Ilan Stavans.
      p.   cm.—(Portico paperback series)
   Includes bibliographical references.
   ISBN 0-8419-1341-2 (alk. paper)
   1. Short stories, Latin American—Jewish authors—Translations
into English.   2. Latin American fiction—20th century—Translations
into English.   I. Stavans, Ilan.   II. Series
PQ7087.E5T76   1997
863'.010892408—dc20

                                                                    CIP

The editor of this anthology gratefully acknowledges generous
grants from the New York State Council on the Arts and The
Lucius N. Littauer Foundation.

Manufactured in the
United States of America

TO JOSHUA

Does a single day go by
without some excitement?

—Anne Frank, *The Diary of a Young Girl*

C O N T E N T S

A C K N O W L E D G M E N T S

This book has been four years in the making—since 1989, when the New York State Council on the Arts first offered me a grant to begin the odyssey. The English versions of the stories are a product of many highly talented scholars and professional translators. My gratitude to each and every one of them for their patience and devotion. Special thanks are also due to the late Gregory Kolovakos, a promoter of Latin American fiction in the United States, who was always prompt in offering me his encouragement and support. Alan Adelson, an editor in his own right and the director of the Jewish Heritage Project, believed in the idea and channeled my youthful energy. Robert F. DiAntonio showed me the path at a time when I thought every single door was closed. Naomi Lindstrom of Austin, Texas, the author of *Jewish Issues in Argentine Literature: From Gerchunoff to Szichman*, read and substantially improved the introduction and bibliography. Saul Sosnowski, at the University of Maryland, the author of *La orilla inminente*, also offered comments and suggestions. David Roskies, professor at the Jewish Theological Seminary and the author of *Against the Apocalypse: Responses to Catastrophe in Modern Jewish Culture*, allowed me to experiment with hypotheses in review essays published in *Prooftexts*, the scholarly journal he coedits.

Segments of the introduction also appeared previously in somewhat different form, in Spanish or English, in journals and reviews such as *The New York Times Book Review*, *The Bloomsbury Review*, and *Judaism;* I hereby would like to extend my debt to the editors. My appreciation also goes to Leonardo Senkman in Israel, Mr. Sosnowski, Ms. Lindstrom, and Edna Aizenberg in New York City, for their lifelong devotion to studying, honoring, and celebrating this branch of Latin American letters about which very few readers know enough. My love to Cynthia Ozick, a friend and guide; and to Chava Turniansky, a Yiddish teacher in Mexico City back in the eighties and now a professor at the Hebrew University of Jerusalem, with whom I discovered the pleasures of reading Mendele Mokher Sforim and Der Nister. Finally, *Tropical Synagogues* would not exist in its present form without the wise and invaluable help of Sheila Friedling, my friend and editor at Holmes & Meier.

Tropical Synagogues

I N T R O D U C T I O N

All that they do seems to them, it is true,
extraordinarily new,
yet it is part of the chain of the generations. . . .
—Franz Kafka

Octavio Paz, a Mexican poet and the recipient of the 1990 Nobel Prize in Literature, in an essay entitled "The Few and the Many" included in his volume *The Other Voice,* wrote that the world is intolerant of the particular. The majority, he claimed, overwhelms and does away with the minority. Perhaps nowhere is this assessment more apt than in Latin America, where the massive population is ethnically mixed, but is generally known, both at home and abroad, as a society that is homogeneously *mestizo,* that is, part Indian and part Iberian. For over five hundred years, waves of diverse immigrants, beginning with the Spanish and Portuguese after 1492, and continuing with the Italians, the Germans, the French, the Dutch, and the Asians, have created a mosaic of racial multiplicity. But the coexistence of different groups hasn't been a happy one, and pluralism has not survived without stumbling. The particular is continually being devoured by the monstrous whole.

The Jews are also part of that particular. Since the time of the Inquisition, in spite of all odds, they have stubbornly remained loyal to their faith and tradition. They have assimilated symbols of their environment and have contributed, albeit silently, to the cosmopolitanism of the region. They have often been the target of anti-Semitic attacks, even violence; left- and right-wing regimes have used the Jews as a scapegoat, branding them a source of social and political distress. Yet their presence has also been valued by democratic, less aggressive forces as a reminder of how freedom can survive through the ages.

The political and economic turmoil has stimulated them to create a literature that bears witness to their deep historical transformation in that environment. That literature, more abundant in the last hundred years, is virtually unknown to North American readers. The reason for this neglect is easy to understand: as a Eurocentric country, the United States did not pay attention to what was written south of the Rio Grande until the 1960s, when a boom of fresh new literary voices from Mexico, Argentina, Peru, and Colombia began to renew the genre of the novel, exhausted after the contributions of Joyce, Kafka, Proust, and Robert Musil. But English-speaking readers failed to notice the less popular, more ethnically focused writers alongside Carlos

1

Fuentes, Julio Cortázar, Mario Vargas Llosa, and Gabriel García Márquez. They saw the universal in Latin American literature, but not the particular.

The twenty-three stories included here belong to various nations and three languages—Spanish, Portuguese, and English. The purpose of collecting them for the first time in one volume for North American readers is to show how these Jewish–Latin American writers think, feel, and nurture their dreams: thus, the objective is at once anthropological and literary. Irving Howe and Eliezer Greenberg wrote in the introduction to their ground-breaking 1954 volume, *A Treasury of Yiddish Literature,* "We have no desire to make extravagant claims: Yiddish literature can boast no Shakespeares, no Dantes, no Tolstoys. But neither can many other widely translated literatures." Well, Latin America has indeed produced extraordinary writers, and the writers in this anthology, I have no doubt, have as much talent as many of their better known colleagues, along with a distinctive ethos and a remarkable style very much their own. Readers who have never before encountered their work are in for a feast.

I use the image of the tropical synagogue in the title because it characterizes the collective personality of this literary tradition. Imagine—somewhere in Patagonia, the Amazon, or a rainforest on the border between Guatemala and Mexico—a forgotten Jewish temple celebrating knowledge and a dialogue with God. The climate is that of magic and revolution. The place is populated by ancestral tribes predating the Spanish *conquistadores* and the coming of Christianity. Frequented by Jews in search of a collective identity, this fecund temple mixes Hebrew paraphernalia and pre-Columbian artifacts, sometimes of Aztec or Quechua origin. Its indefinite age and improbable location, elusive to historians and topographers, speaks to its exoticism: probably founded by Sephardic immigrants escaping the Inquisition, or by Ashkenazi refugees settling in the region before World War II, it has lost its place in memory. Yet the syncretism of its architectural style and interior design is proof of a religious and cultural encounter too rich to ignore. A crossroad linking fantastic surrealism and traditional visions, its enigmatic presence is a unique symbol of the cultural and social experience of Jews in Latin America—an intertwining of the Old World and the New, European and aboriginal, natural and spiritual, primitive and civilized, *lo hebreo* (things Jewish) and the gentile milieu.

Four essential concerns are mirrored in the work of these Jewish–Latin American writers: assimilation and the struggle to retain the Jewish tradition in a modern, secular world; anti-Semitism and the difficulty of being considered distinctive and unequal, which ultimately has a strong impact on the collective

Jewish identity; the violent political reality from 1910 to the 1990s, and Latin America's passive response to the systematic destruction of 6 million Jews by the Nazis; and the supernatural, what critics like Tzvetan Todorov call "the fantastic." The very foundation of this last aesthetic approach may come from the Surrealist movement in Europe, with its dreamlike images; but after a trip to Haiti in 1934, Alejo Carpentier, a Cuban musicologist and baroque writer, claimed that reality in the Caribbean was far richer, more colorful and more imaginative a place than anything European Surrealists could ever fantasize. In a 1984 interview in *The Paris Review*, García Márquez stated that he is nothing but a realist. "Foreigners may think I invent a lot in *One Hundred Years of Solitude*," he said, "but that is because they don't know Latin America." And indeed, several stories here can be taken as examples of this exoticism: a few are set in jungles or decaying cities, while others take place in Prague or Buenos Aires but have a supernatural twist, a "fantastic" aura. They deal with God not as an object of devotion, but as a miraculous force that can suddenly stop the universe's pace. These texts, I foresee, will be retained longer by most readers precisely because this "supernatural" element is now the signature of all the literature produced in the region.

DEMOGRAPHICS

Jews are but a tiny fraction of nonnative population in Latin America. Argentina and Mexico, two countries that first became independent from the Iberian peninsula between 1810 and 1816, and, later, Brazil entered the twentieth century by accepting Jewish immigrants from Russia and Eastern Europe who arrived with the hope of finding prosperity and adapting to a new culture. Most of them were uneducated, Yiddish-speaking inhabitants of the *shtetl*, poor and persecuted. Their odyssey to Latin America proved to be partially successful, at least during the first decades of collective life.

As Theodor Herzl was convening the First Zionist Congress in 1897, Baron Maurice de Hirsch was attempting to place human and financial resources in the agricultural region of La Pampa, thinking the zone would eventually turn out to be the true Promised Land. Actually, Argentina as Zion was for a while a real and concrete challenge to the Zionist dream of resettlement in Palestine. The very first immigrants who settled in colonies such as Moisés Ville in Santa Fé, near the border with Paraguay; Rajíl, in the province of Entre Ríos, at the northeastern border with Uruguay; and others in Rio Grande do

Sul, may have both consciously and by pure chance chosen to travel to Palestine and even to North America, but arrived instead at the River Plate with high hopes for an end to their diasporic wandering. The official census claims that in 1895 there were all together some 6,000 Jews in Argentina; by 1910 the number rose to 68,000, and by 1935 it increased astronomically to 218,000.[1] Compared to other parts of Latin America, the Pampas and Buenos Aires have always been the most populated centers of Jewish life. In 1910, Brazil had some 800 Jews and Mexico 1,000; by 1930 there were some 30,000 and 16,000 Jewish immigrants, respectively, in each of these two countries. Although during the 1950s there was a display of considerable demographic growth of the Jewish population in all of Latin America, since then political turmoil and violence has led many Jews to finally emigrate to Israel and the United States. According to the latest studies, by the late 1980s the Brazilian and Hispanic worlds outside the Iberian peninsula had a total population of over 500 million, of which only 1.2 percent or less were Jews. Argentina held the lead with a quarter of a million Jews, followed by Brazil with some 125,000, and then Mexico with some 50,000. Together, small countries like Guatemala, Costa Rica, and Peru barely counted 10,000. And compared to the world Jewish population, where the United States has 48 percent and Israel 26 percent, pushing the figures in the region doesn't make them reach 4 percent, indeed a minimal number.

Although most of the original Jewish settlers in Latin America were of East European background, quite a few Sephardim, whose roots in the Iberian peninsula predated the expulsion in 1492, arrived in the Americas with and after the four voyages of Christopher Columbus. They were secretly supported, both financially and with crucial cartographic information, by wealthy *conversos* (also referred to as *marranos*) who practiced Judaism in secret, and by New Christian entrepreneurs like Luis de Santánguel, the Genoese admiral's own economic backer and a close adviser to Queen Isabella of Castile, who had wholeheartedly renounced their original Jewish religion. Since 1492, the year of the so-called Discovery,[2] is also the date of the expulsion of the Jews from Spanish soil, a controversial theory supported by the Oxford professor Salvador de Madariaga, the Nazi hunter Simon Wiesenthal, and the historian Cecil Roth claims that the hidden agenda behind the search for a new route to the West Indies was the quest for new lands where the Iberian Jewish population could live in spiritual peace. Be that as it may, a considerable number of Spanish emigrants escaping the cruelties of Torquemada arrived in the Americas and for a while tried to regain control of their ancient biblical faith. Such is the case, for instance, of the famous Carvajal family in Nueva España, later known as Mexico, portrayed in great historical detail and accuracy by Alfonso Toro. But the Church didn't allow for much religious freedom in the colonies, and although researchers have found traces of their path in major capitals such as Lima, Buenos Aires, and Santiago, the Spanish Jews concealed their true identity and eventually vanished. By the time of the 1910 Socialist Revolution of Pancho Villa and Emiliano Zapata, south of the Rio Grande most of the original Sephardic settlers had disappeared. At most, the *converso* methods of secrecy in the New World managed to produce bizarre, anachronistic curiosities: in Venta Prieta, for instance, a small town near Toluca, Mexico, there is an Indian community that practices the Jewish faith and has a synagogue in which it keeps ancient scrolls; although its members cannot read Hebrew or Ladino, most of the male constituency is circumcised. Discovered by a group of North American anthropologists a few decades ago, they claim to be Jewish, although their lineage, as of yet never authenticated, has been put in question by the Ashkenazim.

A new wave of Jewish settlers from the Mediterranean (mainly Syria and Lebanon), many of Sephardic ancestry, arrived in countries like Argentina, Mexico, Brazil, and Venezuela during the 1950s and 1960s. They chose Latin America because of the linguistic similarities between their ancestral languages (Ladino or Judezmo) and modern Spanish and because, as Robert M. Levine explains in his study "Adaptive Strategies of Jews in Latin America,"[3] family cohesiveness meant more to them than the opportunity for upward economic mobility. Their contact with the Ashkenazim has not been easy: the two communities tend to live apart, attend different temples and schools, and rarely intermarry.

The demographics of Latin American Jewry began a trend of decline since the 1960s, as a result of dictatorial regimes and repression. The changes in the sociopolitical fabric made exile and *aliyah*—immigration to Israel—concrete options (some 68,000 immigrants moved to the state of Israel between 1948 and 1983). Generally, as a small, insular, self-contained population proud of its separation from larger society, the overall input of these Jewish communities in Latin America into the cultural mainstream has inevitably gone unrecognized or has not gained the recognition it deserves. Voluntarily or not, their different skin color and non-Hispanic physical appearance, their unique religion, and their educational and economic status have turned them into outsiders. A few of the writers included in this anthology were activists opposing their national governments, imprisoned or forced into exile in Europe, the

United States, and even Israel, distant from their native soil and language, dreaming of a return, writing in a tongue (Spanish) alien to their more intimate milieu. That component of extraterritoriality constantly marks their fiction. Even the inattentive eye can see how their stories repeat, almost in an obsessive manner, a handful of metaphors and images that have to do with alienation: a woman trapped in a bottle; an unloved mother-in-law who prefers to spend her days alone rather than join her estranged daughter and her new husband; a Jewish bride who runs away with a gaucho on the Pampas. Like that of Dr. Jekyll and Mr. Hyde, the identity of these Latin American Jews, judging by their fiction, is full of labyrinthine divisions, accompanied by guilt and anxiety. One gets the impression that a suffocating minority life has created a vacuum, a feeling of seclusion and exclusiveness. Borrowing the words of Danilo Kiš, the author of *The Encyclopædia of the Dead* who himself was adapting a biblical phrase, these writers are "strangers in a strange land." They inhabit a tropical synagogue both as individuals and as a collective: they are the particular in a continent where only the universal matters—or, at least, up until now.

Although the novel and poem are also favored genres (a bibliography at the end of this volume suggests further readings including fiction, nonfiction, and criticism in Spanish, Portuguese, and English), this anthology presents a sample of the most memorable short stories created by Jewish writers in Latin America from 1910 to the present—a window through which we are offered a glimpse of their inner lives and cultural predicament. Although it is my belief that the Jewish experience in Latin America has been remarkably cohesive and interconnected throughout the continent, the particular context of that experience has varied in different countries. To suggest this diversity of environment and sensibility in the face of a generally cohesive ethnic identity, I have organized the volume according to the writer's country of origin; since my approach is at once historical and literary, the stories are arranged chronologically within this framework.

ALBERTO GERCHUNOFF

When talking about Jewish literature in Latin America, one needs to start with the magisterial figure of Alberto Gerchunoff (1884–1950). He is at center stage because he is to this minority literature what Mendele Mokher Sforim [Sh. Y. Abramovitsh] was to Yiddish letters—a grandfather and a cornerstone. Before Gerchunoff, one can find sketches, poems, vignettes, and chronicles of immigrant life, written by Jewish refugees in Russian, Polish, Hebrew, Yiddish, and at times in a rudimentary Spanish. But it is his beautiful and meticulously measured Castilian prose in *The Jewish Gauchos of the Pampas*, translated into English in 1955 by Prudencio de Pereda, a book deeply influenced by Cervantes, that gave birth to the short stories included in this volume, as well as to novels by the same authors.

Gerchunoff's life and craft have to be understood in the context of the history of Jewish immigration to Argentina. In 1891, when the boy was seven, his father traveled from Russia to the Pampas, and the family followed him. Agriculture and cattle raising were the jobs designated for the *shtetl* dwellers, and hard labor was their lot. As expressed in his 1914 autobiography *Entre Ríos, My Country,* published posthumously in 1950, Gerchunoff admired the capacity for hard work of his fellow Argentines. His family was first stationed in the colony of Moisés Ville, but when his father was brutally killed by a gaucho, or Argentine cowboy, they moved to the Rajíl colony. This tragic event and Gerchunoff's later adventures in the new settlement were the inspiration for his early work.

One of the admirable things about Gerchunoff is his polyglotism. Language, after all, is the basic vehicle by which any newcomer must begin to adapt to the new country. Most immigrants improvised a "survival" Spanish during their first Argentine decade, but in Gerchunoff's case, as a child not only did he learn to speak perfect Spanish, but by 1910, at the age of twenty-six, his prose was setting a linguistic and narrative standard. Reading him today, we discover in his writing stylistic forms that were later developed by his followers, among them Jorge Luis Borges. Simultaneously, Gerchunoff's brief biographical sketches of such writers as Sholem Aleichem, Miguel de Unamuno, James Joyce, Max Nordau, and I. L. Peretz, which appeared in newspapers and magazines, and his deep and careful readings of British writers such as G. K. Chesterton, H. G. Wells, and Rudyard Kipling, influenced future artistic generations on the River Plate. Even if he did not fully belong to the popular *modernista* movement budding at the turn of the century in Latin America, many moderns welcomed his literature. The Cuban activist José Martí, the Mexican sonneteer Manuel Gutiérrez Nájera, and other *modernistas* dreamed of reviving all literatures written in Spanish. So did Gerchunoff, although he did not quite share the aesthetic and political values of these contemporaries. His objective was to help Jews become Argentines, to be like everyone else. Following his death, after some two dozen books and innumerable articles, Borges himself praised him as "the writer of *le mot juste.*"

Such a distinction, one should add, is seldom awarded to an immigrant. I can think of only a few others who have achieved it, among them Vladimir Nabokov, Joseph Brodsky, and Joseph Conrad.

I began by speaking of Gerchunoff in relation to Mendele Mokher Sforim because, although the two belong to two different worlds and even different languages, both managed to create a sense of literary tradition and continuity absent before. Mendele was considered by Sholem Aleichem to be the grandfather of Yiddish letters, as Gerchunoff became a cultural mentor and compass for later Jewish writers in Argentina such as Gerardo Mario Goloboff, Mario Szichman, Alicia Steimberg, and Isidoro Blaisten. In fact, the comparison is a clue to the linguistic reality the Argentine had to face: by writing in Spanish, he subscribed to the chain of Spanish and South American letters; Yiddish, the language of most of the immigrants, was left behind after he began publishing, and replaced by Spanish, a cosmopolitan, secular vehicle. Indeed, one has to consider that very few Jewish writers, even if they had some knowledge of Yiddish, could write anything beyond a crude transliterated version. That's why some, including Gerchunoff himself and his successor Mario Szichman, used transliterated Yiddish in dialogue. Besides, a Yiddish-reading audience today is practically nonexistent. Mendele found Yiddish the appropriate vehicle for communication with his people; for Gerchunoff, it was Spanish, the idiom of "exile," that turned them into "normal" citizens of Argentina. The two were equally celebrated as speakers of the collective soul.

During his youth, Gerchunoff had an acquaintance, Leopoldo Lugones, a representative of the *modernistas* in Argentina and paternalistically philo-Jewish and pro-immigrant, who gained access for him to *La Nación*, a very influential newspaper in Buenos Aires. Yet Lugones's last sour years and his own ideological odyssey are symbolic of the attitude of Argentina as a whole toward the Jews: at first a socialist and a liberal, in his mature years and up until his suicide in 1938 he was a fascist and a nationalist. By then the Jews, "alien" people in his eyes, were unacceptable to him as equals because they represented the unwelcome outsider. This hostility has its counterpart. Take the example of Rubén Darío, the *modernista* par excellence and famous Nicaraguan poet who in 1888 wrote *Azul . . .* (Blue), a book whose impact on Hispanic letters was equivalent to that of T. S. Eliot's *The Waste Land* on English poetry. Darío saw the Jews as appealing citizens, paradoxically both symbolic of an eternal voyage and deeply rooted in the Argentine soil. In a beautiful poem entitled "Song to Argentina," he celebrated the biblical heritage and bucolic present of the citizens of Entre Ríos and Santa Fé. Here is a rough, free translation of one of its stanzas:

> Sing Jews of La Pampa!
> Young men of rude appearance,
> sweet Rebeccas with honest eyes,
> Reubens of long locks,
> patriarchs of white,
> dense, horselike hair.
> Sing, sing old Sarahs
> and adolescent Benjamins
> with the voice of our heart:
> "We have found ZION!"

The very same tone is to be found in the twenty-six stories collected by Gerchunoff in *The Jewish Gauchos,* the book to which he owes his fame, a parade of Spanish-speaking but stereotypical Jewish men and women from Eastern Europe adapting to the linguistic and cultural reality of the southern hemisphere. The autonomous narratives that make up every chapter, some better than others, re-create life, tradition, and hard labor in this "new *shtetl*" across the Atlantic. The focus is on relations between Jews and gentiles, the passion to maintain their Jewish religion yet understand and assimilate new customs. What is most striking about the book to today's reader is the political ideology it professes: 1910, one should know, was the centenary of Argentina's independence. Gerchunoff meant his text to be a celebration of the nation's friendly, tolerant, and multiethnic spirit. He had moved to Buenos Aires in 1895 and, beginning in August 1902, contributed regularly to many newspapers, among them *La Nación.* Even after the tragic loss of his father, he stubbornly went on believing that Argentina was a true paradise. He saw the province of Entre Ríos and the cosmopolitan Buenos Aires as a diasporic "holy land" of sorts where the contribution of the Jews would always be welcome in shaping the national culture and where all manifestations of anti-Semitism would ultimately vanish. Needless to say, such optimism flourished for only a single generation. It evaporated even faster than the hatred it stood against.

In the short story "Camacho's Wedding Feast," included as the first entry in this volume, Gerchunoff describes the sorrows of a Jewish family when their daughter, about to be married off to a rich Jew, is suddenly carried off by her gentile lover, Camacho, on the very day of the wedding. To be sure, the motif of the stolen bride is universal, having been used by Boccaccio, Federico García Lorca, and Charles Dickens. Yet note Gerchunoff's selection of the Argentine character's name: Camacho was also part of the cast of *Don Quixote de la Mancha*. With all its literary echoes, the author of *The Jewish Gauchos* is able to create a tale in a style that reminds us of oral storytelling. He does it by having a tête-à-tête with the reader and by shaping an unpretentious, colloquial prose that foreshadows the experimental techniques yet to come in Latin America. Here's the illuminating passage:

> Well, as you can see, my patient readers, there are fierce, arrogant Gauchos, wife-stealers and Camachos, as well as the most learned and honorable of rabbinical scholars in the little Jewish colony where I learned to love the Argentine sky and felt a part of its wonderful earth. This story I've told—with more detail than art—is a true one, just as I'm sure the original story of Camacho's feast is true. May I die this instant if I've dared to add the slightest bit of invention to the marvelous story.

> I'd like very much to add some verses—as was done to the original Camacho story—but God has denied me that talent. I gave you the tale in its purest truth, and if you want couplets, add them yourself in your most gracious style. Don't forget *my* name, however—just as our gracious Master Don Miguel de Cervantes Saavedra remembered the name of Cide Hamete Benegeli and gave him all due credit for the original Camacho story.

> And if the exact, accurate telling of this tale has pleased you, don't send me any golden doubloons—here, they don't even buy bread and water. Send me some golden drachmas or, if not, I'd appreciate a carafe of Jerusalem wine from the vineyards my ancestors planted as they sang the praises of Jehovah.

Three things are evident from this passage: the author's deep and honest love for his new country, Argentina; his parody of *Don Quixote;* and his sense of tradition, both Jewish and Hispanic. This last is crucial: by referring to Cervantes, Gerchunoff, as a member of a cultural minority, nevertheless placed himself in the grand tradition of Hispanic letters. While on the one hand he wanted to forge a link with the great master of renaissance Spain, on the other he sought to relate himself to the Jewish past by referring to such biblical symbols as the wine "from the vineyards my ancestors planted as they sang the praises of Jehovah." Thus two paths intersect in *The Jewish Gauchos,* and the encounter is dynamic and reciprocal. The Jews of Gerchunoff's community of Entre Ríos behave like gauchos, and the gauchos, in turn, inherit from the Jews a set of ethical values. Writing at the moment of Argentina's first centennial, the author sings to a new communion and to a fresh, hopeful love affair. This glorification of assimilation is puzzling. As Naomi Lindstrom claims: "The [novel] assumes that the long-standing Hispanic population of Argentina are the hosts, whereas the new Argentines coming from Eastern European Jewry are guests who must take care not to disrupt preexisting national life with their alien ways."[4] The goal for Gerchunoff's patriotism is to dream of a democratic society where Jews share and actually contribute to the new culture. But was that the goal of the Jewish immigrants as a whole?

Within a few years after 1910, things turned sour in Argentina. And Gerchunoff's perception of the country as a new "Zion" was not left unchallenged. On the contrary, it was opposed and even repudiated by Jewish intellectuals and literati. More than that, his response to a major crisis for the Jews in Argentina was regarded as disappointing for a figure of his stature.

Anti-Semitism reached its height in 1919 with the *Semana Trágica*, the tragic week, an explosion of xenophobic fear that amounted to a full-blown pogrom with numerous injured and dead. (David Viñas, a Jewish novelist born ten years after the tragedy, made use of this sad event, a reminder that the heart of the Americas was not untouched by the same hatred left behind in the old continent, in a novel published in 1966.) The intensification of negative feelings toward the Jews, generated by a wave of nationalism during the administration of Hipólito Yrigoyen, contributed to profound disappointment and skepticism regarding the future of a pluralistic society in Argentina. Though deeply affected, Gerchunoff did not publicly comment on the event. His silence was taken as a sign of cowardly passivity and, perhaps, of self-criticism: some thought he might have come to the conclusion that assimilation was impossible in a country with such profound anti-Semitic feelings. The public would have to wait for a coherent statement. Of course, Gerchunoff was no politician; yet in Latin America the opinions of intellectuals are often the only channels through which deep political and ethical concerns are expressed.

Leonardo Senkman, in his 1983 study *Jewish Identity in Argentine Literature*, discusses the various essays Gerchunoff wrote to articulate and explain his ideas. In response to Adolf Hitler's ascendancy to power in Germany, Gerchunoff's arguments finally became clear in his brief prologue to a 1937 Argentine edition of Ludwig Lewisohn's *Rebirth: A Book of Modern Jewish Thought*. Speaking out against a restriction imposed on Jewish immigration by the Argentine government that limited the quota of immigrants to at least a third of the number in previous years, he openly defended the right of the Jews to live anywhere at any time without prohibitions.[5] It is not difficult to feel in his words a fear of the growth of anti-Semitic literature at the time of the invigorated Nationalist Party, which supported Yrigoyen, and its call for the expulsion or even annihilation of all Jews in Argentina. Yet Gerchunoff's general passivity is palpable when placed in relation to the Zionist struggle for an independent Jewish state in Palestine that was taking place in those years. Though angry, he never advocated any kind of Jewish collective self-assertion. I translate:

> What should we do? Jews and Argentines, we can protest, fight, expose the hidden goals of the policy of cowardice and crime. And it would be proper to set a foundation for the right of the Jew to life, the right of the Jew to go on living exactly in the same place he was born or where he was left by fate, in the name of the following evidence:
>
> (1) No effort in history to get rid of the Jewish element has been successful, precisely because the Jew, anywhere, is irreplaceable when he performs on the stage of the human spirit, and ineradicable even when one tries to dissimulate his physical presence by means of alien dicta forced on him. . . .
>
> (2) It is positively useless to persecute the Jew, take away from him his goods, or place him in a ghetto, because he may accept that circumstance and will find a way through it. He will be resurrected when given the chance, because those same ones that are willing to beat him, eventually will protect him. . . .
>
> (3) When persecuted, humiliated, or molested anywhere on the planet, the Jew will expand his solidarity with other Jews, because precisely in that he finds his dignity. . . . And in that sense, the Jewish character and his diasporic pride will be confirmed when his attachment to other Jews is awakened.[6]

Gerchunoff calls at first for intellectual protests against anti-Semitic acts because he thinks he may persuade his enemy by intellectual means. That persuasion remained a hope, of course, not a reality. As time went on, he sank into disillusionment and silence, and eventually isolated himself from his community. Although he became quite enthusiastic about certain Jewish topics, such as the Talmud, he remained evasive and ambivalent. When Jewish symbols appear in his late fiction, it is always in a remote and distant context, with reference to Heinrich Heine or Baruch Spinoza, never the current scene. His dream of a Promised Land in South America was slowly collapsing, along with other liberal values. At the outbreak of World War II in 1939, about 218,000 Jews lived in Argentina. Yet only a decade later, the country turned into a nightmare for all integrationist hopes.

ARGENTINE ECHOES

The history of Jewish-Argentine literature includes many others considered to be Gerchunoff's successors. Among them is César Tiempo (pseudonym of Israel Zeitlin, 1906–1980), a famous-in-his-time playwright, critic, and poet, who had emigrated to Argentina from the Ukraine. He was highly esteemed as a man of letters and travel writer whose poetry almost uniquely refers to one central metaphor: the Sabbath. This interest is reflected in some of the titles of his works: *Book for the Break of the Sabbath*, published in 1930, or *Joyful Saturday*, which appeared in 1955. He always willingly wrote for a gentile audience and, probably influenced by Israel Zangwill's *Dreamers of the Ghetto*, used the vivid imagery of the Buenos Aires Jewish ghetto to draw an appealing distinction between the Jewish and Christian Sabbaths. As a liberal, Tiempo identified with the oppressed and humiliated, and favored a multiethnic society. His two famous theatrical pieces, *I Am the Theater* and *Creole Bread*, staged in the thirties, dealt with the subject of assimilation and Jewish versus gentile justice. Like Gerchunoff, he was deeply depressed by outbursts of anti-Semitism; yet unlike him, he actively responded with written arguments and oral protests against the racist campaign inspired by the infamous writings of the propagandist Gustavo Martínez Zuviría. The director of the National Library in Buenos Aires, Zuviría, under the pen name of Hugo Wast, had written both *The Kahal* and *Gold* in 1938, inspired by *The Protocols of the Elders of Zion*, the infamous anti-Semitic tract immensely popular, even today, throughout Latin America. Yet despite Tiempo's public complaints, nothing changed. At times even the national press, as if echoing his own writing, denied the presence of racial tension in the country. As with Gerchunoff, the political events, of course, helped develop in him a skepticism about Argentina's democratic future, and they also frightened his young Jewish followers.

Another important Jewish figure in Argentine literature is Bernardo Verbitsky (1907–1979), a prolific realist writer who published long novels dealing with Jewish identity in contemporary Argentina and the world at large. They include *Hard to Start Living* (1941), which, according to the critic Juan Pinto, is an essential text for understanding the cultural situation of Buenos Aires in the thirties.[7] The critic and novelist David Viñas (b. 1929), whom I mentioned in reference to the *Semana Trágica*, in his 1962 novel *Making a Stand* argues for a nation that is at once multiethnic, democratic, and tolerant.

Jewish writers and intellectuals of later generations suffered the horrors of military dictatorship, persecution, violence, and exile. Among them was Luisa Mercedes Levinson, half-Jewish and a close friend and colleague of Borges, who wrote "The Cove"; she is the mother of the Argentine-born New York experimentalist Luisa Valenzuela, author of *The Lizard's Tail*. Another crucial name is Germán Rozenmacher (1936–1971), a talented young man who felt that the constant attempt to participate in the country's everyday life created deep psychological scars among the Jews. The protagonists of his stories, collected in one volume in 1970, are lonely creatures, many of them failed artists with identity problems, who aspire to enter gentile society but are unable to do so. His tenacious belief in assimilation always brings the reader to the conclusion that for him no Jewish existence proud of its accomplishments could flourish in his native Argentina. In "Blues in the Night," perhaps his best short story and included here, Vassily Goloboff, a music professor who once sang in the Moscow Opera and rejected his Jewish name and identity after immigrating to Buenos Aires, returns to religion in his later years. In the tradition of the encounter between Leopold Bloom and Stephen Dedalus, one day he has a sudden rendezvous with Bernardo, a young Jew, in which they share memories about broken families and talk about their enchantment with *I Pagliacci*. But no happiness comes to them in the end.

In the same generation as Rozenmacher are the storyteller Gerardo Mario Goloboff (b. 1939), the author of a trilogy that includes the 1988 novel *Pigeon Keeper*, about rural life in the mythical town of Algarrobos; Humberto Costantini (1924–1987); Pedro Orgambide (b. 1928); Isidoro Blaisten (b. 1933); Alicia Steimberg (b. 1933); Marcos Aguinis (b. 1935); Ricardo Feierstein (b. 1942); Cecilia Absatz (b. 1943); Aída Bortnik (b. 1943); Nora Glickman (b. 1942); Mario Satz (b. 1944); Marcos Ricardo Barnatán (b. 1946); and Mario Szichman (b. 1945). Szichman, the author of *At 8:25 Evita Became Immortal*, is particularly interesting. In the late 1960s he tried to create a family saga that would encapsulate the diverse personalities and viewpoints among Argentine Jews and explore relevant issues such as the community's response to Israel, assimilation, the world of business, and religion. It is quite obvious that not only the works of Gabriel García Márquez, but also Yiddish novels such as I. J. Singer's *The Family Carnovsky*, made a transforming impression on him. He shows some of the stylistic elements of magical realism—a narrative style made popular after the publication of *One Hundred Years of Solitude*, which mixes reality with dreamlike components and uses as its setting the exotic Latin American landscape—but he is more concerned with genealogy and tradition within the family circle. In *The Jews of Mar Dulce* (1971), *The False Chronicle* (1969, revised in 1972), and *At 8:25 Evita Became Immortal*, the Pechof family is followed from their immigration in 1918, their rejection of gaucho agricultural life, and their transition to the urban life of Buenos Aires during the thirties and forties. Although the narrative moves back and forth in time, Szichman stops around 1952, when his characters discover their unacceptable status as Jews in Argentina and desperately struggle to assimilate by changing their surname to Gutiérrez Anselmi. By means of an ironic, self-hating point of view, mixing Yiddishisms with a convoluted Spanish, the author builds a vision of the impossibility of Diaspora life in Argentina as he re-creates the customs and idiosyncrasies of Jewish life in South America with astonishing detail. Unlike Gerchunoff, Berele or Bernardo (Szichman's *alter ego*) is permanently searching for an answer to his father's strange, political death in the city dump. And by deciphering his father's last intentions, Berele discovers the cause of the entire family's dilemma. What is interesting about Szichman's fiction is the way it revises national history. By placing his characters in a variety of periods, from the *Semana Trágica* to the military coups in the forties and the defeated revolution in 1956 (when Berele's father perishes), Szichman makes an unquestionable statement: no regime, no juncture, in Argentine history is good for the Jews because their historical presence on the River Plate is a mistake. If Gerchunoff at one time believed Argentina to be a heaven, Szichman sees it as hell.

JORGE LUIS BORGES

Of the non-Jewish writers in Latin America who have considered Jewish images and themes, such as the Kabbalah, Israel, and the Holocaust, the first and most outstanding figure is Borges, a passionate lover of *lo hebreo*—things Jewish. Mention his name and you conjure up the ability to reduce everything to metaphysical mystery: toenails, much too insignificant for the poet to write about, suddenly become, in one of his odes, the only organic element that resists death; or the world itself, too large for anyone to understand, becomes, in some of the stories compiled in *Labyrinths*, a voluminous book that embraces all possible and impossible knowledge. At once a keen semiotician, a devotee of medieval philosophy, and an innovative *homme de lettres* who was able to invent a distinctive fictional universe, Borges's influence on the international literary scene is very important. Three of his stories are included here in the appendix.

During the 1960s it was fashionable among Latin American writers to start every dissertation, essay, or short story with an epigraph taken from this Argentine fabulist. Only a decade later, one could discover remnants of his style between the lines or plot structures of Gabriel García Márquez or Carlos Fuentes. Today, in Europe and the United States, artists and writers such as Umberto Eco, cinematographer Bernardo Bertolucci, John Updike, and John Barth adore him because of his prodigious knowledge and metaphysical brilliance; others, like Stanislaw Lem, the Polish science-fiction writer, complain that he was a monstrous iconoclast, an egotist and pseudoscholar with a dazzling command of erudition and logic, but incapable of understanding the dilemmas of the modern world.[8] Since 1961, when he shared the International Publisher's Prize with Samuel Beckett and his oeuvre gained international acclaim, becoming more and more the subject of academic study, both sides of the love-hate controversy are expressed in a fascinating showcase of opposites: Borges himself would have said that his detractors are substantially the same as his fans.

Borges's Jewish connection is well documented. Starting with the monumental literary biography of Emir Rodríguez Monegal, to the works of Edna Aizenberg, Saúl Sosnowski, and Jaime Alazraki, much has been written about his attraction to the Golem, "the people of the Book," Isaac Luria and Hebraic mysticism, Kafka, and Spinoza. Borges's mother, Leonor Acevedo Haedo, believed she had some Jewish ancestors, probably *conversos* who came to the Americas after the 1492 expulsion from Spain. It was this possibility that made Borges the target of anti-Semitic attacks in the thirties. The magazine *Crisol* published an article asserting that he was a Jew, and Borges replied in another periodical, *Megáfono* (April 1934), with a response that at once showed admiration and pride toward Judaism. "Statistically speaking," he wrote,

> The Jews are very few. What would we think of someone
> in the year 4,000 who discovered everywhere descendants

of the inhabitants of the San Juan province? Our inquisitors are seeking Hebrews, never Phoenicians, Numidians, Scythians, Babylonians, Huns, Vandals, Ostrogoths, Ethiopians, Illyrians, Paphlagonians, Sarmatians, Medes, Ottomans, Berbers, Britons, Libyans, Cyclops, and Lapiths. The nights of Alexandria, Babylon, Carthage, Memphis have never succeeded in engendering one single grandfather: only the tribes of the bituminous Black Sea had that power.

In the same article he joked about his roots:

Borges Acevedo is my name. In the fifth chapter of his book *Rosas y su tiempo*, Ramos Mejía lists the family names of Buenos Aires of that time to demonstrate that all, or almost all, "descended from a Hebrew-Portuguese branch." Acevedo is part of that catalogue: the only document of my Jewish roots, until the confirmation of *Crisol*. Nevertheless, Captain Honorario Acevedo has made some research I cannot ignore. He indicates that Don Pedro de Azevedo . . . my great-grandfather, was irreproachably Spanish. Two hundred years and I don't find the Israelite, two hundred years and the ancestor eludes me.[9]

Borges's childhood had a duality of languages, English and Spanish (later enriched by Italian and French). He kept saying, even writing, that he first read *Don Quixote* in Shakespeare's tongue, and when a few years later he finally got to the original, he thought it was a lousy translation. His first literary attempts were made in Switzerland, in 1914, where his family had been spending some time. It is there that he enrolled in the Collège Calvin, and developed a friendship with Maurice Abramowicz and Simón Jichlinski, who probably introduced him to Kabbalah. In Switzerland he also studied Latin and German, a language that led him closer to Judaism because it enabled him to read Martin Buber, Gustav Meyrink, and later, obviously, Kafka, in the original. In 1919, on their way back from Europe to Buenos Aires, his family went to Spain.

It was in Madrid that Borges established his friendship with Rafael Cansinos-Asséns, an Andalusian who, according to the Argentine, founded Ultraism, the aesthetic movement that tried to introduce into Spanish the innovations of the European avant-garde—Dadaism, Cubism, Surrealism, and Expressionism. No doubt this was a major event in the writer's life. Cansinos-Asséns wrote several books dedicated to Judaism. His cosmopolitanism sought out the universal resonance in every simple thing. While Spain stubbornly upheld its close ties to Catholicism at the time, he expressed himself openly against orthodoxy and dreamed of being ultranational. In fact, he believed the Hebraic legacy of Spanish culture to lie precisely in the juxtaposition of races intending to abolish all differences. Even more, he thought that implicit in Judaism was an eternally antiestablishment posture. He wanted to do away with tradition, with canonical forms of art. Borges inherited from Cansinos-Asséns not only his rebellious attitude but also a desire to see the Jews in the abstract.

On his return to Argentina in 1921, Borges read the long poem *The Gaucho Martín Fierro* (1872–1879) by José Hernández, a book that deeply influenced him. Perhaps only three important Jewish names were known in the Argentine literary arena of the time: Gerchunoff, Tiempo, and Verbitsky. The first two also wrote for *Proa* and *Martín Fierro*, the two periodicals where Borges published his first pieces. During the Second World War, Borges maintained very good relations with the Argentine Jewish community. He was an antifascist and openly expressed his indignation over Nazi ideology. Zuviría, mentioned above, took advantage of Hitler's rise to power with his infamous novels, published under the pseudonym Hugo Wast, in which he practically called upon the country to exterminate the Jews. Three years later, an Anti-Defamation Committee against Racism and Anti-Semitism was formed by important Argentine Jews and non-Jews, and Borges was one of its strongest supporters. In his fiction, his attitude toward Nazism appears in "The Secret Miracle,"[10] and toward anti-Semitism in "Deutsches Requiem": the first is a tribute to Kafka, the second a dissertation on the evils of Nazism. Similarly, in the forties he openly expressed antimilitary views with regard to the Peronist regime, as a result of which it is said that while Borges's corpse was waiting to be buried at the Plan Palais cemetery in Geneva in 1986, neo-Peronist groups were actively defaming the author's reputation in his own country.

From 1948 on, Borges showed great sympathy for the state of Israel. He traveled there twice, first in 1969 and again in 1971, to receive the Jerusalem Prize. He was an outspoken supporter during the Six-Day War and afterward lectured on the theme of Jewish longing for the Promised Land based on readings of the Bible and Talmud. But his attitude is less sentimental than philosophical and moral: he believed that Israel might be the answer to ancient national goals and desires, but it could also transform the Jew into a simply material being. According to Borges, the Jew has been a polyglot through the ages, a self-made rationalist, a persistent fighter for his right to exist as an extraordinary citizen; he has won a place beyond history and therefore has become almost parahistorical. Israel as a nation may damage the esoteric qualities that have long flourished in the individual; this return to history, he once said, may steal the distinctiveness of the Jews and transform them into politicized creatures, with the same trivial habits as everybody else. One can analyze Borges's oeuvre and argue that, influenced by Cansinos-Asséns, he loved only the ideal image of the Jew: the cosmopolitan, the philosopher, the kabbalist, the polyglot, but never the simple person. Whenever Borges portrayed Jewish characters in his fiction, they were always heroes of the supernatural, champions on a theological and philosophical scale. He never wrote about ordinary people concerned with mundane problems. Something similar happened to his intellectual interests: in reading Spinoza, Borges never let the argument of the Amsterdam Jewish community get in his way; he wanted to see Spinoza purely as a philosophical hero.

There is another example of how Borges preferred the spiritual to the material. When influenced by Gershom Scholem, the foremost contemporary scholar of Jewish mysticism, Borges in his sixties became interested in the Hasidic movement of the late eighteenth and early nineteenth centuries. Yet he never quite understood the theological and social reform it achieved; he saw the Baal Shem Tov only as the master in love with his magic and esotericism, never as a rebel who, like Luther, broke with the medieval conception of the rabbi as an untouchable intellectual genius. Here and there Borges mentions Hasidism, but never in relation to the way the movement brought the ordinary people to the center of the historical arena, replacing the Maimonidean image of the wise man, half prophet and half philosopher; Borges does not mention these features because he was never interested in the actual circumstances of ordinary people. On the contrary, he preferred to look for the metaphysical element, the unseen.

The same thing happens to his view of Israel. After 1971, he never commented publicly on Israeli politics, as he did on other international subjects; neither did he show any interest in literary or intellectual trends emerging from the young state. Yes, he tried to learn Hebrew, but as with Kafka and Walter Benjamin, the attempt proved unsuccessful; the only words that remained in his mind were kabbalistic concepts from the *Sefer Yetzirah* or the *Zohar*. Nevertheless, one should be careful not to read into this a change of feeling: while Borges idealized the abstract Jew, he never felt uncomfortable among Jews, as his adolescent friendship with Abramowicz, Jichlinski, or, later on, with Gershom Scholem proved.

In relation to the Kabbalah, there are many instances where symbols or references appear in Borges's work. Several times he pointed to Meyrink's novel *The Golem* (1915) as a book that attracted him to the world of Jewish esotericism. On his second trip to Israel, he learned from Scholem about such archetypes as the Ein-Sof and the Shekhinah. He even refers to the author of *Major Trends in Jewish Mysticism* in one of his poems, "The Golem."

> *The Kabbalist that officiated as numen*
> *The vast creature he nicknamed Golem;*
> *Those truths are related by Scholem*
> *In a learned place of his volume.* [my translation]

On a more down-to-earth level, Borges contradicts Gerchunoff's mystique of the gaucho as an authentic part of the Jewish experience in Argentina in his short story "The Unworthy Friend," included in *Dr. Brodie's Report* of 1970, as well as in "The Forms of Glory," written by Borges and his friend and colleague Adolfo Bioy Casares (published in 1977). Argentine writers have long worshiped the original gaucho as a national idol, a courageous peasant of the Pampas, everywhere carrying his guitar, his poncho, and his vengeful spirit. Lugones and Ricardo Güiraldes celebrated it as the quintessential national folk myth, and Borges also came close to doing so in "Biography of Tadeo Isidoro Cruz (1829–1874)." Although Borges found in *The Gaucho Martín Fierro* the clearest expression of Argentine identity and a fountain of personal creativity, he viewed the phenomenon of "Jewish gauchos" as a complete anachronism. The term *gaucho judío* achieved prominence with Gerchunoff, yet Borges openly denies that such characters ever existed in real life; Jews were businessmen, merchants, and storekeepers, not cowboys, he argues, and the age of the horseman in the Pampas preceded the Jewish immigration. According to Borges, Gerchunoff portrayed *chacareros*, peddlers descended from the gaucho; thus he confused poor immigrant workers with national heroes like Martín Fierro.

M O A C Y R   S C L I A R

Up until now, I have discussed along somewhat general lines the art of two Argentines, one Jew and the other gentile, both cornerstones in the literary tradition represented in this anthology. There is a third writer, much younger than Gerchunoff and Borges, who is equally important in disseminating and shaping things Jewish in Latin American letters: the Brazilian novelist and fabulist Moacyr Scliar. His fiction owes a lot to his compatriots Jorge Amado, João Guimarães Rosa, Mario de Andrade, Samuel Rawet, and the Ukrainian-born Clarice Lispector, but it is also a direct descendant of Sholem Aleichem, Isaac Bashevis Singer, Rabbi Nahman of Bratslav, and the traditional Yiddish folktale. His characters and settings are Brazilian, but his concerns are the continuity of Judaism, God's relationship with his creatures, and the universe as a sacred space.

Born in 1937 in Pôrto Alegre, Rio Grande do Sul, the son of a business-man who emigrated from Eastern Europe, Scliar is the author of at least ten novels and seven collections of stories, including *The Carnival of the Animals* (1976). His work earned him major international literary prizes such as the Casa de las Américas. Although retired since 1987, he worked as a public-health physician and, like William Carlos Williams and Anton Chekhov, di-vided his time between literature and medicine. His joyful, humorous charac-ters, at times endowed with supernatural powers, are wanderers, soul-searching *marranos*, political activists, or half-Jewish, half-animal centaurs; love, mental disorder, redemption, and the coming of the Messiah are frequent themes. What is Jewish about his writing? His intellectual comedy, his passion for storytelling, his affinity with Yiddish. In *The Strange Life of Rafael Men-des*, for instance, a *converso*, discovering that both the prophet Jonah and the philosopher Maimonides are among his ancestors, immediately takes it as his duty to continue the tradition of wisdom, excellence, and ethics. In *The One-Man Army*, an anarchist tries to build a large communist colony, a New Biro-bidjan (after the so-called Jewish state created by Joseph Stalin near Siberia in 1932) near Pôrto Alegre, but his adventure turns into disaster because of Bra-zil's deep devotion to capitalism. Meyer Guinzberg, the central character, reacts to his defeat by transforming his redemptive fantasy into a frantic love for pigs and horses. Scliar's other creatures indulge in pagan rituals or belong to antinomian sects like that of the pseudo-Messiah Sabbatai Zevi. They are discontented with civilization, unhappy yet looking for answers in philoso-phies and ideologies that are either outmoded or alien to life in South America.

Published in 1978, *The Gods of Raquel* is one of Scliar's best novels and also the most outstanding work in the literary tradition represented in this anthology. An artfully constructed yet stylistically uncomplicated narrative, it tells the story of Raquel, a Jewish girl with existential and religious doubts; her parents are Hungarian immigrants who arrived in Brazil thinking it would be the Promised Land. The setting is Parthenon, a district of lunatic asylums in Rio Grande. Raquel's father, an unsuccessful Latinist, opens a hardware store called *Vulcão* after the Roman god of metalwork. In the context of his business and him sending his daughter to a convent school Raquel's odyssey in search of her own identity takes place. She is introduced to Christianity by friends and teachers, and so strong is this religious influence on her, so omnipresent the Church's rituals and paraphernalia in her daily activities and conscience, that after a few years Raquel is ready to convert. But her leap from one faith to another is not easy: as a Jew, she suffers religious persecution and is often victimized by the nuns in the convent. Besides, eternity frightens Raquel. She believes a choice must be made between Christ and Jehovah and, unable to make up her mind, she denies herself participation in either religion. In her journey, she befriends Isabel, a gentile, who soon becomes a partner in her quests but later turns into a rival when both girls fall in love with the same boy, Francisco. Christianity and Judaism thus become competitors, enemies. Isabel eventually marries Francisco and Raquel engages in an extramarital affair with him. To stress his powerful allegorical message, Scliar inspirits every object in the book, turning it into a pagan deity. His protagonist intelligently concludes that to fully assimilate into Brazil's society, a Jew needs to renounce one's true beliefs. Raquel refuses to do so and her voyage takes a rather fascinating turn: Miguel, a worker at *Vulcão* of native origin, introduces her to sex, and through it to idolatry. His existential dream, we soon find out, is to build a *tropical synagogue*—a sacred altar where Judaism, Christianity, and a number of other pagan cults coexist. Raquel helps him in his endeavor. In a final scene that is at once haunting and unforgettable, she is seduced by Miguel and persuaded to perform bizarre primitive acts involving a variety of religious symbols and terrifying rituals. To my mind, no other Latin American writer has so far managed to describe as successfully as Moacyr Scliar the religious turmoil and confused identity inhabiting the mind of a Jew living in the southern hemisphere.

Perhaps Scliar's most famous work is *The Centaur in the Garden* (1980), a novel in the tradition of Kafka's *Metamorphosis*. Like Gregor Samsa, Guedali Tartakovsky, the protagonist, is a peculiar creature, half-human, half-animal. Yet in his case the grotesque physical appearance, an amalgamation of human and animal features, is not meant to create surprise or terror, but laughter. After all, in the tradition of those monsters found in Ovid and kabbalistic bestiaries or the compelling demons of Isaac Bashevis Singer, he's a centaur— but a fully circumcised, Yiddish-speaking centaur who is also a devoted reader of Sholem Aleichem and I. L. Peretz. Not knowing whether to kill him or have him disappear into the forest, his family hopes to educate Guedali into "a respectable Jew." But they are ashamed of him; feeling frustrated and hurt, he flees his home to become independent. Escape is here the keyword: divisive internal forces are so strong in Scliar's creation that they ultimately tear him apart. At first, to support himself Guedali works in a circus, where he falls in love with a female centaur. They marry and have children. Their dream, of course, is to achieve normality; that is, they hope to lose their distinctiveness. Soon after, they both travel to Morocco, where Guedali undergoes a surgical operation performed by a charlatan. To everyone's astonishment, he becomes human—or almost human: except for his cloven hoofs, he's the same as others. But whatever kind of normalcy he achieves, the transformation turns into such a boring and vacuous routine that he struggles to become a centaur once again, and on his return to Brazil loses all sense of identity. The novel clearly explores the deep and unequivocal desire by the Jewish minority in Brazil and elsewhere in Latin America to assimilate into the milieu, a move that sooner or later destroys its uniqueness and self-esteem. But the story is more than an allegory: the fantastic elements acquire a life of their own as the bizarre is approached in a realistic context.

A satirist, Moacyr Scliar has a marvelous narrative touch that recalls Lewis Carroll as well as Borges. Like the Argentine, he takes upon himself the task of reappraising major historical events with an intellectual inquisitiveness, but also with a *joie de vivre* absent in the author of "Pierre Menard, author of the *Quixote*." What is most interesting is that, although Scliar has chronicled in historical detail the range of Jewish experience in Brazil, his treatment of the Holocaust is relatively spare. Robert DiAntonio, the author of *Brazilian Fiction*, who has studied the novelist's contribution to Latin American literature, is also puzzled by silence on such a critical event in contemporary Jewish history. Scliar's "novels and short fiction," he claims, "have incorporated various, and little known, aspects of Judeo-Brazilian historiography: the settling of Baron Hirsch's agricultural communes in Quatro Irmãos; the Jewish gauchos; the aftermath of the Soviet Union's attempt to establish a Jewish state in Birobidjan; the world of the Jewish Mafia, the *Zewi Migdal*; an anachronistic accommodation of the life of Sabbatai Zevi, the charismatic false messiah; the long history of Brazil's Sephardim; and the Jewish white slave trade in Rio Grande do Sul. However, Scliar, one of Brazil's leading writers and one who has a large and devoted international following, has written very little on the subject of the Holocaust. Perhaps in response to the

Yiddish admonition *M'ken nisht* (one cannot), he felt the subject too tragic to be dealt with. He deals with it only tangentially and from a very unique perspective."[11]

The best example is "Inside My Dirty Head—The Holocaust," a story by Scliar included in *The Enigmatic Eye* (1986) and reprinted here. Told from the point of view of a young boy whose father is a traditional East European immigrant, it describes his puzzlement about Mischa, a Holocaust survivor found sleeping in doorways in Pôrto Alegre. The boy sees Mischa as an alien figure, and the numbers tattooed on his arm as imbued with a perverse magical potency: he dreams of the Holocaust survivor winning the lottery with the numbers tattooed on his arm, yet losing the prize once the number is surgically removed. According to DiAntonio, "The childlike reasoning is a narrative device to express tangibly the sense of guilt of many Brazilians who were personally unaffected by the events in Europe." Scliar suggests that the Holocaust cannot be written about in a literal or conceptual way, perhaps because it is beyond meaning and comprehension.

Other Brazilian writers, like Rubem Fonseca (*Vastas emocoes e pensamentos imperfeitos*, 1988) and Zevi Ghivelder (*As seis pontas da estrela*, 1969), have written about the Holocaust and its consequences. While in North America the theme has become an attractive and sometimes lucrative topic, a sort of unifying, rallying point in the country's Jewish culture, writers in Latin America seldom deal with it. Although the United States had a fundamental role to play in the Second World War, the countries south of the Rio Grande either remained silent and impartial, or their dictatorial governments gave political asylum to ex-lieutenants and soldiers of Adolf Hitler—as well as to Jews. It was often the case that in cities like Asunción, São Paulo, or Montevideo, refugees from Auschwitz or Buchenwald would encounter their German victimizers walking on the street. Yet those horrific encounters never really captivated the national consciousness. The fictional treatment of Holocaust issues in Latin American literature is often apologetic, detached, or sentimental. More often than not, these works explore the aftermath of the massive extermination, but not its causes or specific details. Moacyr Scliar's "Inside My Dirty Head—The Holocaust," which focuses its attention on the mental aftershocks in the mind of a Jew in Pôrto Alegre, differs from the accounts of survivors such as Primo Levi or Elie Wiesel in its preoccupation with post-Holocaust trauma.

BRAZILIAN VOICES

With a population of about 160,000 Jews in 1980, most of them in São Paulo and Rio de Janeiro, the list of Brazilian writers in this literary tradition is not as long as that of Argentina, but it is distinguished: Samuel Rawet (1929–1985), an engineer born in Poland, is one of the most significant early figures. *Tales of the Immigrant*, his collection of stories published at the age of twenty-seven, which includes "Johnny Golem" and "Kalovim," is clearly influenced by Hermann Hesse. Rawet's concern is the Jewish process of assimilation into Brazilian life. By adapting to their new milieu, he suggests, they lose sight of their true identity; using one of his favorite metaphors, they "evaporate." *The Seven Dreams*, a more mature work influenced by Edgar Allan Poe and Kafka, again focuses on misanthropic, obsessive characters tormented by their inner selves. Rawet's obsession with the Jews, whom he perceived as highly intellectual and model citizens, continued in *Ahasuerus' Trip* (1970). But unexpected events changed his mind, suddenly causing him to feel ashamed of his religious and ethnic background. The result was a total rejection of his past. This personal transformation is evident in *I—You—He* (1972), a discursive narrative dealing with larger Brazilian social issues. What is absent in this book is actually more interesting than the subject matter: Rawet wanders around metaphysical and philosophical problems but leaves out his most urgent concern: Judaism. This existential detour ended up tragically, with his suicide at the age of fifty-four. He was incapable of finding an answer to his doubts and ambivalence.

Another Brazilian Jewish writer of note is Carlos Heitor Cony (b. 1926), a well-known journalist in Rio de Janeiro who early in life studied in a seminary, but became disenchanted with religion and turned to politics. His most famous novel, *Pessach: The Crossing*, published in 1967, deals with a novelist who suffers from personal and political doubts but begins to accept his Jewishness when he turns forty, just as he unexpectedly becomes a member of an urban-guerrilla group. Cony is significant because he chronicles the plight of middle-class sophisticates; yet critics such as Regina Igel vehemently refuse to regard him as Jewish, and Cony himself is ambivalent about his ethnic identity.

But the most influential Jewish writer in Brazil, after Moacyr Scliar, is Clarice Lispector (1925–1977).[12] Like Rawet and Cony, she was ambivalent toward Judaism. An engaging prose stylist born into a poor Ashkenazi family in Tchetchelnik, Ukraine, she lived first in the town of Recife, Pernambuco, and at the age of twelve moved to Rio de Janeiro. Her father, a farm laborer, eventually became a sales representative. A voracious reader, she began writing unconventional, unstructured children's stories while still a child; many of them were sent to the *Diário de Pernambuco* but were rejected. In Rio she completed her secondary schooling at João Barbalho School and entered the Faculty of Law, from which she graduated in 1944, just one year after marrying a fellow student who subsequently entered the foreign service. Her husband, Mauri Gurgel Valente, was first posted in Naples, and the couple moved to Italy. All together they spent many years abroad, living in Switzerland and England, and spending eight years in the United States (from 1952 to 1960); not until 1959 did they return to visit Brazil, where Lispector and her husband later divorced.

The author of some twenty volumes of fiction, nonfiction, and literature for children, none of which deal openly with Jewish topics, she gained experience as a journalist, first on the editorial staff of the press service Agência Nacional, then with the newspaper *A Noite*. Her first novel, *Near to the Wild Heart*, published in 1944, when she was still nineteen years old, was an immediate critical and financial success. As translator Gregory Rabassa notes, Lispector's style, deeply influenced by the European modernists, "is interior and hermetic": the action, always subjective, is seen from the point of view of characters involved in the plot.[13] Although critics believe her to be a better short-story teller than a novelist, Lispector continued to write long narratives, including *The Apple in the Dark* (1961) and *The Passion According to G. H.* (1964).

How do we place her in this tradition of Jewish-Latin American literature, if only her origin, but not her themes and concerns, is Jewish? Similar questions are often asked about Kafka, a Jew who created a rich and culturally resonant fiction without ever referring to the word "Jew."[14] Scholars agree that Lispector's distinctly European sensitivity and her worldview have Jewish overtones: the sense of family life and the value of individual existence; a glimpse of a small, wealthy community, with unique religious customs, isolated from the rest of the country.

Clarice Lispector is certainly a pillar, tutor, and promoter of the cultural openness following World War II, when women writers in Brazil, Mexico, Argentina, and other parts of the region emerged not as part of a formal movement but, collectively, as a major literary force. Understandably their themes have to do with their long history of silence and the ensuing struggle to regain their bodies, voice, and soul. Now considered a cornerstone of feminism in Latin America, Lispector recalls Virginia Woolf in her insistence on penetrating the inner life and in her views of domestic affairs from a women's perspective. The piece selected here, from her 1960 collection *Family Ties*, explores the disturbing psychological consequences for a woman of her daily routine.

VIVA MEXICO!

Although Argentina and Brazil have the most significant and sizeable body of Jewish literature, and are thus more represented in this anthology, other Latin American nations, such as Mexico, Venezuela, and Peru, deserve if not equal, at least some attention. In the case of Mexico, although its Jewish community traces its roots to the *conversos* that accompanied and followed Hernán Cortés and his soldiers in the conquest of Tenochtitlán and the Aztec empire, most of today's members of the Jewish community are Ashkenazim who arrived during the 1880s and went on to build a *kehillah*, the traditional Jewish communal framework, organize a sports and cultural center, and establish Yiddish schools with strong ties to the Bundist and Zionist movements. By 1910, there were some 9,000 Jews in the country, most of them in Oaxaca, Veracruz, Monterrey (a wealthy northern city apparently founded by kabbalists, or so the legend claims), and the nation's capital; by 1980 that figure had increased to 37,500.

The first Jewish literary figures in Mexico wrote in Russian, Polish, and Yiddish. They were immigrants such as Jacob Glantz, who shared the tastes and style of early Yiddish modernists such as Moyshe-Leyb Halpern, Jacob Glatstein, and Itsik Manger. They published manuscripts, staged the plays of Abraham Goldfaden, and privately engaged a printer to publish and disseminate their work. But it was the second and third generations, already born on native soil, who, from the 1940s onward, emulated Gerchunoff by switching to Spanish, producing novels, essays, and stories that unequivocally belong today to Mexican letters. One of the compelling features of the literature created by Jews in Mexico is its lack of interest in realism. As the reader will soon find out, most of the Mexican writers included in this volume explore esoteric topics in an abstract style rather than their immediate surroundings or experience.

Also of interest is the fact that the most outstanding Mexican men of letters with an interest in Jewish symbols and themes are gentiles: for example, Carlos Fuentes (b. 1928), born in Panama and the country's foremost novelist.

The son of a diplomat in Washington, D.C., and another true polyglot, he has lived all over the world and is completely fluent in English, a talent enabling him to be deeply involved with North American culture. His passionate interest in Judaism is obvious in three of his books. *A Change of Skin* (1967) concerns symmetries of the struggle between Spaniards and Aztecs in Tenochtitlán and that of Nazis and Jews in Europe during the Second World War. In it a group of four young men and women travel in a Volkswagen from Mexico City to Cholula, a town that has 365 churches, one for each day of the year. As they progress on their journey, reminiscences of their pasts intertwine with the reality of the Mexican soul and its complex history. Two of these young people, Franz and Elizabeth (also called Betele), descendants of opposing groups, have links to prewar Europe and tragic reminiscences of the Holocaust.

The Hydra Head (1978), another one of Fuentes's novels involving Jewish themes, is what Graham Greene would have called "an entertainment." In the literary spy tradition of John Le Carré and Robert Ludlum, it is set against the background of the Israeli-Palestinian conflict and the drama over Mexico's oil. Its protagonist, a James Bond of sorts, is Félix Maldonado, alias Diego Velásquez, a bureaucrat and secret-police agent ready to defend the Mexican oil industry against its enemy, foreign (mainly Arab) invasion. His adventures also allow the author to comment on the insularity of the Jewish community in Mexico City. Finally *Terra Nostra* (1975), a volume celebrated by Milan Kundera as a "masterwork" in the tradition of *Tristram Shandy* and Hermann Bloch's *The Sleepwalkers,* has the Spanish language as its major protagonist, and in a rather ambitious and nonchronological fashion retells the entire history of Spain and the Americas from before 1492 until 1992. Among the Jewish characters are *conversos* and kabbalists like Fernando de Rojas and Samuel ha-Nagid; some incidents of its plot deal with the expulsion of the Jews from the Iberian peninsula just as Christopher Columbus was sailing out of the port of Palos toward the Bahamas.

Homero Aridjis (b. 1931), a poet, novelist, and environmentalist, in *1492: Life and Times of Juan Cabezón of Castile* (1985), describes in rich detail the persecution of Jews and *conversos* in seventeenth-century Spain and examines their hope of sailing to new lands. One of the more illustrious poets and writers in Mexico, himself not Jewish, is José Emilio Pacheco (b. 1939), the author of *A Distant Death* (1967, revised in 1977), an avant-garde novel in the tradition of the French *nouveau roman*. It has an enigmatic protagonist modeled after Dr. Josef Mengele, the Nazi physician who committed atrocities in Auschwitz and who supposedly died near São Paulo in 1984. Although it is set in a downtown neighborhood of the Mexican capital, the novel's Jewish allusions include Flavius Josephus as well as the Israeli secret intelligence. Pacheco is also the author of a famous novella, *Battles in the Desert* (1981), a re-creation of the metropolitan landscape in Mexico City during the sixties. While the narrative explores the naïve love affair between a child and his friend's mother, the larger historical setting intertwines the Six-Day War, Mexico's xenophobia, and its overwhelming nationalism. When compared to other stories of Jewish childhood ("Inside My Dirty Head—The Holocaust," for instance), Pacheco's is interesting for its representation of Jewish childhood and communal life as perceived by a non-Jewish boy.

Among the Jewish writers in Mexico are three women: Margo Glantz (b. 1930), Angelina Muñiz-Huberman (b. 1937), and Esther Seligson (b. 1941). The first, a daughter of Yiddish poet Jacob Glantz and the author of *Genealogies* (1982), is mainly a literary critic and memoirist, whereas the other two are best known as short-story writers. In 1986, Muñiz won the prestigious Xavier Villaurrutia Prize for her collection *Enclosed Garden* (1984), translated into English in 1989, from which "In the Name of His Name" is taken. Her themes are metaphysical: an alchemist's search for God; the inner sexual thoughts of Sor Juana Inés de La Cruz, a nun of the Colonial period who wrote poetry and about whom Octavio Paz published a masterful biography in 1982; and the redemptive quest of a man who is challenged to cross a river. Muñiz is a writer highly influenced by Borges but also by Rabbi Nahman of Bratslav. The author's passionate, lifelong readings of the *Zohar* are evident in each of her resonant sentences. Esther Seligson, a theater critic and the translator into Spanish of the Paris-based philosopher Emile Cioran, is the author of *House in Time* (1982), an attempt to rewrite the Bible. Her narratives, an example of which is "The Invisible Hour," are often metaphorical, obscure, perhaps evasive. Like the creatures of Frida Kahlo (a descendant of Hungarian Jews) and the Surrealist painters, her characters are not bound by the physical laws of time and space and perceive fantastic visions of eternity.

I include myself among the Mexican writers in this anthology. My first attempt to define my literary style and expectations in English came in an autobiographical essay called "In the Margin of Time,"[15] in which I analyzed the stifling Jewish education as well as anti-Semitic manifestations in Mexican culture that pushed me to a self-imposed exile. After it appeared, I won many friends on this side of the Rio Grande but lost most of the old ones in my native land. That essay, my obsession with split personalities, and my desire to understand memory as a form of art were the inspirations for my first novel, *Talia in Heaven* (1979, revised in 1989), written with the Colombian-born, London-based journalist Zuri Balkoff, and a collection of stories, *The One-Handed Pianist* (1992), which includes "The Death of Yankos," a surrealist text that suggests how the universe may be too unreasonable and flat for some.

OTHER   VIEWS

In 1982, Venezuela, with a population of over 14 million, had a Jewish population of 20,000. Two writers of excellence that ought to be listed here are the playwright and sometime novelist of Sephardic descent, Isaac Chocrón (b. 1929), and Elisa Lerner (b. 1932). One of the outstanding contemporary Latin American playwrights, Chocrón is the author of several collections of short stories and novels, including *Break in Case of Fire* (1981), about a young man's search for his Jewish past in the Iberian peninsula and Africa. Lerner, on the other hand, a lawyer and diplomat as well as a playwright, descends from a family of Romanian Jews that settled in the city of Valencia, but moved to Caracas in 1936, when she was four years old. A frequent contributor to magazines and newspapers, she is the author of *A Smile Behind the Metaphor* (1973), the collection of plays *Life with Mother* (1975), and the book of criticism *I Love Columbo* (1979). The story included here, "Papa's Friends," like the art of Clarice Lispector, describes the inner life of a young woman, in this case the daughter of a wealthy Jewish businessman in Caracas; and it also evokes the social life and foibles of the Russian-Jewish immigrant community.

Peru had a population of about 5,000 Jews in 1982, most of whom live in Lima and are a minimal fraction of the total national population of 18 million; nevertheless, Peru has produced a well-known Jewish novelist, Isaac Goldemberg (b. 1945), the author of *The Fragmented Life of Don Jacobo Lerner*, a novel about the conflicts of identity. Born in the small town of Chepén, his career, with its many ups and downs, in a way symbolizes that of most of these Jewish storytellers in Latin America. Having published a collection of poems with the Jewish-Cuban writer José Kozer, his first novel appeared to wide acclaim in 1979, when Goldemberg was thirty-four years old. Critics such as José Miguel Oviedo called it a *tour de force*, a gem. Yet, like Henry Roth after *Call It Sleep* and Felipe Alfau after *Locos: A Comedy of Gestures*, Goldemberg fell into silence. Two other works are *Life in Cash*, a collection of poems, and *Play by Play,* an experimental narrative that has as its background a soccer match between the Peruvian and Brazilian national teams, published in 1984 without much fanfare. It opens with the short story "The Conversion," included here.

In more than one way, Goldemberg's life was re-created by Mario Vargas Llosa (b. 1936), the 1990 presidential candidate and a novelist of international reputation who wrote classics such as *Conversation in the Cathedral* and *Aunt Julia and the Scriptwriter.* His novella *The Storyteller,* published in its English translation in 1989, describes the adventures of Saul Zuratas, a middle-class Peruvian Jew, a brilliant yet unhappy anthropology student in Lima during the late fifties. Zuratas falls in love with his object of study, a band of Machiguenga Indians in the Amazon. He becomes intrigued with the role of the ancient storyteller, the keeper of the tribe's collective memory who travels through the deep jungle from one community to another, enchanting everyone with mythological and, often, iconoclastic tales. As the narrative begins, the starving Indians are declining as quickly as the Amazon forest, and their all-important storyteller has disappeared without leaving an apprentice. So after considerable soul-searching, Zuratas makes the Indians' cause his own, abandons his graduate studies and his aging father, and marches into the jungle to assume the·role of tribal bard. The symbolism is clear: a Jew, a member of a small Peruvian urban minority, is described by the narrator as "the last true redeemer of the Indians in Peru." He takes upon himself the task of saving another minority, and his odyssey is marked by obstacles and defeat. Written in Florence and London between 1985 and 1987, *The Storyteller* contains two parallel stories: of the eight chapters, half are tales told by Zuratas to the Machiguengas, and the remaining attempt a realistic description of his existence prior to his voluntary disappearance in the Amazons—as perceived through the eyes of a mature, accomplished writer living in Italy, Vargas Llosa's *alter ego.* There is a deceptive device in the book's structure: Zuratas is nicknamed *Mascarita,* "Maskface," because of the huge birthmark, from which grows unsightly hair, that covers almost half his face. According to Vargas Llosa, the main character was inspired by Goldemberg, who voluntarily exiled himself from his native Peru and went to live first in Israel and then in Manhattan. Like Zuratas, he comes from a small town in Peru and later traveled to Lima at an early age (as did Vargas Llosa himself); both author and protagonist held similar political views, and their lives must be understood as perhaps desperate attempts to come to terms with their art and their identity; the options available to a Jewish storyteller in Peru result in the fictional protagonist's disappearance into the jungle, an exotic fate that exaggerates, through art, the real novelist's need to escape his country.

Guatemala, which in 1982 had one thousand Jews, less than .01 percent of the total population, has three Jewish writers of importance. The civil war and urban violence have pushed most of them out of the country, but fortunately that has not jeopardized their creative productivity. Guatemala is the original home of Victor Perera (b. 1934), a Jew of Sephardic descent who early in his life immigrated to the United States. His stories have appeared in major New York publications. His is a curious case because having lived most of his life north of the Rio Grande, he switched, as did Gerchunoff, from one language to another—in his case, from Spanish to English. A former editor of *The New Yorker,* he is the author of *The Conversion,* a 1970 novel about a North American student living in Spain who tries to come to terms with his Sephardic Jewish identity. The story included here is part of the delightful *Rites: A Guatemalan Boyhood,* published in 1986 and viewed by Alastair Reid, the poet, critic and translator, as another fine example of how effectively an author can cross from one language into another, bringing all his insights with him. The book, a sum of fictionalized personal recollections of Perera's childhood, is written in a precise, careful language that recalls that of Chekhov and Isaac Babel. The protagonists, their relatives and friends living in Guatemala City during the 1950s love, hate, dream about a better future, engage in business, all in an atmosphere imbued with deeply felt nostalgia. The author's decision to write in English, although perhaps unconscious, is quite meaningful. In the last twenty years, a handful of well-known Latin American writers, among them Fuentes but also the Cuban novelist Guillermo Cabrera Infante, author of *Three Trapped Tigers,* and Manuel Puig, the Argentine playwright and novelist whose works include *Kiss of the Spider Woman,* have switched, occasionally and at times in a consistent manner, into English. Borges himself became all but an English-language author, using his English "translators" as coauthors and at times secretaries and scribes. A motivation behind this cross-cultural maneuver is the desire of writers to attract a wider audience and a more dynamic marketplace. Indeed, the fact that Perera published *Rites* in English, with a trade publishing house, gave the book the attention few others included in this anthology have had so far—or may ever receive.

Also Guatemalan are David Unger (b. 1950), a New York–based poet and translator, and Alcina Lubitch Domecq (b. 1953), who now makes her home in Jerusalem. In 1983, she wrote *The Mirror's Mirror: or, The Noble Smile of the Dog,* a novel clearly influenced by Lewis Carroll and Borges, which described the adventures of an eight-year-old Jewish girl left alone on a battlefield. Her thirty or more stories, including "Bottles," were collected in 1988 in *Intoxicated* and have been published in French, German, and Italian anthologies. Most of her stories—what Irving Howe has called "short shorts"—are hardly longer than a page; yet like those of Nathaniel Hawthorne, her images are breathtaking insights into the complexities of a genealogical past or a troublesome family life. In one story she describes how a widow is surprised by the sudden appearance on her face of her late husband's moustache. In another, a troubled housewife is trapped in a gigantic bottle, as if metamorphosized into a huge Kafkaesque insect. The message is clear: as with the lucid prose of Lispector, the reader is provided with an idiosyncratic view—at times paranoid, often distorted and disturbing—of the claustrophobic reality of women's lives in Latin America.

THE ISSUE OF CULTURAL IDENTITY

How can Jewish–Latin American fiction be compared to the literature created by Jews in the United States or by modern Israeli writers? First and foremost, it is obvious that while writers such as Saul Bellow, Philip Roth, and Cynthia Ozick have acquired a wide international readership, most of the Jewish writers included in this anthology remain unknown, appreciated only by a rather small audience, primarily Jewish. The bridge toward internationalization has been crossed only by a few, among them Moacyr Scliar, Isaac Goldemberg, and two or three others not included in this anthology, such as Jacobo Timerman (b. 1923), the Argentine newspaper editor and journalist who wrote *Prisoner Without a Name, Cell Without a Number,* a personal account of the repression by the military junta during the 1970s. But as a literary tradition, Jewish writing south of the Rio Grande still has little echo. Why? The explanation is complex.

Until the sixties (and perhaps until much more recently) European and North American readers hardly knew anything about Latin American letters in general. It was when Borges won the Publisher's Prize and his narratives began to be translated into many languages that others began to pay attention. A narrative boom followed: in 1967 Miguel Angel Asturias, the Guatemalan author of the acclaimed *Men of Maize,* won the Nobel Prize for literature, and his contribution was followed by García Márquez's *One Hundred Years of Solitude*, Fuentes's *A Change of Skin*, and Vargas Llosa's *The Green House*. What caused this literary phenomenon? As Emir Rodríguez Monegal forcefully argued, there's little doubt that political, social, and economic factors were involved: the end of World War II brought with it the collapse of Western colonialism, and nations in Africa, Asia, and Oceania emerged as new politically independent realities.[16] It suddenly became clear that high culture was not the property of a handful of European intellectuals but could be found as well on the periphery—the so-called Third World. In different parts of the globe but with similar goals, V. S. Naipaul, Wole Soyinka, Derek Walcott, and Chinua Achebe, to name only a few, published their works, and their "marginal" voices began to be heard. The list of new literary voices included Latin Americans, yet only a few of them gained the public's attention in Europe and the United States. The less avant-garde themes and styles were regarded as unimportant, and those writers who were not considered "mainstream" never entered the international arena. Such became the fate of Jewish writers, along with other minorities, in countries like Mexico, Brazil, and Argentina. World readership was interested in "standard," stereotyped views of the region, not in the sum of its heterogeneous parts. The day will come when Asian, Italian, and black narrative voices emerging from Latin America will also be heard, just as today Maxine Hong Kingston and Toni Morrison are recognized as North American writers of excellence.

Because of the tragedy that befell European Jews during the Second World War, but also as a result of the creation of the state of Israel and the dynamism of the American Jews in the United States, the political and cultural balance of power in world Jewry shifted its headquarters from Vienna and Berlin to New York City and Tel-Aviv. Thus, after 1948, early twentieth-century writers such as Abraham Cahan, Michael Gold, Daniel Fuchs, and Henry Roth in the United States, and Sh. Y. Agnon in Israel, gained recognition as important Jewish literary voices. In setting the scene for successors like Saul Bellow, Philip Roth, Amos Oz, and A. B. Yehoshua, North American fiction is particularly important. Stories and novels such as "Defender of the Faith" and "Eli the Fanatic" by Roth, *Dangling Man* and *Herzog* by Bellow, *The Assistant* and *Idiots First* by Bernard Malamud, and "Envy: or, Yiddish in America," "The Pagan Rabbi," and "The Shawl" by Ozick, together with other works by Grace Paley, E. L. Doctorow, and Stanley Elkin, are essential in understanding world Jewish literature today. Their themes have transcended the particulars of Jewish identity to confront universal human concerns. In 1967, Philip Rahv argued, "The homogenization resulting from speaking of [North American—

Jewish writers] as if they comprised some kind of literary faction or school is bad critical practice in that it is based on simplistic assumptions concerning the literary process as a whole as well as the nature of [United States] Jewry, which, all appearances to the contrary, is very far from constituting a unitary group in its cultural manifestation."[17]

And today one can indeed speak of the long list of Jewish writers in the United States not as specifically Jewish, but as mainstream writers who happen to be of Jewish origin. They have managed to jump the gap from the ethnic to the universal through their exploration of issues of selfhood, acculturation, memory, and history. Thus they transcend simply parochial interests, especially as these themes are universalized in an increasingly multicultural North American society. The broad success of Jewish writers from the 1950s through the 1970s (now somewhat eclipsed by the increasing interest in the cultural traditions of black, Hispanic, and Asian minorities) was possible because the North American audience could identify with Jewish artists, as with other ethnic writers, and pursue their development. Moreover, the translating process their works undergo, to be read in Berlin or Rome or Buenos Aires, itself further diminishes their narrowness of outlook. But they are beyond national borders. In part, their success is due to a voracious secular readership, made up of upwardly mobile, well-educated urban Jews in the United States, always eager to explore their identity as cosmopolitan citizens in a technological age. In fact, the heterogeneity that Philip Rahv talks about, together with the relatively large size and cultural comfort of North American Jewry as members of an open, democratic society, has made it possible for their artists and intellectuals to mature and overcome their parochialism. And the fact that Yiddish, both in daily life as well as in journalism and literature, was quickly replaced by English, fundamental to the absorption of any citizen into the so-called North American melting pot, was also a catalyst.

The Jewish writers in Latin America have to be appreciated from an altogether different perspective. First, against Rahv's argument, they indeed form a literary faction or school. Unlike other North American Jewish writers, many partially trace their aesthetic influences directly to nineteenth-century Yiddish writers such as Mendele Mokher Sforim and Sholem Aleichem. And although their idiom is everybody's Spanish, the public at large, even after the contributions of Borges or Vargas Llosa, remains essentially uninterested in Jewish themes. Besides, there is a long tradition of anti-Semitism in Hispanic countries, largely supported by the Church but also, indirectly, by various governments. Still in some minds, the Jew remains an atavistic witness and victimizer of Jesus Christ and an unwelcome member of society. Contrary to their counterparts in the United States, the Latin American Jewish communities are monolithic. They refuse to assimilate, and the broader society also rejects their complete integration. Thus, the Jewish writer's cultural manifestation is either within the community, in which case there is little space for self-criticism, or he or she sooner or later rejects the community, choosing to live outside the country, or at least far from its circumscribed borders. The processes of secularization and acculturation of the Jews in Brazil, Argentina, Mexico, and elsewhere in the hemisphere, because of the unstable nature of the region, do not result from a democratic, free-spirited dynamic. On the contrary, they have evolved dramatically and in the face of immense obstacles. Whereas Roth and Bellow have a secure, if now shrinking following, the number of Latin American readers interested today in the works of Gerchunoff, or even Scliar, is too small to encourage the literary development of those who follow in their tradition.

The case of Israeli writers, of course, is totally dissimilar. Since the founding of the state of Israel, there is a general recognition that the new cultural reality is not a form of Jewish identity but rather a modern national identity. Following the allegorical prose of Agnon, with its Talmudic, biblical, and folkloric resonance, and since independence in 1948, novelists such as A. B. Yehoshua and Amos Oz have taken as their duty to describe, to reflect, and comprehend today's Middle Eastern reality, and especially the Israeli one. Thus, in a moment of crisis and seemingly permanent political turmoil, their mimetic inclination has been toward psychological realism. The Israeli public, highly literate and avid to "escape" the daily routine through the imagination, reads these literary works with enormous interest. Yiddish, once a challenger to become the national tongue, is now the property of an old, dying generation, unknown or ignored by the young and rejected by the intellectuals. Hebrew, with its amazing rebirth, carries pride and denotes courage and renewal. More than anything, what really is at stake now, when it comes to linguistic battles in Israel, is the question of the Palestinian writers' relationship to Hebrew as their own idiom.[18] In terms of the selection of realist topics, while some writers, among them Aharon Appelfeld and David Grossman, trace their roots to pre-Holocaust European culture, and indirectly to Yiddish, the majority has buried the names of Sholem Aleichem and his successors, considering them curiosities of the Diaspora past. Their political life, the permanent threat of Arab-Jewish conflict, the daily contact with Palestinian aspirations, draw their full attention. Being Jewish is not the issue anymore, but rather the quality, and future, of Israeli culture. The collective identity has been reshaped on a concrete, material level. Similar to the personal and cultural transformation of Saul Bellow from Jew into North American, Oz, Yehoshua, and others are now Israeli, not Jewish, writers.

Will the time come when Latin America will be truly democratic and pluralistic, less intolerant of the particular? Perhaps. Meanwhile, the Jews, in Octavio Paz's view "the few" in the universe of "the many," remain the "other voice" that refuses to be devoured by the monstrous whole. Their labyrinthine worldview has been recorded in literature, where they have successfully built, in spite of the climate of revolution and fantasy, a room of their own, a "tropical synagogue" like that of Moacyr Scliar's *The Gods of Raquel*—a hybrid creation intertwining symbols from the Old World and the New.

NOTES

1. The data is taken from Sergio Della Pergola's "Demographic Trends in Latin American Jewry," in *The Jewish Presence in Latin America*, ed. Judith Laikin Eikin and Gilbert W. Merkx (Boston and London: Allen & Unwin, 1987), 85–113. The last official census given by the author is that of 1982.

2. See my book *Imagining Columbus: The Literary Voyage* (New York: Twayne-Macmillan, 1993).

3. In *The Jewish Presence in Latin America*, 71–84.

4. Naomi Lindstrom, *Jewish Issues in Argentine Literature: From Gerchunoff to Szichman* (Columbia: University of Missouri Press, 1989), 59.

5. Leonardo Senkman, *La identidad judía en la literatura argentina* (Buenos Aires: Pardés, 1983).

6. Alberto Gerchunoff, "Prólogo a *Renacimiento de Israel* de Ludwig Lewisohn" (Buenos Aires, Editorial Israel, 1937). Reprinted in *El pino y la palmera* (Buenos Aires: Sociedad Hebráica Argentina, 1952), 75–76.

7. Juan Pinto, *Pasión y suma de la expresión argentina: Literatura, cultura, región* (Buenos Aires: Editorial Huemul, 1970).

8. Stanislaw Lem, "Unitas Oppositorum: The Prose of Jorge Luis Borges" (first published April 1971), *Microworlds* (New York: Harcourt Brace Jovanovich, 1984).

9. "I, Jew," in *Borges, A Reader*, edited by Emir Rodríguez Monegal (New York: E. P. Dutton, 1979), 65. See also Edna Aizenberg's *The Aleph Weaver: Biblical, Kabbalistic and Judaic Elements in Borges* (Potomac, Md.: Scripta Humanistica, 1984). I have made extensive use of the latter in this introduction.

10. See Ilan Stavans, *Prontuario* (Mexico: Joaquín Mortiz, 1992), 105–12.

11. Robert DiAntonio, "Redemption and Rebirth on a Safe Shore: The Holocaust in Contemporary Brazilian Fiction," *Hispania* 74, 4 (December 1991): 879.

12. See the biographical and critical study by Earl Fitz, *Clarice Lispector* (New York: Twayne, 1985).

13. Gregory Rabassa, in *The Apple in the Dark* (Austin: Texas University Press, 1986), x.

14. See Gershon Shaked, "Kafka, Jewish Heritage, and Hebrew Literature," *The Shadows Within* (The Jewish Publication Society, 1987), 3–22.

15. *Present Tense* 15, 2 (1988): 24–30.

16. See the introduction to vol. 2 of his *Borzoi Anthology of Latin American Literature*, edited by Emir Rodríguez Monegal, with Thomas Colchie (New York: Alfred A. Knopf, 1984), xiv.

17. Philip Rahv, Introduction to *A Malamud Reader* (New York: Farrar, Straus & Giroux, 1967), vii.

18. See my "Cynthia Ozick and Anton Shammas: Duel Over the Hebrew Language," *Jewish Frontier* LVI, 4 (1989): 7–13.

ARGENTINA

ALBERTO GERCHUNOFF
(1 8 8 4 – 1 9 5 0)

CAMACHO'S
WEDDING FEAST

*S*et at the turn of the century in Rajíl, a shtetl-*like agricultural town in La Pampa, this lyrical story, first published as part of* The Jewish Gauchos *(1910) and among the best in the volume, evokes the often explosive relationship between gentiles and Jews in the southern hemisphere. It fuses the universal theme of the stolen bride with a narrative voice and incident borrowed from* Don Quixote. *Through the tale's folkloristic tone, which finds pleasure in describing the details of pastoral life as well as Jewish rituals and tradition, the Russian-born author, considered the grandfather of Jewish–Latin American literature, advances his ill-fated view of Argentina as the true Promised Land.*

FOR TWO WEEKS NOW, THE PEOPLE OF THE ENTIRE DISTRICT HAD BEEN EXPECT-antly waiting for Pascual Liske's wedding day. Pascual was the *rich* Liske's son. The family lived in Espindola and, naturally enough, the respectable people of the colonies were looking forward to the ceremony and feast. To judge by the early signs, the feast was to be exceptional. It was well known in Rajíl that the groom's family had purchased eight demijohns of wine, a barrel of beer, and numerous bottles of soft drinks. Kelner's wife had discov-ered this when she happened to come on the Liskes' cart, stopped near the breakwater. The reins had broken, and the Liskes' hired man was working frantically to replace them.

"The soft drinks were *rose* colored," she told the neighbors. "Yes!" she said, looking directly at the doubting Shochet's wife.* "Yes, they were rose colored, and each bottle had a waxen seal on it."

Everyone agreed old man Liske's fortune could stand that kind of spending. In addition to the original land and oxen that he'd gotten from the Administration, Liske had many cows and horses. Last year's harvest alone had brought him thousands of pesos, and he could well afford to marry off his son in style without touching his principal.

Everyone further agreed that the bride deserved this kind of a wedding. Raquel was one of the most beautiful girls in the district, if not in the whole world. She was tall, with straw-blond hair so fine and full it suggested mist; her eyes were so blue they made one's breath catch. She was tall and lithe, but her simple print dresses showed the full curving loveliness of a beautiful body. An air of shyness and a certain peevishness became her because they seemed to protect her loveliness.

Many of the colonists had tried to win her—the haughty young clerk of the Administration as well as all the young men in Villaguay and thereabouts—but none had achieved a sympathetic response. Pascual Liske had been the most persistent of these suitors, but certainly not the most favored, at first. In spite of his perseverance and his gifts, Raquel did not like him. She felt depressed and bored because Pascual never spoke of anything but seedings, livestock and harvests. The only young man she had seemed to favor was a young admirer from the San Gregorio colony, Gabriel Camacho. She had gone out dancing with him during the many times he used to come to visit.

Her family had insisted she accept Pascual and the marriage had been arranged.

On the day of the feast, the invited families had gathered at the breakwater before Espindola. A long line of carts, crowded with men and women, was pointed toward the colony. It was a spring afternoon, and the flowering country looked beautiful in the lowering rays of the sun. Young men rode up and down the line on their spirited ponies, calling and signaling to the girls when the mothers were looking elsewhere. In their efforts to catch a girl's eye, they set their ponies to capering in true Gaucho style. In their eagerness, some even proposed races and other contests.

Shochet is a ritual slaughterer—Ed.

Russian and Jewish songs were being sung in all parts of the caravan, the voices fresh and happy. At other points, the songs of this, their new country, could be heard being sung in a language that few understood.

At last, the caravan moved into the village. The long line of heavy carts, being gently pulled by the oxen, had the look of a primitive procession. The carts stopped at different houses, and the visitors went inside to finish their preparations. Then, at the appointed time, all the invited guests came out together and began to make their way to the groom's house.

Arriving at Liske's, they found that rumors of the fabulous preparations had not been exaggerated. A wide pavilion stood facing the house with decorative lanterns hanging inside on high poles, masked by flowered branches. Under the canvas roof were long tables covered with white cloths and countless covered dishes and bowls that the flies buzzed about hopelessly. Old Liske wore his black velvet frock coat—a relic of his prosperous years in Bessarabia—as well as a newly added silk scarf of yellow, streaked with blue. With hands in his pockets, he moved from group to group, being consciously pleasant to everyone and speaking quite freely of the ostentation and unusual luxury of the feast. To minimize the importance of it all, he would mention the price, in a lowered voice, and then, as if to explain his part in this madness, would shrug his shoulders, saying, "After all, he's my only son."

The Hebrew words, *ben yachid* (only son), express this sentiment very well, and they were heard frequently as many guests expressed their praises of the fat Pascual. Even his bumpkin qualities were cited as assets in the extraordinary rash of praise.

His mother was dressed in a showy frock with winged sleeves, and wore a green kerchief spread over her full shoulders. Moving quickly, in spite of her ample roundness, she went from place to place, talking and nodding to everyone in the growing crowd that was soon becoming as big and fantastic as the fiesta.

Under the side eave of the house, a huge caldron filled with chickens simmered over a fire, while at the side, in the deeper shadow, hung a row of dripping roasted geese. In front of these were trays with the traditional stuffed fish stacked for cooling. What the guests admired more than the chicken-filled caldron, the roast geese, stuffed fish, and the calf's ribs that the cooks were preparing were the demijohns of wine, the huge cask of beer and, above all else, the bottles of soft drinks whose roseate color the sun played on. Yes, it was so. Just as they'd heard in Rajíl, there were the bottles of rose-colored soft drinks with red seals on the bottles.

The music was supplied by an accordion and guitar, and the two musicians were already essaying some popular Jewish pieces. Voices in the crowd were tentatively humming along with them.

The bride was preparing for the ceremony in the house next to Liske's. Friends were dressing her, and her crown of sugar was already well smudged from constant rearrangement. Raquel was very sad. No matter how much the other girls reminded her of her wonderful luck—to marry a man like Pascual wasn't something that happened every day—she remained depressed. She was silent most of the time, and answered with sighs or short nods. She was a normally shy girl, but today she seemed truly sad. Those eyes that were usually so wide and clear now seemed as clouded as her forehead.

In talking about the guests, someone told Raquel that Gabriel had come with other people from San Gregorio. She grew more depressed at hearing his name and, as she put on the bridal veil, two big tears ran down her cheeks and fell on her satin blouse.

Everyone knew the cause of her weeping. Raquel and Gabriel had come to an understanding months ago, and Jacobo—that wily little know-it-all—had claimed he saw them kissing in the shadow of a paradise tree on the eve of the Day of Atonement. . . .

Pascual's mother finally arrived at the bride's house and, in accordance with custom, congratulated the bride and kissed her noisily. Her voice screeched as she called to let the ceremony begin.

Raquel said nothing. She shrugged in despair and stood hopelessly while the group of friends gathered at her back and picked up her lace-bordered train. The future father-in-law arrived with the Rabbi and the procession started.

Outside Liske's house, the guests were gathered about the tables, while inside the house Pascual, who was dressed in black, waited with friends and the father of the bride. When they heard the handclapping outside, they went out to the grounds and the ceremony began.

Pascual walked over to the canopy held up by couples of young men and women, and stood under it. He was joined immediately by his betrothed, who came escorted by the two sponsors. Rabbi Nisen began the blessings, and offered the ritual cup to the bride and groom. Then the bride began her seven turns around the man, accompanied by the sponsors. As she finished, an old lady called out that there had only been six, and another turn was made. The Rabbi read the marriage contract, that conformed entirely with the sacred laws of Israel. He sang the nuptial prayers again. The ceremony ended with the symbolic breaking of the cup. An old man placed it on the ground, and Pascual stepped on it with force enough to break a rock.

The crowd pressed in to congratulate the couple. Her friends gathered around the bride, embracing and kissing her, but Raquel was still depressed. She accepted the congratulations and good wishes in silence. Other guests gathered around the long table and began to toast and drink.

Old Liske proposed some dancing before they sat down to supper, and he himself began by moving into the first steps of the characteristic Jewish piece, "the happy dance," to the accompaniment of the accordion and guitar. At the head of the long table, the bride and groom stood together and watched the growing bustle without saying a word to each other. Facing them, standing very erect and pale, was Gabriel.

The guests called for the bride and groom to dance. Pascual frowned anxiously and shook his head. He did not dance. The calls and applause receded, and everyone stood waiting in embarrassment. Gabriel stepped forward suddenly and offered his arm to the bride. The accordion and guitar began a popular Jewish polka.

Gabriel tried to outdo himself, and he was a superb dancer. At one point he said something to Raquel, and she looked at him in surprise and grew still paler. People were beginning to whisper and move away. Israel Kelner had taken the arm of the Shochet as they both stepped away from the watching circle.

"Gabriel shouldn't have done this," Kelner said. "Everybody knows that he's in love with Raquel, and that she's *not* in love with her husband."

The Shochet pulled at his beard and smiled. "I don't want to offend anyone," he said. "I'm a friend of Liske's and he's a religious man—but Pascual is a beast. Did you see how mixed up he got when he was repeating the *hare-iad* pledge during the ceremony? Believe me, Rabbi Israel, I feel sorry for the girl. She's so beautiful and fine. . . ."

Little Jacobo took Rebecca aside and talked to her in Argentine *criollo*—he was the most gaucho of the Jews, as demonstrated now by his complete gaucho dress. "Listen, *Negrita*," he began. "Something's going to happen here."

"A fight?" Rebecca whispered with interest.

"Just what I'm telling you. I was in San Gregorio this morning. Met Gabriel there. He asked me if I was going to the wedding—this one, of course. I said yes, I was, and he asked me about doing something later. . . ."

"A race?" Rebecca interrupted. "You mean to say that you made a bet with Gabriel? Oh, you men! And they said that he was heartbroken!"

"Oh, well," Jacobo said. He shrugged his shoulders. "As they say: Men run to races."

As night began to fall, the paper lanterns were lit, and many guests walked off a distance to see the effect of the lights. It was a special privilege of the rich to have such lights, and the last time they'd been seen here was during the visit of Colonel Goldschmith, a representative of the European Jewish Committee.

The next item was dinner, a banquet that bars description. The guests were seated and the bride and groom served the "golden broth," the consecrative dish of the newlyweds. Then the platters of chicken, duck and fish began to circulate; and the wine was poured to a complete and unanimous chorus of praise directed to the hostess.

"I've never eaten such tasty stuffed fish."

"Where could you ever get such roast geese as this?" the Shochet asked.

Rabbi Moisés Ornstein delivered the eulogy and added: "I must say that no one cooks as well as Madam Liske. Whoever tastes her dishes knows that they are a superior person's."

Fritters of meat and rice, wrapped in vine leaves, were served next, while more beer and wine quickened the spirits of the guests.

The bride excused herself, saying that she had to change her dress. She left the party accompanied by her friends. Her mother-in-law had started to go with them, but Jacobo stopped her. "Madam Liske!" he said. "Sit down and listen to your praises. Sit down and hear what we think of this wonderful banquet. We'll be mad if you leave," he said, when she seemed reluctant to stop. "We're enjoying ourselves very much and we want to share this with you."

"Let me go, my boy," she said. "I have to help my daughter-in-law."

"Rebecca will help her. Sit down. Sit down. Rebecca!" Jacobo turned to shout. "Go and help the bride!"

The old lady sat down—everyone about had joined in the urging—and Jacobo brought her a glass of wine so that they could drink a toast.

"When one has a son like yours," the Shochet said to Madam Liske, "one should be glad."

The toasts were offered and drunk, and this clinking of glasses, lusty singing, and music could be heard over all the grounds. The sky was full of stars, the atmosphere lightly tinged with clover and the scent of hay. In the nearby pasture, the cows mooed and the light wind stirred the leaves.

Jacobo got up and excused himself. "I have to see about my pony," he explained. "I think he might need a blanket."

"I'll look after my mare," Gabriel said, as he stood up to go with him.

They moved away from the group, and Jacobo took Gabriel's arm: "Listen, the bay is saddled and waiting by the palisade," he said. "The *boyero*'s kid is watching him and the gate is open. At the first turn there's a sulky all set. The Lame One is watching there. Tell me, have you got a gun?"

Gabriel did not seem to hear this last point. He patted Jacobo's arm and started to walk towards the palisade. After a few steps, he turned to look back. "And how will Raquel get away from the girls in there?"

"Don't worry about that. Rebecca's there."

When the girls who were with the bride did return to the party, Madam Liske asked for her daughter-in-law. "She's coming right away with Rebecca," they told her. Then Rebecca returned alone, and gave the old lady still another excuse. Jacobo was doing his best to distract Madam Liske with toasts. Others took it up, and there was a great clinking of glasses and mumblings of toasts. The musicians continued to play and the guests to eat and drink. The jugs of wine were being refilled continuously, and no one's glass was ever low.

Pascual, the groom, looked fat and solemn and said nothing. From time to time, he would dart a quick look at the bride's empty chair. The gallop of a horse was heard at that moment, and then, soon after, the sounds of a sulky starting off.

Jacobo whispered into Rebecca's ear: "That's them, isn't it?"

"Yes," the girl whispered back, "they were leaving when I came away."

The continued absence of the bride was worrying her mother-in-law and, without saying anything, she slipped into the house to see. She came out immediately.

"Rebecca, have you seen Raquel?" she said.

"I left her in the house, Señora. Isn't she there?"

"She's not."

"That's funny. . . ."

The old lady spoke to her husband and to her son, Pascual. The guests were beginning to whisper among themselves. They saw that something had gone wrong. The accordion and guitar went silent. The guests began to stand up; some glasses were tipped over, but no one paid any attention. A few of the guests moved towards the house. Others asked: "Is it the bride? Has something happened to the bride?"

The Shochet of Rajíl asked his friend and counterpart from Karmel about the point of sacred law if it was true that the bride had fled.

"Do you think she has?" the Shochet of Karmel asked.

"It's possible. Anything is possible in these situations."

"Well, I think that divorce would be the next step. The girl would be free, as would be her husband. It's the common course."

Meanwhile, the excitement was growing all around them. Old Liske grabbed the Gaucho's little son. "Did you see anything out there? Out there on the road?" he said.

"Yes. Out there, on the road to San Gregorio. I saw a sulky, with Gabriel—he was driving it—and there was a girl sitting with him."

"He's kidnapped her!" Madam Liske screamed. Her voice was close to hysteria. "Kidnapped her!"

Shouts and quick talking started all over the grounds now. Most of the crowd were genuinely shocked and surprised. When old Liske turned to abuse the father of the Gaucho boy, the man stood up to him, and they were soon wrestling and rolling in the center of pushing and shouting guests. The table was overturned, and spilled wine and broken glass added to the excitement. The Shochet of Rajíl mounted a chair and shouted for order. What had happened was a disgrace, he said, a punishment from God, but fighting and shouting would not ease it any.

"She's an adulteress!" shouted the enraged Liske, as he sought to break out of restraining hands. "An infamous adulteress!"

"She is not!" the Shochet answered him. "She would be," he said, "if she had left her husband 'after one day, at least, after the marriage,' as our law so clearly says it. This is the law of God, you know, and there is no other way but that they be divorced. Pascual is a fine, honorable young man, but if she doesn't love him, she can't be made to live under his roof."

The Shochet went on in his usually eloquent and wise way, and he cited similar cases acknowledged by the most illustrious rabbis and scholars. In Jerusalem, the sacred capital, there had occurred a similar case, and Rabbi Hillel had declared in favor of the girl. At the end, the Shochet turned to Pascual: "In the name of our laws, Pascual, I ask that you grant a divorce to Raquel and that you declare, here and now, that you accept it for yourself."

Pascual scratched his head and looked sad. Then, in a tearful voice, he accepted the Shochet's proposal.

The crowd grew quiet and the guests soon began to leave, one by one, some murmuring, some hiding a smile.

Well, as you can see, my patient readers, there are fierce, arrogant Gauchos, wife-stealers and Camachos, as well as the most learned and honorable of rabbinical scholars in the little Jewish colony where I learned to love the Argentine sky and felt a part of its wonderful earth. This story I've told—with more detail than art—is a true one, just as I'm sure the original story of Camacho's feast is true. May I die this instant if I've dared to add the slightest bit of invention to the marvelous story.

I'd like very much to add some verses—as was done to the original Camacho story—but God has denied me that talent. I gave you the tale in its purest truth, and if you want couplets, add them yourself in your most gracious style. Don't forget *my* name, however—just as our gracious Master Don Miguel de Cervantes Saavedra remembered the name of Cide Hamete Benegeli and gave him all due credit for the original Camacho story.

And if the exact, accurate telling of this tale has pleased you, don't send me any golden doubloons—here, they don't even buy bread and water. Send me some golden drachmas or, if not, I'd appreciate a carafe of Jerusalem wine from the vineyards my ancestors planted as they sang the praises of Jehovah.

May He grant you wealth and health, the gifts I ask for myself.

Translated by Prudencio de Pereda

ISIDORO BLAISTEN

(b. 1 9 3 3)

UNCLE FACUNDO

Like E. L. Doctorow's "Willie" and Jorge Luis Borges's "Emma Zunz," this story by the author of South of Dublin (1980) is about revenge. Told from the viewpoint of a candid boy, it details the unsettling of happy domestic life when an unexpected visitor suddenly arrives. Facundo, a mysterious relative attached to Entre Ríos, like Rajíl one of the Jewish agricultural colonies in Argentina in the early decades of the century, drinks and gambles. And the morality of the apparently functional family of four that reluctantly embraces him in Buenos Aires is immediately transfixed. Blaisten devotes this surrealist exploration to the conflict between older and younger generations, between rural and urban settlements, bourgeois assimilation and marginality.

JUST SO THAT YOU CAN SEE WHAT MY FAMILY WAS REALLY LIKE BEFORE WE decided to kill off Uncle Facundo—I mean, before Uncle Facundo arrived— let me tell you what each of us used to say.

Mother would say:

Dogs can always tell when their master is about to die, there's nothing worse than having an operation when you're running a fever, penicillin gobbles up your red corpuscles, she'd say, children dehydrate in summer, she'd say, boys are usually on their mother's side and girls on their father's, she'd say, children of split marriages are always sad, she'd say, Jewish doctors are the best, she'd say, mothers always love the wicked sons more, she'd say, those who have the most are those who spend the least, and some poor soul . . . she'd say, to think he walked around with that cancer inside him, she'd say, wallpaper collects bugs, she'd say, in the old days people used to die of the flu.

Father would say:

Swimming is the only real sport, the Germans lost the war in Russia because of the cold, soldiers and sailors have unfaithful wives, and travelling salesmen as well, nothing shaves as close as an old-fashioned razor, a good glass of red wine is great in the winter, beer in the summer, thin women are really hot, red wine should never be drunk cold, black tobacco is healthier than blond tobacco, no doctor operates on his own wife, all that the workers want is one hot meal a day, they go begging in the streets and have a savings account in the bank, thieves should have their hands chopped off and be hung in the public square, the best fertilizer is horse shit, the only money is in farming, barbecues should be eaten standing up, countryfolk have no problems, a few potatoes, a couple of eggs, kill a chicken and that's that.

My sister would say:

There's nothing nicer than going to the movies when it's raining. A lonely bird will die of a broken heart. Blond people go red in the sun, dark people don't. They go from man to man and then. I hate films that make you cry. I adore studying and learning and studying and—. I won't be like those who get married in white.

I would say:

You really have to take your hat off to the German economy. All Japanese are traitors. Swimming softens your muscles. Grumpy people get over their anger very quickly. No steady girlfriends till I get my degree. I want to study. No politics in class.

This is what my family was like until Uncle Facundo arrived. Father worked at the railroad, Traffic Bureau, Retiro Terminal. He would get up at five in the morning, sip his *mate* while reading the paper from beginning to end, and then walk the seven blocks to Saavedra Station. Mother looked after the house, watered the plants, and watched television. My sister did decorative wood-burning, had a job as a teacher, and studied to be a social worker.

I was studying economics and working as an accountant's assistant at Bonplart Textiles.

I remember that when we were kids, my mother and father would talk about Uncle Facundo in whispers. When I or my sister came near, they would interrupt their conversation.

On summer nights father would bring out the wicker chair for mother, the low stool for himself, the Viennese chair, which I used to turn round, for me, and the deck chair for my sister.

On those nights it always happened that when father, after commenting on the state of the backyard wall, would tell us again about how they had published his letter to the editor, mother—I don't know why—would talk about Uncle Facundo.

Uncle Facundo was mother's brother, and also the brother of Aunt Fermina. Neither father nor I nor my sister had ever met him. When mother got engaged to father, Uncle Facundo had already disappeared. When we were old enough to understand, mother told us that Uncle Facundo had got married in a town called Casilda and that his wife had died under mysterious circumstances. Evil gossip and Aunt Fermina said that Uncle Facundo had done away with her.

Uncle Facundo was the black sheep in mother's family. Aunt Fermina said that she no longer thought of him as her brother and that his behaviour had sent grandma to an early grave.

One day we received the following telegram from Uncle Facundo:

> Dear brothers, sisters, nephews and nieces:
> Arriving Friday 10. International train, Posadas.

Father was against allowing him into the house but mother said that in spite of everything he was her brother, and that the poor boy must be feeling very lonely, and that if he had chosen our home instead of Aunt Fermina's, there was probably a good reason.

So on Friday 10 at a quarter to midnight, we all sat expectantly in Chacarita Station. The train was almost two hours late and while we waited in the restaurant we fell into an argument.

Father said that Uncle Facundo was a bum, and that if he wanted to stay for a few days with us, fine, but that he shouldn't imagine that father was going to keep him for the rest of his life. Mother and my sister said that as soon as a man is driven to the edge, someone will step on his fingers rather than come to the rescue. I said nothing. Then the train arrived.

We had difficulty finding Uncle Facundo. The only one who knew him was mother, so we just stared into her face. At last she saw him.

He was standing against a column, clutching a parcel that looked like a large shoe box.

And then, as I stared at him, I had the impression that I had always known him—all my life. Uncle Facundo gave everyone that impression. And when we were next to him, he lifted mother into the air and kissed her, hugged father till he made him cough, took Angelita in his arms as if she were his bride, and me, he just put a hand on my shoulder without saying anything, a conniving sparkling look in his eyes.

"Come on, let's have a drink!" he shouted. "I want to show you a few things."

Father said that first we should get the luggage. But Uncle Facundo had brought no luggage—only the shoe box.

In the restaurant he ordered white wine for everyone. Mother and father glanced at each other. With the exception of father (just a little with lots of water) no one at home drinks at all. But my sister, who seemed to be walking on thin air, desperately wanted to see what Uncle Facundo had brought for her. The truth is, we were all very much intrigued, and we gulped down the wine and even had a second round. Mother seemed transformed, laughing out loud like mad, especially when Uncle Facundo lifted the lid off the box and placed in her hands a Paraguayan shawl knitted in *ñanduti* lace by the Indians. It was beautiful, done in wonderful colours. It was something mother had longed for all her life.

And that night Uncle Facundo charmed us all. We each got things which we had always longed for. Father received a box of Havana cigars. Havanas from Havana. The best, the most expensive, not the stinking cheroots Michelini brings him from Brazil. Havanas.

He gave my sister a ring and a matching necklace. The links fitted one inside the other, growing or diminishing in size, and when they all came together you could see an aquamarine hanging between the gold and silver. My sister jumped up and kissed him.

When he gave me the penknife I think I felt faint. It was a Solingen blade, with a silver handle inlaid with gold, wrought with the finest craftsmanship I have ever seen, either before or since.

We had another round of drinks. Father paid and we drove home in a taxi. And that night no one, except Uncle Facundo, managed to sleep.

That was the first battle Uncle Facundo won against us. Sometimes I think, what good did it do him? But I also wonder what good did it do us to have killed him. What good did it do mother to have smothered him with a pillow, father to have strangled him, myself to have dug the little penknife between his sternum and the main arteries, while my sister cut his veins with a disposable razor blade?

What good did it all do us, I wonder, if Uncle Facundo is still there, embedded in the backyard soil, sideways, like a swimmer, shrunk perhaps, or perhaps leaving nothing but a hollow shape there where his flesh once was, while the cement continues to bake in the sun, and Uncle Facundo's spirit haunts the wall. . . . But all that was later, much later, when we had no choice but to kill him.

On the day after that memorable night, Uncle Facundo was the first to get out of bed. And this also became a memorable event, because in all the time he stayed with us, up to the very day of his death (and especially on that day) it was necessary to shake him for hours to wake him.

It was a Saturday. Uncle Facundo went into the backyard and, next to the wall that was to be his tomb, found a few empty tar tins, and a bunch of tools. With those he built mother a kind of shelving for the den, and then went inside to wake her up with a *mate*.

At midday, when we all got up and saw what Uncle Facundo had done, we expressed admiration for his handicraft; and I remember he said that real work was the work done with the hands, and that all the rest, papers and numbers, were a charade and chicken-shit.

Lunch was like a party. Uncle Facundo told us all about the time he had harvested rice in Entre Ríos and stories about the ranches he had worked on in Corrientes. But the funniest part was when he told us what he had done when he had worked as a gravedigger in Casilda. At that point, he sent my sister out to buy two more bottles of wine. Mother, her eyes gleaming, suggested a game of bingo, but Uncle Facundo said poker was better, and we all looked at each other because none of us knew how to play and we only had a pack of Spanish cards.

Mother asked what poker cards looked like. Uncle Facundo told her, and mother rummaged around in the closet and appeared with an unopened box that had a set of dominoes, a top, two packs of French cards and plastic chips, which she had bought on sale at Gath & Chaves. "Are these the right ones?" she asked, taking off the cellophane wrapping. Luckily they were, and Uncle Facundo taught us to play. Poker turned out to be the most wonderful, prodigious game we had ever played. At first the chips had no set value, but then we agreed they would be worth ten pesos each, and then fifty, and then a hundred, and father sent my sister for two more bottles of wine. Uncle Facundo called after her that two of rum would be even better. As Angelita was about to leave, Aunt Fermina appeared.

When Aunt Fermina saw what was lying on the table, she almost died. She didn't even bother to greet Uncle Facundo after so many years. She insulted him, called him names. Mother, who seemed a little drunk, spoke up for him. Father shook his head as in a daze, saying, "Peace, my dears, peace."

Suddenly father stood up and slapped my sister across the face from the other side of the table, scattering the chips and the money, and yelling at the top of his lungs: "So what are you waiting for, you idiot! Go get that bloody rum!"

It was the very first time I saw my father hit my sister.

Angelita ran away to the shops, and Uncle Facundo got up and went into the backyard, and stood by the wall, smoking, watching the stars that were beginning to come out.

Now that I think of it, it seems as if Uncle Facundo had a marked fondness for that wall in which he's now trapped, sideways and surrounded by bricks, the mouth and eyes full of cement. . . . Perhaps there's only air around the skeleton. . . . Well, you'd have to tap the wall to see.

In the end Aunt Fermina left, and at first no one seemed willing to eat a thing. But then Uncle Facundo started telling jokes, and sent my sister out for two more bottles, and taught mother how to cook *saltimboquis alla romana,* and we all had a royal banquet, drank the two bottles of rum and the wine, and went on playing poker till six in the morning.

Next morning the neighbours complained about the noise, and father, who skipped work for the first time in his life, almost hit Michelini.

And that's how it all began. Father and Uncle Facundo started going every Saturday and Sunday to the racetrack, and mother would give them her savings to bet on the horses.

Angelita brought home her girlfriends, also teachers, and Uncle Facundo taught them how to dance tango and then took them to bed with him. Mother was as happy as a lark and at night she'd go downtown with a young poet. Uncle Facundo approved wholeheartedly, saying it was healthy and part of life and that in life things had to be killed off by living them to the hilt, that beauty and sex should go hand in hand, and that people's real problem—when there were no wars to worry about—was that they were all bored out of their minds. That's why—he would say—neighbours stand at the door all day long living the life of others, that gossip was a form of frustrated romanticism, and that people gobbled up crime and pornography because they needed them, because they supplanted life, because real life was a whirlwind.

I brought over the guys from the university to hear him.

Up to there things could have worked out quite well. Father, who had always been someone incapable of harming a fly, had punched up almost every one of our neighbours. First they began by respecting him, then they became his followers and crowded along after father, admiring his paintings.

Father had discovered his "hidden vocation," as Uncle Facundo called it, and his pictures now littered the house. Michelini used to come and stare at them for hours on end. Sometimes Michelini's eyes would cloud over, he'd pat father on the back, and leave without saying a word.

I had changed: I felt a new, personal magnetism. The girls in my class adored me and dropped by to see me at all hours.

We all felt alive. There was not a moment, not the slightest crack in time for us to wonder what to do. At night we danced, we played poker, we listened to Uncle Facundo; mother would read the young poet's latest stuff, father would paint, go over the racetrack papers, fight with the neighbours. We were alive.

But my sister began putting on the airs of a left-wing intellectual, and the "political awareness" bug bit her fiercely. First she started off with the "stultification of the bourgeois sensibility," and then she carried on with the "Catholic-Marxist dialogue." Father wanted to beat the shit out of her. So Angelita sided with Aunt Fermina.

Aunt Fermina spent her time chewing on her anger. Since Uncle Facundo had appeared she had tried once or twice to come to our house and preach at us, but she was afraid of father who threatened to cut her throat every time he saw her. Now was her big chance.

The first thing Aunt Fermina did, helped by my sister, was creep into the house one Sunday morning while we were all asleep and, with the palette knife, rip father's paintings to shreds.

Poor father. He looked like the portrait of Dorian Gray. I remember his face when he saw the slaughtered canvases, the empty tubes of paint, the trodden frames. He said nothing, not a word. But on Monday he was again as he had been before. He got up at five, sipped his *mate*, read the paper from one end to the other, and in the evening just sat outside the door, on the low stool, while we all danced indoors, played poker, and listened to the young poet's poems.

And then father also became "aware of the facts." In no time at all he joined forces with my sister and Aunt Fermina. One thing is clear: even before Aunt Fermina took her next step, even before she convinced me (because mother was the last to give in, in spite of becoming the most vicious one of all—smothering Uncle Facundo with the pillow), even before father was won over by Aunt Fermina, something had to break, something that made things easy for Aunt Fermina. It was the sorry sight of father, walking around like a Martian, different, drifting among us, explaining to us how the Germans lost the war in Russia because of the cold, while those of us who remained on the side of Uncle Facundo continued to live on, regardless.

After that, it wasn't difficult for Aunt Fermina to win me over: I'm easy.

Life began to decline. But mother was as firm as a rock. She was the mistress of the young poet who, according to Uncle Facundo, saw in her both the ideal woman and a mother figure. The boy was crazy about mother and would write her the most wonderful verse. But mother was left on her own. And that's how Aunt Fermina achieved her goal. She grabbed hold of mother and put the question to her:

"You're the last one. Either we kill Facundo or we kill the poet."

Love triumphed. That night we decided to do away with Uncle Facundo. We found him asleep, an unforgettable smile on his lips. Father strangled him and I plunged my knife in between the sternum and the main arteries. My sister cut open his veins with a disposable razor blade. Aunt Fermina supervised everything.

We had trouble dragging mother away; she insisted on keeping the pillow pressed against his face.

Then we stood him up sideways and built another section of the wall around him. And that's all.

Now Uncle Facundo is there dead, inside that wall for ever, baking in the sun, and I can't stop looking at the wall with a certain sadness, especially on summer nights, when father brings out the wicker chair for mother, the low stool for himself, the Viennese chair, which I turn round, for me, and the deck chair for my sister, and mother says dogs can always tell when their master is about to die, and father says the only money is in farming, and my sister says a lonely bird will die of a broken heart, and I say all Japanese are traitors.

Translated by Alberto Manguel

ALICIA STEIMBERG
(b. 1 9 3 3)

CECILIA'S LAST WILL
AND TESTAMENT

T*his haunting tale by the author of* Musicians and Watchmakers *(1971) can be read in at least two different ways: as a parable of the unknown fate of the* desaparecidos *in Argentina during the dictatorship, and as a ghost story. As Chilean poet and editor Marjorie Agosin has said, the story is about "the thousands of people who continue to occupy physical and emotional spaces" in the consciousness of the Americas. But the suggestion that Cecilia lives in a building not unlike that of Julio Cortázar's "House Taken Over," a prison inhabited by untrue memories, is also a plausible interpretation.*

I FOUND THESE PAPERS ON TOP OF THE PIANO, IN THE HOUSE WHERE CECILIA lived for so many years, after she had already left. I had the keys to the house and used them to get in after nobody answered the bell. It was a summer night. The window was open, letting in a sultry breeze that smelled of the earth and promised a storm.

I always thought that people who write their last wills and testaments do it because they feel that death is near, be it from old age, from an incurable disease, execution, or suicide. As you will see, Cecilia was not facing any of these. I suppose that she was merely thinking about her death. Or perhaps about the death of an era, of a part of her life.

The storm ceased to be a threat and became a real storm: the wind whipped the curtains on the windows and the leaves of the trees in the garden, and rain pattered down, a delight to hear from the apartment. I sat in Cecilia's armchair, lit a lamp, and began to read.

Buenos Aires/January, 1978

I want to set down here my last will and testament. I have no idea as to how these things are supposed to be written, but I am sure that whoever finds these pages will take the trouble to contact my heirs and carry out my wishes. I don't believe it should be necessary to undertake any legal proceedings. Nonetheless, I have made certain arrangements as regards particular matters, such as my burial. I will begin with my testament.

To Pepe, I leave the last ten years of my life, with their corresponding pleasures and pains (more pains than pleasure, Pepe would say). However, and he knows it, these were not the worst years of my life. Quite the contrary. The last two or three in particular were without question the best. I came to feel so satisfied with things that an epitaph occurred to me. It does not appear among these things here willed because, on account of a remark Pepe made, I changed my mind and decided not to use it. After the conventional "Here lies . . . ," the inscription I had in mind said: "Do not be sad. Or, if you must, be sad, but know that in life I did what I wanted to do." Pepe looked at me pityingly and said:

"They'll kick the stone over."

He feels it's preferable not to show too much happiness over nothing to avoid making others envious.

To Francisco, whom I stopped seeing so long ago I can hardly remember him, but with whom I also shared a number of years of my life, I leave that unforgettable dream about the Chacarita. More than a cemetery, the place seemed like the Edwardian interior of the Molino Café. At the counter there was a fat man counting money; in the following scene I found myself in a place that looked more like a cemetery, beneath a dome supported by columns. From the roof of the dome there was a thin tube of rubber suspended. As I drew close to see what it was, a torrent of money came out of the tube, while a voice echoed down from above, saying: "Let's say forty-six to keep it twenty-seven."

I have no notion what those numbers mean: I leave the problem to Francisco. It may not be very nice to bequeath a problem to someone, but he left me a number of them, and I had no say as to whether I accepted them or not.

On the other hand, nobody is obligated to take something left to him in a will. He can keep it or throw it in the trash, or donate it to charity.

To Sergio, who has stuck by me unfailingly for nearly twenty years, and who never abandoned me, I leave all the moments of freedom from my life, but especially one night when I opened an exquisite box of French-perfumed body powder (this is quite an extraordinary bequest, because it was the only time in my life that I used body powder), and then went to meet him. I wish I recalled whether we got drunk or just a little tipsy. What Sergio should know is that I was happy that night, because it was important to him, and still is important to him, that I am happy.

To José, I leave all my literary prowess, in honor of the heroic enthusiasm with which he embraced my first efforts. I say heroic because, knowing José, it's impossible to imagine him showing enthusiasm for anything. It took all the cunning I could muster to find out that behind the profound melancholy of his face, that aqueous, funereal gaze that seems to set a stone on whatever it touches, there was enthusiasm, I would say almost great enthusiasm for those early pirouettes of mine. José is such a pessimist that he doesn't believe in anything in the future. Every time he announces something, he adds:

"If nothing happens. . . . If something doesn't come up. . . . There are always those unforeseen kinds of things. . . ." And a terrifying silence falls in which anyone would start to doubt everything.

José's childhood is an absolute secret, but I'm sure that horrifying things happened to him and he prefers not to remember. Maybe he was hungry; maybe they beat him with a whip; maybe they shut him up in a dark, windowless room.

Just in case, I leave him as well my recurrent fantasy that I am locked in a kind of safe made of stainless steel, like a modern bank under construction might have. The safe is quite spacious, with no right angles: the joints of the walls with the roof and floor are all rounded. It is hermetically sealed, impregnable, but I know I will be held there only for a limited number of hours. I must remain calm, I think, tomorrow they'll come to take me out of here. All things considered, the best thing I can do is sleep. I lie down on the stainless steel floor; I try to find a comfortable position and can't. The worst thing is that the space is lit, and I don't really know where the light's coming from. Finally, I curl up on my side and open my eyes. If they are open, I have to look at the steel walls, and I'm very frightened. I'm incapable of thinking of absolutely anything, of filling my head with whatever, like I can in everyday situations. Ideas, memories, random thoughts, imagined conversations with different people, everything empties out of my head like water through a colander. I have a brain full of stainless steel; I close my eyes again and trying counting to a hundred. If I make it to a hundred I will sleep; and I will only wake up when they open the door to let me out of here. But, really, why am I here? Am I trying to rob the bank? Or did I wander in here by mistake, distracted, thinking it was an elevator, and then it shut automatically behind me until ten o'clock next morning? I can't remember why I'm here, and the terror reaches a point that I decide to abandon this particular fantasy, and replace it with other, more pleasant thoughts.

I leave this fantasy to José. From the perennial torment he wears on his face, I figure he'll know what to do with it. Besides, I'm leaving on a trip and don't have room for much useless baggage.

To Silvana I leave my spotty wardrobe. She, like me, suffers from that peculiar lack of confidence in any outfit not consisting of designer blue jeans and a plaid shirt. With my closet, she won't have to shudder before diaphanous dresses or high-heeled sandals. I always wanted them, and only now that I'm leaving this house forever can I permit myself to buy them.

To Matilde I leave the tremendous collection of uninhibited screeching I kept boxed up year to year, ever since she started to lay that kind of thing on me. I never knew why I saved any, given that it was made up almost entirely of reproaches, insults, and bitter complaints about her own unhappiness, for which I honestly believed myself somehow responsible. It was with considerable surprise that I realized that Matilde would have been miserable even without me, because misery is her profession and her destiny. Maybe I saved all that yelling so I could return it to her sometime. It might give her a certain satisfaction to remember. It would be nice if Matilde recalled that when I was first the object of that yelling I was only a little girl, and some of that I wasn't able to stuff into the box I'm leaving her. Some echoes eternally in my ears. I also leave her a rare moment of calm in which I, with the innocence appropriate to my tender years, believed in a lasting peace between the two of us. We were walking together, one sunny afternoon, along the Avenida Juan B. Justo. We came to a humble little house with a wooden door painted blue. Matilde rang the bell and a fat, freckled woman with bright red cheeks opened the door, revealing a long corridor of black and white tile. Matilde and the woman exchanged a few words I didn't hear. I was absorbed in the tiles of the corridor and in a chicken coop I could see in the back. The woman left us waiting, clumped heavily down the hallway, and opened the wire door of the chicken coop, causing great confusion among the birds. She soon returned with something wrapped in her apron: three recently laid eggs. Matilde allowed me to carry them in a little paper bag. They were warm. Back at home, we whipped one of those eggs with port and sugar. I drank the heavy mixture in great gulps and felt a pleasant warmth and a light sleepiness. A brief happiness, and the illusion that it would last forever.

To Eduardo, I leave the poems of incomprehensible words we composed between the two of us; it was he who said that in them we had captured our madness, so we might look at it fearlessly in the dark days of our infancy. Thank God we had each other. It wasn't long ago that somebody ran into us at a party and asked if we'd been introduced.

"Not exactly," I said. The first time they presented me to Eduardo, he refused to recognize my presence, did not reply to my hello, nor pay me any attention at all.

Surprised, the mutual friend who had wanted to introduce us remained silent. Then I explained to him that when I was presented to Eduardo, he was in a cradle in the maternity ward of the hospital.

Our friend laughed, but I don't know if he really thought the joke was all that funny. I think he finds me a bit complicated, but I always have to find something that distracts me from the horror of being buried alive in that safe made of stainless steel.

To Marisa, I leave all those songs we sang till dawn in harmony when we were twenty, especially "By the Bridge, Janey," which went "By the bridge, Janey, not by the stream." We conjectured about that phrase, and reached the conclusion that if Janey went by the bridge she'd keep living, whereas if she went by the stream she'd drown. We might have come up with other notions, for example, what if Janey could swim, but we were fixated on the idea of suicide and suicides seemed very interesting. Around this time a friend of Marisa shot herself in the heart and lived. Marisa respected her almost to the point of veneration, as did I, because I based my sentiments on Marisa's, given I couldn't copy her seductiveness, her beauty, or her utter disregard for everybody in the world except herself. I never met the suicide, and I may have had some different ideas about her, but I was very careful not to let on so Marisa wouldn't make fun of me. I leave her as well that kind of fun, carefully classified and labelled as: wounding phrases, deprecatory glances directed at me, deprecatory glances directed at others and shared with me, the way she could curve those beautiful lips in a rictus of disgust, the toe-pointing practiced when she had one leg crossed over the other. She will find them in a box that originally contained sandalwood soap, a masculine aroma she liked so well, hidden beneath a tiny reproduction of a work by her beloved Chagall.

I know that it is unusual to leave things to someone already dead, but the next time somebody goes to put flowers on Ignacio's grave, please put along with them all the ingenious or intelligent phrases I ever said that he always used to marvel aloud at. With that, he managed to convince me early on that I was quite an exceptional sort, with unique gifts. The blows of life (why not) have busied themselves convincing me that if, indeed, I am able to make invisible cats scamper across roofs drawn out of air, for many other things I'm a hopeless idiot, something Ignacio would never have admitted. Also put on his tomb a leaf from a children's book that I read over and over when I was small. It talked about honey, and showed a bee, a honeycomb, a jar of honey, and a boy sitting at a table, spreading honey on a piece of bread. The text spoke of the various applications of honey, and whenever I read this page I remembered Ignacio, who was so fond of me and never yelled at me, and who so shortly after left this world that an incurable astonishment remained with me ever since.

Ana: To you, who certainly will find these pages on top of the piano, I leave everything you will find in this house, from the furniture to the ghosts, and including the contents of various drawers. Study each letter carefully, every photograph. Don't be alarmed if, upon opening a door, you feel suddenly like you've gone back thirty years. This house was remodeled several times, and in the back there is a patio of uneven tiles, a bath, an unused kitchen, full of old appliances and cookware, and a tiny room with a very small window separate from all the other bedrooms. When I was little I desperately wished that that were my room, but I would never have dared suggest it. When the servant girl had a bed, it was her room. When she didn't, it was the ironing room. But it was a refuge to which I could flee for brief periods. There you will find many of my dreams and adolescent fantasies, a photo of Carlos Gardel, and a wave of violent perfume that its last occupant slathered herself with to go out on Sundays. They are all yours, Ana.

It embarrasses me to give away old knick-knacks, but maybe you will find among all the trash in the back of the house a little shelf that once hung on the dining room wall, with the following miniatures on it: a Lilliputian edition in two volumes of *Don Quixote*, a free gift from Escasany Jewelers, bound in Russian leather and printed on onionskin, that includes only the chapter about the windmills, and a little, very fat bronze doll called Billiken, that had some sort of importance as an amulet.

From the old bathroom, you might want to take: "Life offers three great gifts: health, wealth, and love . . ." and "Sorrento" in the rendition of Aunt Rosita who sang it every time she took a shower. Also, my face as a girl reflected in the mirror of the medicine chest, and the tube of mascara with which Matilde used to blacken her lashes every morning in an act as mechanical as brushing her teeth. Also, the extreme cruelty of her eyes as she applied the mascara.

Finally, in that closed-up kitchen there is a pile of children's books full of educational and macabre stories, like the one about the unfortunate girl who lodged some poor relatives in her house, who ended up poisoning her, and who, as she writhed around in her death throes, repented of their crime and so *confessed it all to her.* And the dying girl was so, so very good that she managed to forgive them all before rocketing off to Heaven.

When you make your pass through the modernized part of the house, notice that in the bathroom there are a number of toothbrushes, more than there were ever people in the house. Every time that I picked up my toothbrush I was amazed at the presence of all those anonymous toothbrushes. I would be completely absorbed, nearly hypnotized, by my own inability to remember where they came from. However, I never got around to throwing them all away, as if I were afraid of loosing some curse. There's a very old one of antique design that looks like it was used to clean dentures, and that always drew forth a particular repugnance from me. But I wasn't even capable of tossing that one out. What will you do with all those toothbrushes, Ana? And with all the liqueur glasses up on the top shelf in the kitchen? Maybe you can use one for eyebaths, like Gramma did. She filled the little glass with some mysterious liquid and then—pop!—she planted it with one quick, agile movement over her eye. One nice thing about Gramma was that she didn't mind me sitting there looking at her with my mouth open when she pressed an empty bottle of cod liver oil to her face. Through the remnants of the liquid and the glass, her eye acquired extraordinary dimensions, and after she had held it there for a while she smiled at me, triumphant, and I looked at her, fascinated.

In the back of the closets are shoes, Ana, the kind I ought to have thrown out years ago, but they're still there. I don't think they'll be of interest to anybody. I ask only that you take them up on the balcony of the top floor and throw them, aiming as best you can, into the vacant lot in front. For years I lived in this house complaining bitterly of the antisocial monsters who threw things in the vacant lot. I accused them of being mentally defective. I never did anything like that. But now I want to give myself the chance, even if it's by proxy. One old shoe, another, another, ready, aim, fire.

As for the rest, you can decide its destiny, except for the piano that I will have sent to my new house. I never knew how to play, but it's a memento of Aunt Rosita who could only play "Fuer Elise."

And now, my Last Request:

I want to be buried without ceremony (though I wouldn't mind flowers, which I've always liked) in the cemetery of the Chacarita in Buenos Aires. I have always lived in Buenos Aires, and the Chacarita is Buenos Aires. It has its ugly neighborhoods, and its pretentious ones, the prettier neighborhoods where the members of certain of the foreign communities live, or die, or are dead. There are the walls of niches, with the dead piled up just like the living in apartment houses. People choose the place they want, or that they can afford, within the cemetery.

Never bring calla lilies, I hate them. Nor carnations, nor jonquils, which are funeral flowers. I like roses, jasmine, sweet peas.

I declare that in the moment of this writing I am in good health, I work hard, and am looking forward to enjoying life.

—Cecilia

As I finished reading, I noticed the rain had stopped. I leaned out the window to think. I had never met any of the people that Cecilia mentioned in her will, so it would be impossible for me to parcel out her inheritance. To comply with her last wishes, I would need legal authorization, that supposing, of course, that Cecilia died before I did, something utterly unpredictable. As far as I know, she never had family, except her grandmother who died long ago; Aunt Rosita must have been some invention of hers.

She actually always wanted relatives. She was fascinated, almost hypnotized when she spoke to me about the secretaries that take the buses out to the suburbs every afternoon, and, arriving at their humble homes, find an old mother, bent, a shawl she's crocheted herself over her shoulders, who has dinner waiting. Then she would go on to describe the dinner, and her face would take on the vagueness of delirium. Dinner was invariably prepared from leftovers: stew from the roast, bread-pudding with scraps from the whole week. The mother and her daughter moved from room to room over the slick floor on scuffs made of wool scraps. Night after night, the two together ate those meals made from leftovers. The problem, the insoluble enigma that cost Cecilia more than one sleepless night, was what the original meal had been, the one that provided the first leftovers. But Cecilia was sufficiently sensitive to turn away from that dead end. Just as she slipped out of that stainless steel safe without anybody's having come to open the door, she circled around the quiche made with last night's greens, and spent half-an-hour thinking about surfing.

"It's a sport that now I'll never have a chance to take up, and I regret it," she said.

She admired the bronzed, triumphant bodies shooting across the crest of a wave. Surfing was the symbol of all she had never done or known in her life. When a physicist tried to explain the notion of the infinite in terms utterly incomprehensible to her, she shook her head sadly and said:

"That and surfing, no chance."

She was tough-minded about her limitations, and I think she exaggerated them.

But I don't know why I'm talking about Cecilia as if she were dead. It's that eccentricity of hers that drove her to make out this will.

I will take these pages with me. They have no legal value and Cecilia won't be able to be buried as she wishes until we find the. . . . But this has to be handled delicately. It doesn't seem particularly nice to hurry things along where a case like this is concerned. Besides, I don't know when I'll see her next, since she says she's not coming back. But I know she'll be back. As long as I live, Cecilia will be back.

Translated by Christopher Leland

GERMÁN ROZENMACHER
(1 9 3 6 – 1 9 7 1)

BLUES IN THE NIGHT

In the tradition of soul-searching literary odysseys best exemplified by James Joyce's Ulysses, this tale by the author of "The Black Cat," first published in 1971, is an exploration of immigrant life, urban identity, and the cultural link between Eastern Europe and South America. Vassily Goloboff is introduced as the first tenor of the Moscow Opera, a maestro; Bernardo as a sensitive, intelligent, artistic young man in Buenos Aires. Set within the confines of a circumscribed Jewish neighborhood, their rivalry and existential plight makes for a memorable story about the multiple meanings of exile.

"NU? WHAT DO YOU THINK?" MAMA SAID, PEERING THROUGH THE WINDOW. "There he is again," she grumbled, and looked at the gold watch hanging from her woolen jacket. "He had lunch here. Fancy that. It's four o'clock and he's already back for a cup of tea," she muttered bitterly.

Bernardo lifted the feather eiderdown, thick, white, soft, with large buttons, and in his underpants he jumped off the bed into the warmth of the gas stove.

"These artists are a pain in the neck," Mama said. She was wearing those glasses with horrible tiny pearls and curlicues which Jewish women love so much. Looking over her head, Bernardo peered through the window to where the old man was standing, three floors below, braving the fierce wind, in the radiant cold of a Saturday afternoon.

He seemed as still and straight as a general, struggling to hold himself up, terribly fragile, pushed along by the gusts of the wind, the brim of his straw hat twisted from so much bending that it gave him the air of a worn-out cowboy.

Corrientes Street was empty; the lights of the Pasteur subway were burning pale, orange, unnoticed in the pure, cloudless icy blue of this last Saturday of July. It was as if for the lamplighter, the wintry day was merely an accident, a fiction of light, between nine in the morning and five in the afternoon, and as if the July night was the only certainty. His father's snores came to him from the bedroom like a sonorous, steady sigh punctuated by snorts and moans. And Bernardo was so lanky, with those burning eyes, and so timid; his beard, too heavy for his seventeen years; his nose, rotund and heavy, and his almost rabbinical stoop, the way of swaying he had when he studied, like an inverted pendulum. Bernardo was curious about seeing that old man who was crossing Corrientes Street in the solitude of a Saturday afternoon. It was so frosty and windy.

"Don't open," Mama said, moving away from the window. "When he rings the bell don't open. We are not in. We are dead. We've gone away. We've gone up in smoke," she said. Then she cleaned the misty window panes where there were still some smudges with her fat fist, the nails short on her stubby fingers.

"But he'll notice," said Bernardo. "Our shutters are open. He'll know that we don't want to let him in."

Only then did Mama look at him. "How come you are in bare feet?" She hurried and bent down, kneeling to pull the slippers from underneath and in this position waited for him, like a bullfighter for the bull, waving them provocatively, saying, "Take, here they are, put them on, the cold is bad for you." But Bernardo stood there looking at her, in the very high room, yellowed with age and covered with old photographs of bearded ancestors inside their round bronze frames carved with leaves and flowers against the wallpaper of small faded roses.

Bernardo went over to the tall chair with frayed upholstery, where his trousers hung. He grabbed them and put them on, believing that the old man would be about to enter the house.

"Where are you going now?" Mama moaned, stupefied. He snatched the blue turtleneck sweater which was on the rolltop desk, and under it he found his shoes, among the volumes of the Pijoan encyclopedia. Putting on his fur-collared leather jacket, he left his apartment, dashed along the corridor, and rang for the elevator. When he opened the rusty door, there he stood.

"Is Papa in?" asked the old man, apathetically, as he came out of the elevator.

"No, no one's in." Bernardo could feel the old man's disbelief and his humiliation as he scrutinized the boy's face; there was bitter surprise and disappointment at being unable to gorge himself, as he used to, on the heaped plates of Mama's cookies.

"What? Today, Saturday, he went out?" exclaimed the old man. And then, recovering his composure, he said, "All right he did tell me to come. . . . But it doesn't matter. It's just as well. I have so many things to do. . . ." And he coughed, covering his mouth with ceremonial aplomb. Bernardo saw the ring with the big black stone that he wore on his little finger, which was freckled and wrinkled, like the rest of his hand. They went down in the reddish light of the shaky cage, each bar of iron creaking in its own way.

"I came out because I was hungry," said Bernardo, as if there were somebody else speaking inside him, irresistibly attracted by that old man, who did not even look at him, so small and so absurdly stiff, as if he were absorbed in problems of state. "Mama went out to a WIZO tea. You know, those ladies who have birthdays and get a flower for a present. . . ." The old man nodded but Bernardo knew that he really had not swallowed the pill.

"And Papa?"

What could the boy invent now? "Papa went to see a Mr. Shreiber, or Shneider. . . ." The old man looked at the small elevator bulb and nodded. Bernardo knew that the old man could practically hear Papa's snores.

"Ah, yes . . . Shneider, an engineer, no? A millionaire, great friend of mine," he said irritably, as they left the building. Bernardo, with a kind of anguish, put his hand on the sleeve of the old man's black coat, and he saw that the velvet collar had been darned over and over, and he pictured the old man in long johns, utterly lonely. And then, pulling his sleeve, he ventured without knowing how. "Aren't you hungry, Professor? I'm dying for a cup of coffee. I'll treat you." The professor did not answer and Bernardo feared that he had been clumsy. "Where are you going?" he asked, even more clumsily, because the old man had already begun to walk away. Now I've really humiliated him, Bernardo said to himself, lowering his head and hurrying to catch up with him. He moved indecisively, with the gangling, awkward legs of a boy not fully grown. He cleared his throat timidly, as he always did when he had to say something. "I'm walking this way too." I weigh on people,

Bernardo said to himself. My God, why am I always such a nuisance? And what do I say to him now? It's terrible to walk like this, as if I were a bundle of sticky hay that clings to people. My God, when will I be a man once and for all?

The two were pulled along by the very pure blue wind, like dry crackling leaves, golden leaves of winter afternoons, flying over the streets, clear and sharp, like a Renaissance canvas which the cold, cloudless afternoons in Buenos Aires sometimes have, awakening wistful memories of spring.

"Clouds," said the old man, pointing with his gloved finger. He had produced, like magic, a pair of faded, yellowing gloves. Bernardo saw a bare finger through a small and unmistakable hole.

"Clouds?" Bernardo said, and he looked at the sky, nodding then with that exaggerated gesture of boys searching like faltering, disoriented birds, for somebody to love them amidst the fury of things.

"Do you know something?" Bernardo suddenly blurted out, leaning over, hating himself for clinging so hard, pressing his damp feelings, roughly, on the old man. "I want to sing," he said, resting his head on the old man's shoulder, sensing at once that the old man did not like to be touched. But Bernardo continued to hold him as if he were an old school friend, or his dear younger brother. He was a head shorter than the thin and clumsy adolescent.

The old man stood in exactly the same way as when Bernardo, from the balcony, had seen him come from the temple every Saturday at midday, walking arm in arm with Papa, chatting, taking their time, stopping every few steps, gesticulating and occasionally taking off their hats and pressing them down again mechanically, Papa over his forehead, and the old man over his eyes, walking, stopping every few steps, talking freely, at their age. And at times they would walk with their hands behind their backs, just as the old man was doing now.

"Ah, yes?" said the professor, looking curiously into the boy's eyes.

"Papa spoke to me a lot about you, Sr. Goloboff. Couldn't I . . ." Bernardo swallowed, "Couldn't I study with you, Maestro?"

The old man arched his brows. "Well . . ." He shrugged his shoulders skeptically. "I don't know if I'll have the time. You know . . . I have so many students. Hugo del Carril, Virginia Luque. I would have to look at my schedule. . . ."

These lies were what annoyed Mama the most. She was so jealous of the friendship between Papa and the old man, Papa moved by compassion for him, ever since the day when he had casually invited him home for lunch after they left the synagogue together. Papa, a tall Jew, stooped and bald, so dark, with his great nose and large eyes, who, during the week and even on Sunday mornings, worked at the Baratillo, the sort of variety store that overflows into the street with its piles of cardboard suitcases, cheap trousers, long johns and raincoats, ties and toys. There in the Azcuenaga area, in a shop with dusty floorboards, with Papa behind the counter in his terrible silence, eyes accusing, looking at him wearily.

"I want to study music." The old man shrugged his shoulders. Bernardo remembered the endless after-dinner chats with Papa which so annoyed Mama, the two men would sit together hardly exchanging a word. In the dark dining room—facing the damp, gray interior patio of the building, with clothes hanging in space, and children shouting—when all that was left were scraps of food and empty tea glasses, Papa felt like an amateur patron of the arts when he would ask the old man: "And do you remember how Tito Schipa sang in the last part of *Pescatore de Perle?*" And standing by the sideboard with the somber European air—which it owed, perhaps, to its marble top—the old man sang an aria, while from the front room came the clatter of the TV that Mama had turned on.

Papa had once said, "He was a great performer."

"But now he's past it, poor chap," Mama had added.

But his father had made no comment. He respected his friend; that is why he fed him. And he would listen to him with his eyes closed, in the same way as he would listen to the Sunday operas transmitted from the Colón, tucked into bed with his transistor radio, the billowing eiderdown covering everything up to his ears. The day would be dying and through the somewhat moth-eaten curtains on the windows facing Pasteur Street, the blue turned a sort of purple, Bernardo could almost taste the sadness of Monday in the warmed-over, tasteless *gnocchi* that Mama brought to Papa in bed.

"Because I can play the trombone a little," said Bernardo, "and besides, I can imitate all the instruments."

"Ah, yes? Is that so?" asked the old man. "Let's hear." And right there, in the wind, in the semideserted street, Bernardo sang "Tenderly" for the old man. And then he tilted his head over his left shoulder and played the violin, and a moan came out of his body while with his right hand he moved the bow—which was only air, only wind. And at that moment Bernardo was a great violin, completely self-absorbed, playing himself in the middle of the cold winter. And then he bent over a little, and with his right hand he pinched the air, and the grave tones of a cello filled the street. And then he made a fist with his right hand, that moved back and forth from his lips, following the melancholy rhythm of a trombone, music squeezing out of his swollen lungs. And then he scratched his belly and a guitar was born, and then his hands covered his mouth and pressed against his nose and all of a sudden a horn began to wail very slow, muted barking sounds.

"My heart belongs to Daddy," the old man said suddenly and melodramatically, with phlegm in his throat and with the tragic air of an actor of the old school, and he began to sing, filling out the light melody with moans and gasps and absurd intensity. And the two of them went on walking and Bernardo played the horn with his mouth, and sometimes with faint whistles he conjured up the delicate tones of a flute.

"That is a bit out of tune," the maestro said. "Where do you know that from? I mean, where did you first hear it?"

"At the circus," Bernardo lied, "when I was a boy and we lived in Bahía Blanca. I ran away with a circus. Three weeks on a truck all over the province with the orchestra leader. He was phenomenal. He could play almost thirty instruments." (And the truth was once he had run away for two hours to go to the circus. That was all.) "And what's more, I can really play the trombone."

"How did you learn?"

"With the firemen, in Bahía. Where else could I learn to play the trombone? With a fire chief. I was only this big . . . until Papa couldn't afford to pay for the lessons anymore."

All of a sudden Bernardo felt he had run away from home again for two hours, like when he was eleven. He remembered the silent, suffering look on Papa's face. He wanted Bernardo to be what he would never be: a great Zionist leader of the community, whom everyone in the family would admire; the Jewish paper would photograph him, and he would fly to America and would even manage to marry the daughter of some big industrialist. He swallowed. It would never come true. And now he had run away from his father's Baratillo shop, and from the painful silences and the mutual recriminations and complaints that filled his house; and now the scatterbrained professor—as Mama used to call him—he was going off where fortune led him.

Because Bernardo, after the circus episode, had never left home again. He didn't even have friends. But at night, in bed, he would hum very softly to himself, imitating all the instruments.

"All right. But out of tune. Sometimes out of tune," the professor said with his hands behind his back.

"Not with the real instrument." And Bernardo thought—as if *he* did not go out of tune when he started singing liturgical songs.

Papa and the old man also admired the same cantor in the synagogue, a man from Cangallo Street. And they would go to hear him every Saturday, like the fans of the Boca soccer team. And that was another reason why they were friends. Because the old man used to remember little scraps of melodies that the cantor had interpreted that morning. Once Papa said to the professor: "Now we must be patient with him. Who knows if my son will have patience for me when I am that old." And Papa had looked at him.

"I have a trombone at home," said the professor.

"No!" the boy exclaimed with wild joy. He slapped him on the back so hard he almost knocked him over. "Please," he said, "let me play it, Maestro."

"It is half broken," said the old man shaking his head.

"Please," begged the boy, "do it for my father." It was a low, sly blow, but what else could he do?

The professor sighed, hesitating, indecisive. "Your Papa is a sensitive person," the old man said, still undecided.

Bernardo felt that the old man was embarrassed. He did not quite know what it was about. "Have you ever been in a circus?"

The old man recoiled, scornfully. "Circus, shmircus! I am a serious artist."

Suddenly, the sky turned dark. The anguish of Saturday night made Bernardo's heart ache. He would be alone, like last week, like next week, dreaming of parties to which he would never be invited, frightened at the thought of being pulled by the crowd of Lavalle Street. And he felt that the old man was perhaps even more frightened than he.

"Wait," he said, and he went into a deli. He bought pastrami, pickles, and black bread, although he would have preferred to buy a slice of pizza; but he thought the old man was too old-fashioned for that kind of food. And then they took the trolley and the gas lights of the subway stations were burning—this time at least with some purpose, since it was night along Corrientes—and they were pressed against elegantly dressed women and young men with blue suits and shiny ties, going to parties with girls laughing hysterically, because they were only fourteen.

There, standing in the trolley that rattled more than tramcars, the professor said to him, with a distant happy expression that lit up his sad, dull eyes, "You know? Once in St. Petersburg it was winter and we were in the opera. Circus," mused the old man smiling benignly. "In the first act of *Madame*

Butterfly, I had a headache. And then, Chaliapin came and he said to me: 'Micha, what's the matter, Micha?' And he served me, with his own hands, a cup of tea."

"Chaliapin himself?" asked Bernardo.

"Of course. He was my intimate friend. He said to me: 'You'll go far, Micha.'" And the old man became silent. They did not speak until, at the corner of Donato Alvarez and San Martin, the old man said as they got off the trolley: "Par-r-don us, señor-res," rolling all the *rr*s in the world.

Bernardo reflected on how far away from their house the old man lived. On Saturdays, between lunch and tea, he must have hung around downtown, getting cold in the square, falling asleep at the matinee movie, killing time before returning to the boy's house to eat great piles of cookies and to say, "What a nice family, Sr. Katz; such tasty cookies Señora, God bless your hands."

They walked along Donato Alvarez until the boy saw the reason for the old man's shame. A gray house, with a broken balustrade on the terrace, barely lit by the street light, with its tin shade rattling in the wind like broken plates. They entered the courtyard where the wind blew even harder than outside, and behind the three or four shuttered doors came the noise of spoons against plates, and televisions—one in each apartment—and some child crying. The old man opened one of the shuttered doors, which had some slats missing, turning the key in the padlock that held a chain.

"What could they steal from him?" Bernardo thought, looking at the broken tiles and at the enormous plant pots set against the very tall wall enclosing the patio and facing the rooms. The wall was peeling, rotten with dampness, oppressive.

"Come in," said the professor. A head peered out of the room next door. The professor had gone in to put on the light.

"Listen," said the head, softly. "Ts, ts," it called out. It was an Italian head with a lot of gray hair and thin strands of noodles in its handlebar mustache, a tired head with bags under its eyes, of a peddler of groceries. "Are you the son, the grandson?"

Bernardo said that he wasn't.

"Never mind, tell him to stop banging."

"To stop banging?"

"Yes. When are they taking him to the old-age home? He gets up in the middle of the night and starts banging little nails into the walls." The Italian was almost whispering. Bernardo looked through the shuttered door and saw a very ugly woman, with a huge masculine face, sparse hair, swaying gently in a rocking chair covered by blankets, watching TV. Meanwhile, over a little iron stove, something with a nasty smell, maybe cabbage, was brewing in a brown enamel pot, with a large tin lid that did not fit. In a corner, next to the closet, was an empty pushcart.

"Don't you see, young man? He grabs a hammer and boom, boom, booms away. Please tell him. Look at my eyes from lack of sleep. We are working people here. . . ."

From another louvered door two small boys in overcoats came out, their parents behind them.

"That man is a turner. He can't sleep either. Ask him. . . ."

"Sr. Katz!" the old man shouted from inside his room.

"Yes, tell him, young man," begged the turner, who was very dark, with hair heavily plastered down with oil, like a dandy, a stiff shiny curl covering his narrow forehead groomed perhaps for some movie on San Martin Avenue.

"Tell him, tell him," the children chimed in.

"Come in here!" the old man shouted again from inside, this time in Yiddish, suddenly upset, on the verge of tears. As he went in Bernardo could tell that despair had overcome the old man's nerves and his voice was strangely contorted.

"There is nobody to talk to in this place."

Dry leaves swirled in the courtyard. Inside the old man took off his coat. "I don't even say hello to them anymore. What's the good? Who are they anyway? Do they know, maybe, who they are talking to?" said the old man, and he closed the louvered door, and then the glass door. The windows and the door were curtained, because the room faced the street. The fringes must have been hand sewn by his late wife some twenty years before.

"The trombone is on top of the closet," said the old man, and he turned on an old electric heater. The boy did not take off his jacket. His nose was still as cold as it had been outside, and the whole day's frost seemed to have concentrated in that room; so much so, that his stomach was beginning to ache.

"With those goyim, better not to have any dealings," said the old man. Bernardo wanted to disagree, but there was no point.

"Israel is the only place," he said. "One of these days I'll go," he added, as he took off his old-fashioned jacket, black with thin stripes. "But I ask myself, what can an old man do there? They need young people like you." He seemed so small to Bernardo in the middle of the room, lighting a cigarette, with trembling hands, dreaming about things he would never do, alone in that house where he did not talk to anyone, offended by those who did not recognize his past glory.

"You have to go there," the old man insisted, with that nagging obsession which dominated his thoughts and his actions, an obsession shared by Mama.

"No," said Bernardo childishly, tall and gangling, sucking his cheek through his teeth, his hands in his pockets, looking at the wooden floor.

"What do you mean, 'no'?" said the old man, without anger, smiling affectionately, as if he had to explain something elementary to a small child. And Bernardo felt bad: Papa dreamt of being buried in Israel. His eyes would shine at the thought. He would be willing to die there and then to achieve such perfect peace and happiness.

"No," said the boy, and he felt that he understood the longing of the old man because he had felt it himself.

He was not the kind of Jew that Papa wanted him to be but he had never played ball with the boys in the street either, because Mama did not let him: He was like a leaf blown in the wind, and as rootless, and he was neither here nor there, and Papa's dark and unpronounced curse would follow him with a respectful silence. And he searched, torn, in the night.

"What is there to talk about?" asked the boy, and suddenly he stroked the old man's cheek roughly. "I really like you, professor, because we are both artists," Bernardo said. And once he started talking, he could never hold himself back: "My goodness, how can I blurt it all out like this?" He felt like one of those carriages that moved along in violent, erratic jerks.

The old man looked at him: "The trombone is on top of the closet," and he put his cigarette in a holder. And Bernardo stood on the peacock-shaped wicker chair, and he saw it, covered with dusty old newspapers: It was a band-trombone, like the ones used by the firemen. They wrapped themselves round your body when you picked them up to play. And it seemed as if their music flowed from a strange act of love among muted notes, the air, and your body. He sat upon the great double bed, which the old man had occupied alone for heaven knows how many years. He thought not of the present but rather of the time when the old man, after having slept a whole life with the same woman, must have stretched out his hand and found nothing there.

The old man unwrapped the gray paper on the vinyl tablecloth and, grabbing a primus stove, he lit it and put a kettle over it. Bernardo's foot hit upon something. The chamberpot. Of course. If he went out to the bathroom at night, he would drop dead on the spot. He looked at it. It was strange. It had a floral design, and besides it was not empty.

"Pardon," the old man said, without blinking. He took it out while the boy played some notes softly, familiarizing himself with the instrument. It was an unexpected encounter, in that the whole episode had begun all of a sudden when something had made him come down to meet the old man. It was all happening to him, who had never left home, who had never gone to bed after 10 P.M. and who had felt that he had to ask permission even to go out to buy the paper. He would not go out because he would feel a strange fear about walking alone in the streets. He had always been like a whipped dog; he would get into bed and pull the covers over his ears; and he would think "My God, I'm going to be seventeen." He felt he was so young; and he thought of the women who passed by without looking at him. Why should they? Who would look at a melancholy giraffe?

"A little sandwich?" asked the old man. "What will your father say when he knows you've been here? Because it's not right to come like this, suddenly, to a stranger's house, without letting him know."

"I won't tell them I came here. I'll tell them we went to the movies."

"Movies!" the old man said, while gobbling huge chunks of black bread and pastrami. "The last time I went to the movies I saw one with Jeanette MacDonald. . . ."

"And . . . ? Who is she?"

"Of course. . . ." He spoke with his mouth full, without wasting time, as if he did not care any longer if the boy found out it had been a long time since he had a good meal. "What do you know about good actors? Those were real stars. And they had such voices. . . . It's not that I haven't been to the movies for a long time, but I go to see old movies, always the same ones, that I have seen before. Why go see these modern ones? Are they going to teach me anything?" He arched his brows. "I know it all already. Besides, there aren't any good ones today. Although Palito Ortega was a student of mine."

"Really?"

"Of course. He came a few times. He couldn't modulate his voice. He sang like this. . . ." And he emitted a guttural sound from his throat. A roar. "Gooooah. . . . And so I taught him how to do it." Closing his eyes, his hand over his chest, and wrinkling his brow, he uttered a melodious falsetto: "Aahhh."

Over the damp wallpaper, under the bulb that hung from a long cable, Bernardo saw the walls covered with photographs and drawings, the old pencil cartoons of the thirties in which the head looked enormous and the body like a dwarf, and they were all of the old man. The story of a whole life. According to what he had heard from Papa—who never told him anything directly, so he had to find out through Mama—the old man had sung at the Moscow Opera during Imperial times, when he was just a boy. And since they wouldn't let Jews do it, he had changed his surname to Goloboff. So perhaps his real name was Meyer, or something like that. Bernardo imagined him very young, as in one of the portraits on the wall, the most yellowed one from the 1880s. He looked handsome, like Lord Byron, with a long thick mane, a formal suit with tails, and a cravat with ruffles.

"Here I play the leading role in *La Bohème*," said the old man in passing, seeing him looking at the sketch.

Goloboff, who never stopped using that name—Vassily Goloboff—when the Revolution came, entered the *Proletcult,* the Department of Culture. And Bernardo thought with surprise of the ease and even the trace of affection with which his father had pronounced that word; although he now remembered the Revolution with revulsion, Goloboff had run away from the *Proletcult* after some love affairs. He had large, tragic eyes, whose beauty could still be discerned, although they were misted over now: large melodramatic actor's eyes, that surely must have captivated women. And then he came to Argentina . . . and began to travel around in second-class carriages, giving concerts and recitals, always with others, of course, because he knew that nobody would come to listen to him alone. And during the High Holidays he sang as a cantor in some colony in Entre Ríos, because although he had kept the name Goloboff, he now recognized himself once again as a Jew—it was useless to pretend otherwise. Or perhaps because he felt terribly alone. And Papa used to tell Mama at the table (all they ever said to Bernardo was "Pass the salt" or other such things) that since his wife's death Goloboff had become increasingly religious and had gradually withdrawn into himself with a sombre obstinacy, covering his loneliness and insecurity. He had met his wife soon after his arrival from Russia, another emigré just like him, and they lived together and became closer and closer, although he had occasional affairs with ever-younger girls.

"And these?" said Bernardo. There was a pile of *Radiolandia* covers.

"Autographed for me," said the old man, without attributing much importance to them. "All those singers, they took classes with me. . . ." He took a large sip of tea. "Don't you want to eat anything?"

"No." But it was a rhetorical question anyway.

The old man was eating as hungrily as ever. "They call on me every day. . . . But what can I do? It's too much for me. From Chaliapin to Palito Ortega. . . . I even had to remove the plaque from the door."

A good singing teacher. At least that is what Papa used to tell Mama. And since he was so pushy, he had managed to get some stars to come to him, although they may have come only once or twice, to take lessons and give him their autographs. That was Papa's version. Who would ever know the real truth? But Bernardo had his own idea of how the bronze plaque was nailed to the wall: "*Vassily Goloboff. Advanced Professor of Singing. First Tenor of the Moscow Opera.*"

Bernardo could picture the Italian with the large mustache dirtying the plaque with tar, and the old man cleaning it, until he gave up and hung it in the room. And he imagined Hugo del Carril's face—if he had come—entering the tenement and the kids pressing in at the door, listening to him singing the scales, and Bernardo even felt the old man had brought the actors to impress the neighbors. Or perhaps not. Perhaps he had gone to the actors' houses, putting on his air of a duke in exile. And that would make more sense. Bernardo would never know. And then he would let the less celebrated students come to his house, those who showed up at the tango contests that took place in the barrios. Or perhaps at the salon "Argentina." Perhaps the old man would hang around the Paternal Neighborhood talking about the autographs he had. Bernardo could not tell how it came about, but there, on the wall, were the autographs, genuine or false. And he imagined the poor student singing the scales, while outside, in the patio, children played ball against the wall, which was scaling as if from leprosy from the different coats of paint which never covered the wall itself, and were always gray with dried-up streaks of moisture. He imagined there the ball bouncing against the wall like muffled cannon shots, and the shouts of the neighbors, and the radios at full blast; and there, inside, with the doors closed and the tuning fork striking against the vinyl surface of the table, in the darkness, with the little bulb shining among so many portraits over the faded flowers—the old man and his students would sing arias, or practice a dance, or perhaps sing "Granada."

"Pardon," the old man said and he went out. He returned with the floral chamberpot and put it next to a leg of the bed. Bernardo heard the rain. He looked through the window, moving the curtain. A fine rain, like mist, was falling in the night, and the curtain seemed to come apart in his hands, and the opaque dampness covered the windowpanes like a caress, like the saliva left behind kisses, like warm moisture, like a great maternal hug that removed him from the cruelty of the street where it was now raining harder, a solid flood of rain, as if water was the only thing the world had ever known or would know.

"Let's see how it's going," said the old man, and the boy grabbed the trombone and began to play very softly "Since You Went Away," rocking with the dull, flat notes, swaying, sitting at the edge of the double bed, as if a wind inside him was moving him, rocking him. And he felt as if he were coming down the Mississippi and he was black, and he had lived in 1880, and he was sinking in a river of his own blood, and was howling with all his might.

"I know it a little," said the old man, and he stood next to the closet with the three mirrors that exposed his back, and in an operatic style, with his hands wide open and a blank look in his eyes, he sang, very slowly, "Since You Went Away."

And the trombone came in like a circus, with its jarring, off-key notes, setting the rhythm, and the water dripped from the ceiling, and he never found out how the rest of it all happened. But the old man opened the closet and took out a straw hat and then a walking stick, and he said, "Let me teach you a few things. How was it now that Molly Picon did it? That one which goes. . . ." And he began to sing: "A little bit of peace and joy, No money? Get used to it! *Abi gezint darf men glicklech zein.* If you are healthy, it's enough to make you happy." And the boy played the tune from the operetta, which was as tired as the old man, who was now sitting, facing the mirror. He had taken out a box of pencils and powders and was making up his face. And the boy discovered all of a sudden that he was doing it for his sake, for Bernardo, while the old man hummed with an unexpected happiness.

"I'm going to give you a show," he said, and he hummed the melody to himself. And while the boy tried not to notice what the old man was doing, he closed his eyes and accompanied him with the flat, sad, slow notes of the trombone. When he opened his eyes, he realized the old man had put on makeup to impress him, there between the cupboard, the table, the bed, in the very tall room. And it was as if the whole world had disappeared. And all those faces—always the same faces—more and more wrinkled, looking down from the walls, smiling at him in monstrous grimaces: the professor's eye paint enlarging his eyes, and talcum powder covering his wrinkles, and a little lipstick on his lips.

"Picaresque repertory," the Maestro announced. "In the style of Aaron Lebedeff." And he began to take vaudeville steps, singing about girls looking for men, and he rested his hands on his knees, and he made them float from knee to knee without lifting his feet off the floor. Then he kicked one foot after the other nearly as high as his waist and began to run around and dance, with his incredible seventy years, with the feeble remains of his vitality in a pathetic vaudeville.

"There's no business like show business," he announced, and the boy went at it frenetically, with his muted trombone. The old man screeched with the tremulous air of a showman from another era, singing there was no business like show business, you smile when you are low. And he knelt like Al Jolson. And there was more to come, when the old man took off his hat and threw it away and announced, gasping, "Catari," and put his hands over his flat stomach; forgetting about all the singing lessons he had given throughout his life, he sang with what little voice he had left in him, with his hands, with his body, with everything. And the boy accompanied him with his trombone, one single note after each phrase, badly, clumsily, like in the shabbiest circus on earth. The truth was that the old man no longer knew the tunes. So he did not care because nothing registered anymore. So he went on, deliriously. It was his own show, the last show he would ever give. In fact, he had never before given such a show. And now when there was nothing left anymore, now, before this one single spectator—his entire public—the performance was taking place. And not in Saint Petersburg, nor at the Colón, nor on Broadway, but in that one-story house on Donato Alvarez, with all the rented rooms, while outside it rained steadily in the night.

"And when I sang this," the old man stuttered breathlessly, "it was then Chaliapin caressed me," he said, softly stroking the boy's cheek without seeing it, without seeing anything, as if he were dreaming while awake.

"And then he brought me a glass of tea." A gentle nostalgia mixed with euphoria when he spoke. But now it was not he who was talking, but Chaliapin through him.

"'Micha, what's the matter, Micha?' Don't you see, Sr. Katz? He, Chaliapin, with his own hands, with his very own hands, served me a glass of tea. . . . I was still singing in the chorus. I was not successful then, as I became later. And I felt that his gesture would last me for my whole life. Even if nothing else happened to me, that was enough to fulfill a man's destiny."

And Bernardo felt, "My goodness, it's true." And the old man announced, breathlessly, "I Pagliacci. The clown's death. Here, there was always a lot of clapping for the aria and the bravura." The Maestro began to cry, and with the tears that made his makeup run, and with the wrinkles, and with the painted lips, he tried desperately to sing, but he could hardly get out the sounds. And when he was supposed to fall down dead, he looked down at the floor, first fell to his knees, touched the floor. Then threw himself down, "Il sono morto!"

A tense, heavy, terrible silence fell upon them. The old man lay gasping on the floor, and Bernardo gently put the trombone down on the bed; he began to applaud at first softly and then harder and finally with frantic intensity. The old man stood up, he made a ceremonial bow without looking at him, as if he was in the theater, and then he said, "The show is over."

With a towel he slowly began to remove his makeup. He gasped. He walked over to the bed, he took out a suitcase and opened it, there were buttons and also thread and combs and bottles. From under the clutter he took out a book bound in red velvet with torn, musty pages. It was a prayer book. He leafed through it and took out a large grayish page, well thumbed, ornamented with curlicued designs.

"Today the actors play," said the old man, and he handed it to Bernardo. "And here is a ruble from Tzar Nicholas. The only one I have," he said, and he smiled at the boy with his enormous, crazy, perverse eyes that were beginning to disturb Bernardo. The old man came up to him. Bernardo felt his pressured breathing on his face; the greasepaint around the border of his eyes ran down his cheeks.

"We could do a tour together," the old man said, and Bernardo noticed that he was crying. "We could travel the country. . . . We could do many things together. . . ." Bernardo got up. "Stay, Sr. Katz. It is still early. Let us make plans. We have the night ahead of us. . . ." He was pleading with him, trembling. He was in tears. "It is still early, take another cup of tea. . . ." said the old man. And all of a sudden he embraced him. *"Hob rakhmones!* Have pity on me!"

And then Bernardo ran toward the door, he opened it, shaking with fear, and he ran away from the old man forever, toward the night, toward the rain, toward the savage city. The old man remained, standing in his room, asking for pity, and he was alone.

Translated by Nora Glickman

GERARDO MARIO GOLOBOFF
(b. 1 9 3 9)

THE PASSION
ACCORDING TO
SAN MARTÍN

*I*nfluenced by Borges's prose style and Julio Cortázar's nostalgia, this autobiographical story, set in the late 1940s and early 1950s, is a re-creation of Argentina under tyranny—a tour de force detailing the small-scale adventures of a Jewish adolescent in search of himself and his role as citizen in a provincial town where Juan Domingo Perón and his followers ramble the streets. Part of a generation torn between political activism and exile, the author explores the meaning of friendship, loyalty, ethnic relations, and first love.

Children, beware of idols.
—First epistle of Saint John, 5:21.

THE NOTEBOOKS CARRIED HER NAME, AND SO DID THE PENCIL BOXES, THE pens, the erasers, the dust covers. Besides, the entire morning she was before us, hanging at the center of the main wall of a huge classroom with three high windows that overlooked the street and from where one could hear the daily rumors, the voices of the fruit vendors and passers-by.

My pages were dirty, full of ineradicable spots. At first, my goal was to keep them almost untouched, but as the week went by I saw how they would be wearing out from the multiple crossings-out. I was also a sad boy, and perhaps that's why I couldn't stop the slow corruption of these promising white notebooks.

In any case, the figure of the "Great Captain" adorned the first page. In that sixth grade, we were asked to start (and finish and populate) everything with him: exactly a hundred years ago he had died in a site in France with a name, of strange pronunciation, suggesting the sea and exile. I made that first beloved page my own, and with my sharpened, self-centered pencil and my best wishes, I would begin my immeasurable attempt to reproduce in lines and silhouettes what was undoubtedly beyond my patriotic ability.

His virtues were so grandiose they escaped the improvisation of a child; nevertheless, time and again I insisted. I would start with his upturned nose, then descend to the fine mouth. Later, tenuously and decisively, I would reproduce the solitary chin where the design couldn't hide the ugly features, continue with the neck, and return to the shadow of the face and the curved ears and infinite sideburns; I would entertain myself with the arabesques of his visible uniform, and would leave the eyes, the forehead, everything from the top, to the deferred, inescapable end. Those eyes meant the worst to me. I was never able to place them in a precise location nor could I find the exact size, the adequate form, the color, not even the eloquent and clear expression— the inimitable independent spirit that led him to his victory.

I found myself alone in unmatched combat. Nobody was around. The other boys had departed as if in a feverish dream. The eyes of the "Condor of the Andes" scrutinized me from on high. I penetrated them until I swallowed them up, but then my pencil improved on their form and the true lines of my drawing would vanish.

In the end, I would finish in any way possible. The bell that announced intermission liberated me and led toward the exit. But then the expression on the face of the teacher approaching my bench would appear, screaming: "Finish once and for all! You can't spend the entire morning creating that disastrous portrait." And, truthfully, when I opened the workbook at home, I would shamefully contemplate my oeuvre: the portrait was a caricature, as removed from the original we had in front of us in the classroom as from any human figure.

Wasn't I a good enough patriot? Didn't I feel the same as everybody else? Or as some claimed, did I draw such garbage because I was Jewish and didn't love Argentina? This last question emerged from the mouth of Miss Bileto in the silent class, astonishing me and everyone else as a mere possibility. Ana María (I knew later on, when I returned to school after a brief illness) was the only one who answered no, or the only one who at least answered something, arguing that I was a bad painter and that was all: she knew I loved my country more than any other, and that I had never said anything bad about the "Saint of the Sword" or, for that matter, any other general.

Those years were difficult—perhaps every single generation in our inhabitable world can claim the same. And probably it's true. But everyone must give account of the conflicts that have consumed him, and perhaps by adding together all those sufferings one could find the meaning of a certain truth, and through limited truths (in an uncertain future) understand the vastness of history. Ours started before the titanic eyebrows of the *Libertador* in a town school, when we were eleven or twelve, and ended much later. Or perhaps is only now finishing at forty-something, when I try to paint, without artifice other than the simple word, a face that escaped me—that of Ana María.

She was among the best in the class. She was the only daughter, an adopted child (it was a well-known secret) of a woman who was the school's guard. Hiding with decorousness her humble origin, she was loved and respected because of her spirit of comradeship. "Conduct" was as important a grade as any other, and although she got high marks, her power in the classroom depended on the few carefully selected occasions when she spoke out. She would do it tenderly, to make herself heard; she would create an oasis in the midst of our noise and endless disorganization. Naturally brief, naturally fair, naturally Catholic in a town where exceptions were few, her somber defense of me that day ended forever Miss Bileto's poisonous hostility against me. And at the same time it opened for us a road we had never explored before: one in which I expressed my gratitude, our mutual solidarity, which not even age or time or the harsh obstacles that the years would bring could diminish.

I mentioned how that period was difficult; the circumstances, nevertheless, never succeeded in diminishing our increasing fraternity. That's how I need to describe it since I couldn't really say we were friends: the gender differences were much more important at that time than today, and visiting her more often would have been unthinkable. Neither did we know the possibilities of love: perhaps our dreams came close at one time, but I'm afraid only mine were the ones that looked for her, and in that case I would be dishonoring her memory if I went into detail narrating them. Besides, I'm not writing to talk about me or of my nights; I'm doing it to portray a dream that doesn't belong to me—an unattainable breath, her childish face against the storm.

No, we didn't love each other, nor did we lose each other: the idols took care of all that. The idols and my difficulty in worshipping them.

Once sixth grade was over, I registered in the National School and she in the Commercial; I slowly became accustomed to and enjoyed the company of street friends and hooligans; I remember wanting, and having, some success with women. Fortunately, Ana María remained apart from those relationships and from those frantic contacts. Once in a while we would meet at a secret corner, keep up an innocent dialogue about our respective companions and studies, and leave knowing that we lived right here, in a universe still visible, present, routine.

In the year 1952 I saw her parade down the naked streets of our town surrounded by huge crowds; sad men and women were marching behind and in front of Ana María—peasants, construction workers, workers in the only oil refinery in the area, modest wage earners, maids. They mourned the image of Eva (for them, "Evita"), recently deceased but already eternal. All were indistinguishable under the silence of leafless trees. A movie with Sterling Hayden and Jean Hagen was playing that night at the Rex Cinema: I thought I would miss it, never to find out what happens "when the city sleeps," because this one, mine, never slept; it was living a nightmare that was just beginning, that would eventually overwhelm us all. The spectacle seemed grotesque; protected behind the living-room window I smiled. When I saw Ana María again, this time next to her mother, her pain was painful to me, as was my having to smile. I was unaware of the evil human beings are capable of, and I played with other people's mourning like a perverse god.

The long-awaited storm began in June 1955. By then we were feeling suffocated even in our own home, and not even in front of Francisca (who since my birth worked for us) were we able to speak up. The uprising had failed, but even during those brief hours of patience Dad signaled to me not to discuss anything with her. The good woman, in her simple words, explained the disgrace the country was experiencing and how everybody was against "those selling our country out," those same ones who, in an incoherent screenplay, "had killed Moreno and Belgrano, San Martín and Evita." Out of compassion, out of esteem, we allowed her to talk. Also out of prudence: the official radio didn't wait long to synchronize its revenge, and at home the lights in the dining and living rooms were turned off.

September brought long-awaited freedom. The tyranny fell and with it the statues. Indeed, as students of the Fifth National School we destroyed the biggest and most ridiculous of them all, the one at the ugly Prócer Plaza. I had already begun to write during that time and would discover (or others would help me discover) the innate simplicity of oratory. Encouraged by the misguided adolescents around me, I gave feverish speeches in favor of victory, and I also spoke a few tempting sentences about my own work at the semester-end party. Ana María was there, the representative of the Commercial School, and naturally heard all of my grievances. For a while that didn't bother me, and I didn't even get close to her; perhaps during my speech I had given vent to my indignation regarding the nation's blindness; perhaps my heated fury angered a few.

A little while later there was a ball complete with two orchestras. Although I've always been timid about waltzes, I danced to Mexican songs and loose rock-and-roll melodies. At a certain moment, stumbling and losing my balance (a few drops of alcohol had helped create such state), I saw her. I thought she was looking at me, not dancing, next to two friends. Defiantly, I crossed the dancing platform, and when I saw myself close enough by her side, disloyal, ostentatious, I was afraid of a possible rejection. She greeted me without much enthusiasm, introduced me to her friends, and invited me to share a table. I told her I preferred to dance, and she consented. I sensed she didn't need an explanation because she knew the secrets of men.

We danced. One, two, three numbers. The singer made a mistake in the lyrics of "Garúa" and I quoted them to her: "Nobody can be seen crossing the corner. The row of street lights illuminates the asphalt dying on the street. And I walk without paying attention, always alone, always by myself, remembering you." She praised my talent for memorizing and my ideas; that gave me the poise that perhaps not even she possessed. Ashamed, I looked her straight in the eyes and heard: "Don't be afraid, some day all this sadness will turn into happiness." I forgot that we were dancing, I forgot where we were, I forgot my feverish speeches; but I didn't forget it was the first time I was embracing her.

We talked about unimportant subjects, and also about her and me. But we never discussed, as if by tacit agreement, the possibilities that could lead to our separation. Our understanding was there, fresh, still untouched, a gamble against corrosion.

The memories that immediately follow that incident belong to an improbable maturity. I abandoned my native town for a cold city where the streets made my confusion more profound: they were like the dreams created by a bizarre and hermetic tyrant to provoke false perceptions. I walked through those streets anxiously looking for clues to my own childhood, but neither the houses nor the people were the same, and I learned to understand myself as a mutable creature in a vulnerable world.

Once in a while I would return to my hometown to see my parents; the encounters were difficult and hostile. I was already engaged in that examination of consciousness typical of my generation, and had begun analyzing the abyss that separated us from what was referred to in those days as "the masses." Intellectuals without a soil, we were searching for a place in history, and to find it we needed to perceive the past both with our eyes and heart. Dad blamed our discussions and confusion on the university and "on who knows what other type of company."

I looked for her during those trips. I was anxious for something more than an encounter and the return of a lost dialogue; something more than the mere recovery of a lost face and an expression I hardly managed to remember; something more than the fantasy of an impossible affair. Undergoing deep changes in my ways of perceiving the country and our destiny, I needed her agreement, now possible, and her immeasurable forgiveness.

I couldn't see her. She and her mother had also moved away from town, and nobody knew (or wanted to give me) her address. Somebody told me that her mother had died in Buenos Aires; somebody else insinuated the possibility of "dangerous" militant activities in the northern provinces. But nothing was certain. Years have gone by and blood has been shed in a savage way. Today the whole country is nothing but a pile of ashes, and the few pieces of wood feeding the fire belong to tyranny. Most probably Ana María succumbed; she had only one body to carry her message, and perhaps she had to give it up, letting it flow into the pollen nurturing the flowers and the water feeding the plants. I have never known for sure what her fate was, and perhaps I don't want to know. I look for her name here and there but I've never seen it, and that gives me a slight hope. Deep inside I know she is no longer among us. She has passed away like a shadow or the wind in the trees. Others have loved her and followed her. In our painful south, in our deserted pampa, in our immense salty dunes, in the obscure paths of the city or in the hungry valleys, they must have witnessed her silent communion, her sacrifice, her good spirit. I portray her from the vantage of miniscule, endless diaspora—me, always a stranger, always small in scale. I'm uncertain about her silhouette, about her complexion, and about the events that enveloped us; but I am sure about the setting. She touches my hand with a childish sweetness, and sings instead of crying over the motion of the seas.

To Oscar Terán

Translated by Ilan Stavans

NORA GLICKMAN
(b. 1 9 4 4)

THE LAST EMIGRANT

Frist published in its English translation in 1982 in the New York City Zionist monthly Jewish Frontier, the setting of this tale is the province of La Pampa. The female narrator, a Yiddish-speaking girl, is infatuated with Baruch Leiserman, a businessman who witnessed the Russian Revolution before settling with his sick wife in Argentina. In re-creating the life of East European immigrants who dream of Israel while labor unrest sweeps neighboring Buenos Aires, Nora Glickman charmingly evokes the failure of an entire generation of Jewish settlers to accept, or at least understand, their South American environment.

OLD LEISERMAN IS DEAD, THE EMIGRANT, BARUCH LEISERMAN. THE NEWS shook loose memories of my hometown in the province of La Pampa. I remembered how much closer he was than my grandfather, or any uncle for that matter.

As the days grew longer, Mama would take me along on visits to see him and his wife, Sara. Around five, Dad might be engaging a customer in some interminable discussion about renewing an insurance policy and Mama would take advantage of the opportunity to escape from the office and would go to look for me at home.

It was just a few blocks away, we walked. Lanuse's bar exhaled its beery and smoky breath that followed us as far as the corner. The Viners and the

Shames would set up their wicker chairs next to the entrances of their respective stores to be able to kibitz with each other. The women seemed older than the men; they rocked slowly and chatted in Yiddish mixed with Spanish. Then we would pass Litner's bakery where a furry, dirty dog stretched out and blocked the sidewalk, undoubtedly paralyzed by the languid, penetrating aroma of freshly baked loaves. Or perhaps by age. Anyway, Mama would buy a few pastries there and Mrs. Litner would keep her posted on the rheumatism that was swelling her knees as well as on her mother who lay dying in the room in back. Mama always listened quietly: things seemed to worsen at a comfortable rate, and there would be months and months to enjoy the same pastries and the same conversation.

Sara Leiserman would treat us to a tureen full of toasted sunflower seeds, with *leykach*, honey cake, and *prekuske*, Russian tea, and we bit on lumps of sugar as we drank the tea. I liked to dip the sugar a little bit at a time and watch it turn brown in the hot tea. Then Sara would take a nap. She was always tired, and Mama stayed to chat with Baruch. I went to the storehouse in back, cradling corn in my dress and feeding it to the chickens around the patio. Sometimes I threw a handful as hard as I could just to see them run and cackle a little. Other times I chased them and plucked their feathers. Baruch's old roan always stood by the water trough; he scratched his neck against its rusty edge, though he never cut himself. I would fill a bag full of grass for him and hang it on his neck to see him through the night.

Mama would still be talking when I went back in the house. I listened to them while going through Sara's shoe-box full of yellowing photographs. Baruch talked about the Russian Revolution, the ear infection he inflicted on himself to avoid the draft—it still acted up now and then—and the labor unrest in Buenos Aires. Mama commented on articles from the Yiddish newspaper. She was big on Israel, Zionism, and the kibbutzes, although Baruch didn't see any advantage in a Jewish homeland. "It's better for them to hate us separately; a Jewish state surrounded by Arab enemies won't last very long as a democracy." Just to needle him, Mama would make me sing *Wir furn kayn Eretz Israel** and then sing along even louder than me. Then it was *Zog mir shvester Leybn, vos ich vel dir freign†* where Leybn declares her intention to grow oranges in Israel and forget about the Diaspora. Mama put everything into

---

*We are traveling to the Land of Israel.—Ed.
†Tell me, sister Life, what I want to ask you.—Ed.

those songs; she seemed to feel herself nearer to Israel, free of the burden of the *goles,* the Diaspora.

Baruch made fun of her, grimacing with an impatient *Achhh,* waving away the songs with his thick and hairy hand. Then all of a sudden, he would grab me around the waist and say *"Danushka mayns, zing mir 'unter'n vigele,'"** which was his favorite song. I complied willingly and sang that and other songs while they hummed along in time. Baruch had a certain way of closing his eyes and arching his thick, bushy eyebrows, creating a magic, irresistibly appealing space in front of his forehead. When he opened his eyes again, it was as if he had woken up with a shudder. I don't know if it was pleasant or not, because he usually preempted discussion with some mundane observation.

It was during these visits that Mom did Baruch's bookkeeping, and there was always an argument. She would marshal two or three figures and show how he could replace the carriage with a used pickup, how if the outer hall were blocked off—the one leading to the grapevines—the house wouldn't get so cold during the winter, how it was better to have one laborer year-round rather than employ three just for the harvest. . . . Baruch would raise his hands to his cheeks, pressing them hard, telling Mama how the plague of grasshoppers had ruined everything two years before, and how when the Perels' fields went up in smoke just before the harvest, his was saved only because the wind changed direction; how another fire like that, or perhaps hail, like in '51, could leave him penniless, and then, what would become of him? You always needed to keep something in reserve.

Mama would get exasperated: "My daughter is right—you're just an old tightwad and you'll never invest in anything, you old hardhead, you'll never get anywhere that way." Then, a few minutes of truce during which nothing could be heard except the crackling of the fire. Sunflower-seed husks piled up on the checkered tablecloth, or fell to the floor.

Back in the office, Dad would be grouchy, doing sums, tearing up sheets of paper and tossing them into the wastebasket—somehow he never missed, although he never seemed to try very hard. "You left Blanca alone at the cash register and she made some mistakes again . . . you left without posting the balance." "It's not as if I'm your employee," Mama replied. "Blanca gets paid to be a cashier, not me." Dad kept on crumpling paper into little balls and

---

*"My Danushkea, sing 'Under the Cradle' to me."—Ed.

looking over his notes. There was no more discussion, though she stayed and worked until the evening. How could she just drop everything to go and see that *shlimazl*, that poor, lazy Baruch? What did she see in him? But she stood up for him—"He's got *seykl*. He thinks. He reads more than all of you put together, he should never have stayed in this crummy little town, this Bernasconi Bernashmoni." And then, *shoyn*, that's enough! and the matter was closed.

But Dad did feel sorry for Sara. She was stuck with Baruch. She survived the pogrom in Russia, she lived through it all in Vilna by a miracle, though now, in Argentina, her luck had run out. She used to tell how she was the only one to hide in time when the Cossacks broke into her uncle's house; she saw everything and forgot nothing. The hooligans broke up the furniture with their sabers, tore up the comforters and the pillows and filled the room with feathers. They gutted Sara's uncle, a large man, and filled him with the feathers. Her aunt wailed and they tore her eyes out before killing her. I can't remember exactly what they did with the girls. Sara was an orphan and lived with them. After the pogrom my *zeyde** brought her to Argentina, passing her off as her daughter. Sara was quiet and withdrawn. She seemed to rub her complaints off her veined hands by rubbing them into her apron. According to Dad, Baruch never even looked at her before taking her to wife—and probably never looked at her after, either. His first wife died while giving birth to her fourth child and the others were still small. It was clear that he couldn't handle them by himself, and there was Sara, available, submissive. Mama says that people are just the way they are, and if Sara wanted to be a martyr, she got what she wanted.

We had moved several years before to Bahía. Every summer we passed through Bernasconi, but just because it was on the way to the farm. Sometimes we dropped in to say hello to the Leisermans, but it just wasn't the same anymore. Dad came along with us, and the visits were always cut short so we could see as many friends and relatives—and offend as few—as possible.

Baruch's accident happened at his farm, a short distance from the town. He apparently saw the tornado coming; nobody better than he could read the pinkish streaks in the clouds—like an old-time gaucho he understood the menace implicit in the motionless air, suspended like in a photograph. So Baruch must have anticipated the inexorable advance of the dark column that swal-

---

*Grandfather—Ed.

lowed everything in its path and he, Baruch, the headstrong emigrant, had to thwart it, defeat it, just long enough to get his four panic-stricken cows into the barn; he went out alone to close the gates and protect his cattle.

The farmhand just happened to be in town that day. When he returned the following morning, he found Baruch among the wreckage, a hundred yards from the barn, in the middle of a huge puddle left by the storm. Baruch rolled into the mud, dragging with him all the plants he ever seeded during his life there. What would he have been thinking? About the cows that wouldn't make it? Whether he had enough supplies in reserve? The unfinished business? No: he probably just closed his eyes, just like when he liked a song, and then knitted his brow and let himself go, carried away in his magic poncho.

Translated by John Benson

AÍDA BORTNIK
(b. 1 9 4 2)

CELESTE'S HEART

The protagonist of this brief tale by the award-winning screen-writer of The Official Story (1985), published for the first time in 1989 in Alberto Manguel's translation, is a rebellious Jewish girl in an authoritarian milieu. Forced to act against her will, against common sense, she slowly and courageously speaks out, expressing her valor not in grand-scale historic events but in silent resistance toward the most conventional of daily acts.

CELESTE WENT TO A SCHOOL THAT HAD TWO YARDS. IN THE FRONT YARD THEY held official ceremonies. In the back yard the Teacher made them stand in line, one behind the other at arm's distance, keeping the arm stretched out straight in front, the body's weight on both legs, and in silence. One whole hour. Once for two whole hours. All right, not hours. But two breaks passed, and the bell rang four times before they were allowed back into the classroom. And the girls from the other classes, who played and laughed during the first break as if nothing had happened, stopped playing during the second break. They stood with their backs to the wall and watched them. They watched the straight line, one behind the other at arm's length, in the middle of the school yard. And no one laughed. And when the Teacher clapped her hands to indicate that the punishment was over, Celeste was the only one who didn't stretch, who didn't complain, who didn't rub her arm, who didn't march smartly back into the classroom. When they sat down, she stared quietly at the Teacher. She stared at her in the same way she used to stare at the new words on the blackboard, the ones whose meaning she didn't know, whose exact purpose she ignored.

That evening, as she was putting her younger brother to bed, he asked once again: "When am I going to go to school?" But that evening she didn't laugh, and she didn't think up an answer. She sat down and hugged him for a while, as she used to do every time she realized how little he was, how little he knew. And she hugged him harder because she suddenly imagined him in the middle of the school yard, with his arm stretched out measuring the distance, the body tense, feeling cold and angry and afraid, in a line in which all the others were as small as he was.

And the next time the Teacher got mad at the class, Celeste knew what she had to do.

She didn't lift her arm.

The Teacher repeated the order, looking at her somewhat surprised. But Celeste wouldn't lift her arm. The Teacher came up to her and asked her, almost with concern, what was the matter. And Celeste told her. She told her that afterward the arm hurt. And that they were all cold and afraid. And that one didn't go to school to be hurt, cold and afraid.

Celeste couldn't hear herself, but she could see her Teacher's face as she spoke. And it seemed like a strange face, a terribly strange face. And her friends told her afterwards that she had spoken in a very loud voice, not shouting, just a very loud voice. Like when one recited a poem full of big words, standing on a platform, in the school's front yard. Like when one knows one is taking part in a solemn ceremony and important things are spoken of, things that happened a long time ago, but things one remembers because they made the world a better place to live than it was before.

And almost every girl in the class put down her arm. And they walked back into the classroom. And the Teacher wrote a note in red ink in Celeste's exercise book. And when her father asked her what she had done, and she told him, her father stood there staring at her for a long while, but as if he couldn't see her, as if he were staring at something inside her or beyond her. And then he smiled and signed the book without saying anything. And while she blotted his signature with blotting paper, he patted her head, very gently, as if Celeste's head were something very very fragile that a heavy hand could break.

That night Celeste couldn't sleep because of an odd feeling inside her. A feeling that had started when she had refused to lift her arm, standing with the others in the line, a feeling of something growing inside her breast. It burned a bit, but it wasn't painful. And she thought that if one's arms and legs and other parts of one's body grew, the things inside had to grow too. And yet legs and arms grow without one being aware, evenly and bit by bit. But the heart probably grows like this: by jumps. And she thought it seemed like a logical thing: the heart grows when one does something one hasn't done before, when one learns something one didn't know before, when one feels something different and better for the first time. And the odd sensation felt good. And she promised herself that her heart would keep growing. And growing. And growing.

Translated by Alberto Manguel

MARIO SZICHMAN
(b. 1 9 4 5)

REMEMBRANCES OF THINGS FUTURE

Critics concur in viewing the author of this sardonic tale as the true Latin American inheritor of the tradition of self-denigrating Jewish humor. His famous novel At 8:25 Evita Became Immortal *(1981), which won the Ediciones del Norte Prize, describes the three-decade-long pilgrimage from immigration to assimilation of the Pechoff family in Buenos Aires, complete with their change of name to Gutiérrez-Anselmi to hide their Jewish identity. Set in Poland in 1939—according to the Hebrew calendar the year 5700, a time when Argentine Jews, victimized by the* Semana Trágica *pogrom and other blunt anti-Semitic attacks, were beginning to recognize the nation as incapable of sustaining democratic values and tolerance—the plot of this comic story, published here for the first time, deals with the bombing of Jewish schools, both progressive and Orthodox, and the response of government authorities to Jewish resistance. The narrative viewpoint is that of the mother of Shmulik the galley-proof messenger, a poor woman unable to understand the political implications of her son's unexpected disappearance. The implicit themes, of course, are the Holocaust and Jewish self-hatred.*

◇

AT THE TIME THAT THE PEOPLE IN PINYE OSTROPOLER'S TOWN BEGAN TO
search for the whereabouts of their family members, the postman got into the
habit of calling twice at first, and three times by the end, until there was no
one left in any condition to receive the mail.

Every morning of that hazard-filled year of 1939, the postman would
show up in his impeccable gray suit, and with a smile he would present the
good news. In the afternoon, he would show up rigorously attired in mourning clothes, to deliver the instructions to one of the neighbors. It never failed
that someone in town would think, "I am sure that someone in my neighbor's
family must have done something to deserve these instructions." And those
suspicions were usually confirmed. The instructions would order the neighbor
to go to the town's century-old tree and pick up a message left atop the fourth
branch from the bottom; thus he would find out that his relative's whereabouts
had been lost after becoming an infiltrator. It was signed "A friend." Usually,
after reading the letter, the neighbor would pack up his bundles and take a
chartered ship to other lands—ridden by guilt but never by fear, for Poland
was a country endowed by laws of a profound humanist content, a beautiful
tradition went hand in hand with its population, and may God grant you
peace.

One of the few occasions on which this routine was broken happened
with Shmulik's mother—Shmulik was the galley-proof messenger. Until re-
ceiving the instructions and finding out that his whereabouts were lost after
having become an infiltrator, the woman had been proud of her Shmulik,
because his official whereabouts had been a calendar factory in the mountain-
ous region of N. The woman had thought that such whereabouts were immutable, for she had told her Shmulik the fable of the naughty boy who was
kidnapped by the monkey after having taken his hands out of his pockets; and
so, her son never dared to play around with his own buttons or his salary,
thus reaching a position where he earned money by the fistful.

When the poor woman received the instructions, she asked Pinye to come
along with her to the tree because she did not know how to climb it. Pinye
collected the message and that is how the woman found out that it seemed as
if her son's whereabouts had been lost. "If you had shown concern for your
little treasure's whereabouts, you would have known by now that he is taking

his hands out of his pockets. It takes only one step from that to becoming an infiltrator," said the message, signed by the usual friend.

"How did I go wrong?" wondered the poor woman. Perhaps she had given her Shmulik a secular education? But that had been the only way to keep him out of the fun and games. Other kids of his generation had decided sometime in their puberty to take their hands out of their pockets, and there you have it now: they spend the entire day with their noses stuck in some Talmudic scroll, trying to find their whereabouts in an unattainable past of splendor, while their women take food out of their own mouths to keep the children fed. But not her Shmulik. Deprived of the use of his hands, Shmulik had to rely on his nose to find the right way to go, and from having used it so many times to steer the sled during the winter, its shape was now aerodynamic. Besides, at the Hebrew calendar-printing shop where Shmulik worked, they were not interested in the past but in the years to come. This was something that, in that year of 1939, the Jews demanded to see in block letters, since they considered it beyond reach. That is why all the members of the community would fight to get calendars; they wanted to lay their hands on a tomorrow riddled with seasons and ceremonies evocative, first, of their martyrs, and then of their heroes, sure that the massacre at the hands of Chmielnicki would always be rescinded by the victory of Bar-Kochba.

The calendar-printing shops could not keep up with the demand, and Shmulik's capacity to maintain his hands in his pockets was highly valued, because his long arms allowed him to create huge openings that the typographers would stuff with galley proofs. And, with a slight turn of the head, Shmulik could follow the direction of the wind at twice the speed of other galley messengers.

The owner of the calendar shop rewarded such skill by depositing 200 zlotys in Shmulik's cap every month. This allowed him to pay for his room and board with a family whose members were in charge of putting the spoon in and out of his mouth, unbuttoning his clothes, and mending his pockets; even so he still saved 120 zlotys, which he sent his mother through Nusn, the water carrier.

Shmulik had won eight prizes for best messenger of the month, and the medals clinked proudly on his cap. The owner of the calendar shop had even hinted that there was a possibility of making him a partner. And out of the blue, all this was about to be thrown out the window because the selfish child decided to take his hands out of his pockets—such was the mother's lament to Pinye. Instead of feeling guilty on account of the message in the tree and packing up her bundles, the mother decided to search for her son's whereabouts so she could reproach him for his sudden decision to ruin his own life.

Pinye listened to the woman's grief and counseled patience. Maybe Shmulik had no further need of a whereabouts.

The poor woman, however, was not ready to resign herself. Everyone must have a whereabouts, ran her argument. Pinye suggested that perhaps her son had taken his hands out of his pockets to reach for a bottle and, stupefied by the alcohol, had awakened the next day married to a Gypsy. One of these days, while the mother was needlessly worrying, the son would be getting ready to give her the great *nakhes* [happiness] of making her a grandma.

The woman reproached Pinye for his insensitivity. It was clear that he had not been the one to give up his life to provide her Shmulik with an education, she told him. Her son was incapable of doing such a thing to his mother.

To placate her, Pinye recommended that she treat her son not only as a youngster who is respectful of tradition, but also as an ingrate about to lose his whereabouts. The poor woman, disturbed by such words of consolation, sent a letter in the next morning's mail to the calendar shop where Shmulik worked, demanding to know his whereabouts. She was one of those old-fashioned mothers whose only concern was to devote her whole life to her son, the letter stated.

When the poor woman received a reply by telegram indicating that the company could not furnish such information and asking her to please not compromise them further, she decided to modify her strategy by sending her reproaches written directly on the envelope. She had the habit of addressing her complaints to "The Ingrate Who Is About to Lose His Whereabouts." None of her letters received a reply.

The poor woman came back to Pinye for advice. What did he suggest she do? She did not intend to rest until she found out her son's whereabouts. Wouldn't it be best to go to the police and search in the Missing Persons Bureau? Pinye pleaded with the poor woman not to involve any of the authorities until she knew what to expect. Could she have possibly forgotten about Gitele? She, too, had searched for a half-brother who had been accused of becoming an infiltrator. And what happened? When the authorities finally discovered where he was, Gitele remembered that she had had a whole brother before his disappearance. Pinye recommended that the woman wait for a while. The best thing would be to carry out some discreet inquiries. He could take care of the matter.

The woman thanked Pinye for all the trouble he was taking, and this time sent her letter in the afternoon mail, addressed to the owner of the calendar-printing shop. In it she worried about the whereabouts of her son, so respectful of tradition but an ingrate about to ruin his own life. In the postscript she implored the heavens to let there be no suspicious contents in the packages her Shmulik carried.

The owner of the calendar-printing shop received the woman's message, went to the town's century-old tree, collected the letter, and read it, fearing that he had sullied his family name because of some infiltrator. He rolled it up into a ball, threw it into some bushes, packed up his bundles (among which were several boxes with brand-new calendars), left his house in the late hours of the night, and took off for other lands in a chartered ship, the *Cracow Baroness*. The ship obtained denials of asylum in Southampton and Reykjavik and wound up stranded in the Sargasso Sea. Some of the calendar packages were jettisoned to sea when the captain decided to lighten the load on the ship, and they ended up washing ashore in Calais. The cryptographers of the French intelligence service analyzed the calendars and determined that they were texts in code from German spies confirming the invulnerability of the Maginot Line.

Meanwhile, the letter sent by the poor woman to the owner of the calendar-printing shop was found by a park ranger who unfolded it, smoothed out its creases, examined it by flashlight, adjusted his cap, scratched his head, thought that "he must have done something to deserve this message," and immediately notified the authorities.

The following day, the police were ordered to discreetly surround the printing shop in order to capture the poor woman's son. They knew the infiltrator's description very well: he generally walked around with his hands in his pockets and carried around packages suspicious in nature, as attested by the postscript in the letter written by his mother and the hurried departure of the printing-shop owner.

That afternoon, the police investigation met with success. A stranger, his cap covered with medals, crossed a checkpoint on his sled, carrying two suspicious-looking packages under his arms. When asked about what he carried, he replied that they were galley proofs from over there, pointing toward the printing shop with his aerodynamic nose, since he had his hands in his pockets. The policemen exchanged knowing glances and allowed him to infiltrate the place.

Not ten minutes had gone by when the bomb squad arrived and placed an explosive charge among the suspicious packages, blowing them up. A hole in the shape of the foundation was left where the printing shop had previously stood. And exactly in the center of that hole were the remains of a sled, a cap covered with medals, and two suspicious-looking packages, somewhat tattered but able to be collated. They contained galley proofs full of foreign-language characters.

The chief of police, fearing a conspiracy, called an expert in ancient languages, who confirmed his worst suspicions. Someone, in 1939 in Poland, was sparing no effort to fire up the minds of the Jews, filling them with nonsense about the future. And what a future! In a few months they expected to reach the year 5700. The chief of police ordered barricades built on the main access roads to the printing shops to prevent the presence of new infiltrators.

The next day, the poor woman was informed of her son's death in a confrontation with the forces of law and order. Inside the medals on his cap they had found microfilm strips detailing a conspiracy on the part of some Hebrew calendar makers, whose intentions were to sow dissent.

That night, fearing that they had inadvertently sown dissent, the three most important Hebrew calendar makers packed up their bundles, among which were some boxes of brand-new calendars, left their homes in the late hours of the night, and took off to other lands in a chartered ship, the *Countess Petrovia*—ridden by guilt but never by fear. The passengers obtained refusals of asylum in Hamburg and Oslo, and their ship finally ran aground in Antwerp, where they were interned in a concentration camp as prisoners of war. Some of the packages were analyzed by cryptographers of the Belgian intelligence service, who determined them to be messages in code from German spies recommending respect for the neutrality of that country.

Meanwhile, in Pinye's town, the police were able to quell dissent by blowing up suspicious-looking packages, which Shmulik had dropped off at the doorways of various printing shops before his confrontation with the forces of law and order.

When there wasn't a printing press left untouched, the Hebrew calendar makers met in the barn they were allowed to use as a synagogue to undertake the analysis of their current historical juncture. Might it be that anti-Semitism was happening in their region, they inquired. But a delegate from the Jewish Congress asked them to pipe down, because it wasn't as if they lived (a) in Germany, where the official policy was to stick a yellow star on every Jew; or (b) in the Ukraine, where the official policy was to drag out the Jews into the main street, chained by the neck, and make them fight the bear while the stationmaster refused to sell them tickets to travel, not even on the roof of the train; or (c) by all means not in Russia, where the Czar's official policy was to deny any participation of the Black Cossacks in the pogroms, while Rasputin went around curing all his children, turned into hemophiliacs by the Jewish Conspiracy. Given that anti-Semitism was not an official policy, the best thing was to turn to the local authorities, recommended the delegate from the Jewish Congress while pulling up his lapels, since the heat radiated by the gathering of malnourished bodies could not sufficiently counter the cold that entered through the hole where once the roof had been.

Pinye then told the delegate about the disgrace heaped upon the poor woman. One of her messages had fallen into the hands of the local authorities, with results known to everybody. Her ignorance of her son's whereabouts had begun to get every printing shop blown up.

"Couldn't it be that her darling little treasure had been mixed up in some mess?" asked the delegate. "'Cause there are printing shops, and then there are printing shops. It isn't the same to have an Orthodox printing shop as a *progressiver* one." Take the Jews of Tarov, for instance. Their schools started to get blown up. But there are schools, and then there are schools. It is not the same to have an Orthodox school as a *progressiver* one. They could ask Lubcek, right there in the flesh, how the Jews of Tarov confronted their situation.

Lubcek, the Hungarian, explained to the gathering that the blowing up of Orthodox schools caused the children to go back home, while the blowing up of *progressiver* schools caused the children to be twice lost. "When they blow up one of our schools," said Lubcek, the Hungarian, "our children stay home and play all day. They don't get tired of playing, the little blessings from God. Oh, how they play! Then we feel remorse, we go to the synagogue, the rabbi reads some chapters of the Talmud where the prophets have foreseen that this would come to pass by reason of the sins we have committed, and we rebuild the school in double shifts so that our children are not deprived of their education. The government sends a communiqué, addressed to the noble and suffering Hebrew Community, promising a deserved punishment to whoever is held responsible, and Father Zozim, chaplain of the local chapter of the Black Cossacks, comes to the reopening of the facility. On the other hand, when the *progressiver* schools are blown up, all the students go underground, the government uncovers a conspiracy to have the throats of its most distinguished citizens brought to the guillotine, and one of the subversives always winds up murdered at the hands of one of his own comrades so that they can pin the blame on the police."

The people attending the meeting decided to send a petition to the authorities begging for their case to be considered. After all, they were Orthodox calendar makers, not *progressiver.*

The calendar makers were met with open arms by the mayor; the blowing up of their printing shops had deprived him of the 20 percent levy on alien activities. The mayor offered them tea with lemon and they all celebrated when he drank it in the Russian manner, clenching a lump of sugar between his teeth. After praising the noble and long-suffering Hebrew Community and announcing a new luxury tax to be collected by his son on the first and fifteenth days of every month, the mayor ordered the chief of police to extend any and all necessary protection to the calendar makers. And more.

Regrettably, the overzealousness of the police was detrimental to the activities of commerce; with their eyes ruined by the profusion of searchlights looking for clues in their facilities, and their behinds injured by poorly trained guard dogs, the majority of the calendar makers decided to leave in a chartered ship, the *Monrovia Duchess.* The travelers were able to obtain denials of asylum in Havana and Barranquilla, they crossed the Strait of Magellan, and from there the ship went straight to the Sargasso Sea, where it ended up stranded next to the *Cracow Baroness.*

Meanwhile, six Hebrew calendar makers who had been unable to take the ship on time with the rest of their colleagues were summoned by the chief of police to his office. On the functionary's desk was a cookie jar that read "Citizens for Responsibility Fund." The chief of police said that he had called on them to exhort them to renew their labor. He reminded them that their country was endowed by laws of a profound humanist content, a beautiful tradition went hand in hand with its population, and may God grant them peace. No one was forced to embroider a yellow star on their clothes, nor were they forced to go out on the street to fight the bear, and, moreover, stationmasters allowed Jews to travel on the roof of the train. They were living in the year 1939, this was Poland, and, moreover, the noble and long-suffering Hebrew Community expected to reach in a few months the year 5700. The indigenous population thought this difference to be an unfair privilege. Why not try to make the Hebrew calendar gradually come to match the Gregorian one? If they could find a way to bridge that gap, he would be very grateful to them. He appealed exclusively to their sense of duty. Indeed, he considered them to be responsible citizens. Or at least responsible. Discussions about their citizenship would come later. By the way, any contribution of two hundred, five hundred, or a thousand zlotys was entirely left up to the donors.

The calendar makers, mindful of the appeals from the chief of police, decided at that moment to begin producing calendars with increasingly lapsed dates in order to bridge that gap. The victory of Bar-Kochba continued to be marked, but the massacre of Chmielnicki was abruptly deleted, eliminating in one blow four hundred years of *tsuris* (misfortune). One of the makers even proposed to follow the suggestion of an expert on Delaporte calendars to limit each month to twenty-eight days. He figured out that this way, in a thousand years the Jews would be able to accomplish a history almost as wretched as that of the Polish people. But the proposal was discarded, since it meant that every year would begin exactly on the same day, obviating the need to make new calendars.

Afterward, the calendar makers began competing with each other to see who could avoid the most years of calamity. For instance, when one of them decided to cancel 1321 because that was the year of the Chinon Massacre, another responded by eliminating with one pen stroke the years 640 and 1096, thus wiping out the campaign of forced conversions in Byzantium and the Crusaders' massacre in Ratisbon. Each time they were able to eliminate a few years from their calendars the makers would appear before the chief of police, proudly demonstrating how the gap between the Hebrew and Gregorian calendars was decreasing. "We have already reached 4383, but that won't be all, that won't be all," the spokesman for the calendar makers would inform the chief of police. "It is my belief that, within a short time, we will be able to achieve even less history than the Swiss."

Clearly, the zeal that went into excising their past would sometimes limit the horizon of the calendar makers, like the time they discarded 1492 to eliminate the expulsion of the Jews from Spain and were left with the Americas yet to be discovered. But the dwindling Jewish Community did not complain about such potholes. The calendars had returned happiness to them, and they did not wish to lose it by clinging to historical rigor, for life itself already is full of sorrow.

Meanwhile, the poor woman who had lost her son's whereabouts in the confrontation with the forces of law and order received 120 zlotys from Nusn, the water carrier, accompanied by a newspaper clipping reporting the strange presence of a man with his hands stuck in his pockets ten minutes before the printing shops were blown up in places as remote as Radom, Kielce, and Piotrkow. The latest conflagration, said the reporter, had propelled the stranger toward the *Monrovia Duchess,* a ship scheduled to make stops in Havana and Barranquilla.

Mad with joy, the mother ran to show the clipping to the chief of police, who, upon seeing the reappearance of the likeness of someone who had died in a confrontation with the forces of law and order, searched in the Missing Persons Bureau, removed one name from the list, inserted it in the list of people who had died in a confrontation with the forces of law and order, placed the poor woman's son in the list where that recently found person had just been, and decided to apprehend the infiltrator dead or alive.

Initially, the chief of police had thought of continuing to quell the pockets of dissent with the help of the bomb squad. But immediately afterward, torn between the need to deal with the purveyors of social schism and the problems of the Internal Revenue Service, he decided to convene the calendar makers and ordered them to immediately report to him the presence of any infiltrator with his hands in his pockets. Furthermore, he informed them that as of that moment, they were to mark the national holidays in their Hebrew calendars, which carried a 10 percent tax on indigenous activities. And until the new collecting office could be set up, they would be able to deposit their tax payment in his personal account.

The Hebrew calendar makers gladly accepted those demands. They had no problem in reporting the presence of infiltrators, since they had been informed that the latest whereabouts of Shmulik's likeness was reportedly aboard the *Monrovia Duchess,* near the Sargasso Sea. As for the other part, they were enthusiastic about sharing their calendars with the Polish people, since that could only increase their sales.

However, upon inspection of the indigenous Polish calendars, the makers stumbled upon an unexpected difficulty. It might have been that those calendars were made in poor-quality printing shops, or perhaps it was due to negligence on the part of the historians, but the fact was that the majority of the national holidays coincided with the celebration of some pogrom.

The Hebrew calendar makers were in a real quandary. If they entered the national holidays they would lose all their Jewish clients: if they left them out, the protection offered by the local authorities would cease. Perplexed and undecided, they opted to ask for an appointment to see their protector.

The chief of police received them in his office and told them he was at their disposal. When the calendar makers presented him with their dilemma, the Chief of Police responded that they lived in a free country. There was no prior restraint, mail was not opened, there were no special laws or suspension of constitutional guarantees, a beautiful tradition went hand in hand with the population, and may God grant them peace. If they wished to continue making calendars without mentioning those dates on which the precious blood of the Polish people had been spilled, well, that was up to them.

That night, five of the six calendar makers tossed their few belongings into their trunks and took off aboard the *Moscovia Princess,* intending to join their old colleagues. The travelers were denied asylum in Valparaiso and El Callao. Even the Bolivian authorities offered to reject them, despite the fact that their nation lacked any access to the sea. Finally, the ship stumbled upon the *Cracow Baroness* and the *Monrovia Duchess* in the Sargasso Sea. The emaciated passengers of the *Cracow Baroness* and the *Monrovia Duchess* were transferred to the *Moscovia Princess.*

After meeting with denials of asylum in some minor ports, the *Moscovia Princess* ran aground in Antwerp, near the *Petrovia Countess.* While the combined passengers of all four ships were being interned in a prison camp, the Second World War broke out and they were liberated by the Nazis, who mistook them for Croatians. The calendar makers gathered their dwindling belongings and fled on to France. The war caught them by surprise over there, and they were forced to hide in caves and survive on wild truffles and strawberries. When the Liberation took place, they were put in front of the firing squad, first, because they spent the years of hardship living like Persian kings, and, second, because the code messages in their calendars had proclaimed the invulnerability of the Maginot Line, allowing their French patriots to rest on their laurels.

With respect to Shmulik's mother, every month she continued to receive 120 zlotys through Nusn, the water carrier, during the first two years of the war, and 200 zlotys from the last calendar maker left in town. The only thing that the calendar maker asked for in return was confirmation of Shmulik's definite absence from the town.

Armed with the newspaper clipping provided by the poor woman, and hoping to stay in business, the calendar maker decided to make use of the infallible recourse of currying official favor by plastering his calendars with previously forgotten national holidays safely distant from the dates of the pogroms. Everyone was happy, especially the Polish people, who for the likes of them had never imagined the existence of so many victories.

Nonetheless, even with the greatest of effort it was impossible to find a full supply of national holidays. Some months had to be fixed by including the Miraculous Apparition of the Virgin. For other months, the calendar maker would add mottos such as "Do not forget that next month we have a bounty of national holidays," or "There are only fifteen days left, how much can two weeks matter when we already have an important national holiday coming up?" But then came a recalcitrant month. There wasn't a single national holiday that could bring about any popular enthusiasm, nor was there a single Miraculous Apparition of the Virgin, and the next month marked a patriotic victory that had left the nation with 62,500 square miles of unredeemed territory provisionally occupied by Germany and Russia.

The calendar maker thought and thought about it, and finally arrived at what he supposed to be a good way to solve this. "Fortunately, as soon as next month's victory goes by, we will have something to celebrate," he wrote. But he would not be in any condition to do so.

Conversely, Shmulik's mother was able to celebrate her reunion with her son. One day she received a letter from Shmulik that announced his return and detailed his odyssey, starting with his escape from the explosions and ending with his arrival in Spain. The first detonation, he explained to his mother, had blasted him a distance from the shop, making it impossible for him to collect his cap filled with medals. After getting away from that place, he had been very busy dropping off Hebrew calendar galley proofs in the doorways of other printing shops, but the explosions kept throwing him farther and farther away, until he ended up without a job. At that moment, he discovered that there was no further purpose in going about with his hands in his pockets. He tried other fields of endeavor, but word had been getting around that his nose was like a magnet for the bomb squad, so he chose to get away, for a while, from everyone he knew. That was the reason he went aboard the *Monrovia Duchess*. Until things cleared up, the poor woman's son said, the best course of action was to travel, to be at one with nature, to spend each night under a different sky. In order to avoid new temptations, he had decided to begin proofreading captain's logbooks written in unknown languages. He was particularly interested in ignoring the language used in the logbook of the *Flying Dutchman*. But the log was sewn together with a grammar of the Bru language, the tongue of an Austro-Asiatic people, and Shmulik had become so fascinated by its complexity that he gave up all suspicion and studied it until he became an expert. Did his mother know that the Bru language had forty-one vowels? Thanks to that newly acquired knowledge, he was able to find out in the captain's logbook the way to free the ship that had run aground and pilot it over to Amsterdam, where a mine sent them flying through the air. Holding on to a piece of wood, Shmulik had floated all the way to Copenhagen and was able to seek refuge inside a windmill. He now figured that it would take him two more days to reach his hometown. Perhaps, he told his mother, they could get together under the century-old tree.

This time, the poor woman decided to seek Pinye's advice before taking action. Pinye suggested to her that there were sons, and then there were sons. It wasn't the same to have an Orthodox son as a *progressiver* one. The problem was that Orthodox children would return home in difficult times. On the other hand, *progressiver* children died twice. Why didn't she consider her son to be *progressiver* and thus lose him a second time?

The next morning, the poor woman went in tears to the *Free Tribune* news office and announced that she no longer had to know her son's whereabouts, since she had found out that he was dead. That very night the poor woman put her meager belongings in a trunk and left to meet with her son. The reunion was a tearful one.

The next day, the mayor read in the *Free Tribune* that the poor woman's son had been assassinated by one of his own comrades anxious to pin the blame on the constitutional authorities, and demanded the resignation of the chief of police for falsely attributing his death to a confrontation with the forces of law and order. Furthermore, as a Draconian measure, he decided to increase the postman's rounds to three a day, seeking to make up for losses of tax revenue by confiscating the property of absentee landlords.

Translated by Iván Zatz

bRAZIL

MOACYR SCLIAR
(b. 1 9 3 7)

INSIDE MY
DIRTY HEAD—THE HOLOCAUST

*P*rolific and prodigious, Scliar has a lighthearted style and an enchanting voice that recalls the art of Sholem Aleichem. But the tone in this extraordinary tale from the collection The Enigmatic Eye *(1989) is dark, ironic. As in Victor Perera's "Kindergarten," events are told from a child's point of view. At its center is an obsession with the tattooed concentration-camp numbers as a sign of personal identity, and also a sense that, after the Holocaust, the world has been invaded by impostors. Compared with Szichman's "Remembrances of Things Future," the focus here is, in Joseph Brodsky's words, "the dance of the ghosts of memory."*

INSIDE MY DIRTY HEAD, THE HOLOCAUST IS LIKE THIS:

I'm an eleven-year-old boy. Small, skinny. And dirty. Oh boy, am I ever dirty! A stained T-shirt, filthy pants, grimy feet, hands, and face: dirty, dirty. But this external dirt is nothing compared to the filth I have inside my head. I harbor nothing but evil thoughts. I'm mischievous, I use foul language. A dirty tongue, a dirty head. A filthy mind. A sewer inhabited by toads and poisonous scorpions.

My father is appalled. A good man, my father is. He harbors nothing but pure thoughts. He speaks nothing but kind words. Deeply religious; the most religious man in our neighborhood. The neighbors wonder how such a kind, pious man could have such a wicked son with such a bad character. I'm a disgrace to the family, a disgrace to the neighborhood, a disgrace to the world. Me and my dirty head.

My father lost some of his brothers and sisters in the Holocaust. When he talks about this, his eyes well up with tears. It's now 1949; the memories of World War II are still much too fresh. Refugees from Europe arrive in the city; they come in search of relatives and friends that might help them. My father does what he can to help these unfortunate people. He exhorts me to follow his example, although he knows that little can be expected from someone with such a dirty head. He doesn't know yet what is in store for him. Mischa hasn't materialized yet.

One day Mischa materializes. A diminutive, slightly built man with a stoop; on his arm, quite visible, a tattooed number—the number assigned to him in a concentration camp. He arouses pity, poor fellow. His clothes are in tatters. He sleeps in doorways.

Learning about this distressing situation, my father is filled with indignation: Something must be done about it, one can't leave a Jew in this situation, especially when he is a survivor of the Nazi massacre. He calls the neighbors to a meeting. I want you to attend it, he says to me (undoubtedly hoping that I'll be imbued with the spirit of compassion. I? The kid with the dirty head? Poor Dad).

The neighbors offer to help. Each one will contribute a monthly sum; with this money Mischa will be able to get accommodation in a rooming house, buy clothes, and even go to a movie once in a while.

They announce their decision to the diminutive man who, with tears in his eyes, gushes his thanks. Months go by. Mischa is now one of us. People take turns inviting him to their homes. And they invite him because of the stories he tells them in his broken Portuguese. Nobody can tell stories like Mischa. Nobody can describe like him the horrors of the concentration camp, the filth, the promiscuity, the diseases, the agony of the dying, the brutality of the guards. Listening to him brings tears to everybody's eyes. . . .

Well, not to everybody's. Not to mine. I don't cry. Because of my dirty head, of course. Instead of crying, instead of flinging myself upon the floor, instead of clamoring to heaven as I listen to the horrors he narrates, I keep asking myself questions. Questions like: Why doesn't Mischa speak Yiddish like my parents and everybody else? Why does he stand motionless and silent in the synagogue while everybody else is praying?

Such questions, however, I keep to myself. I wouldn't dare ask anybody such questions; neither do I voice any of the things that my dirty head keeps imagining. My dirty head never rests; day and night, always buzzing, always scheming. . . .

I start imagining this: One day another refugee, Avigdor, materializes in the neighborhood. He, too, comes from a concentration camp; unlike Mischa, however, he doesn't tell stories. And I keep imagining that this Avigdor is introduced to Mischa; and I keep imagining that they detest each other at first sight, even though at one time they were fellow sufferers. I imagine them one night seated at the table in our house; we're having a party, there are lots of people. Then suddenly—a scene that my dirty head has no difficulty devising—someone suggests that the two men have an arm-wrestling match.

(Why arm wrestling? Why should two puny little men, who in the past almost starved to death, put their strength against each other? Why? Why, indeed? Ask my dirty head why.)

So, there they are, the two, arm against arm; tattooed arm against tattooed arm; nobody has noticed anything. But I have—thanks, of course, to my dirty head.

The numbers are the same.

"Look," I shout, "the numbers are the same!"

At first, everybody stares at me, bewildered; then they realize what I'm talking about and see for themselves: Both men have the same number.

Mischa has turned livid. Avigdor rises to his feet. He, too, is pale; but his rage soon makes his face and neck break out in red blotches. With unsuspected strength he grabs Mischa by the arm; he drags him to a bedroom, forces him to go in, then closes the door behind them. Only my dirty head knows what is going on there, for it is my head that has created Avigdor, it is my head that has given Avigdor this extraordinary strength, it is my head that has caused him to open and shut the door; and it is in my head that this door exists. Avigdor is interrogating Mischa, and finding out that Mischa has never been a prisoner anywhere, that he is not even a Jew; he is merely a crafty Ukrainian who had himself tattooed and who made up the whole story in order to exploit Jews.

So, once the ruse is exposed, even my dirty head has no difficulty in making Avigdor—and my parents and the neighbors—expel Mischa in a fit of fury. And so Mischa is left destitute, and he has to sleep on a park bench.

My dirty head, however, won't leave him alone, and so I continue to imagine things. With the money Mischa gets from panhandling, he buys a lottery ticket. The number—trust this dirty head of mine to come up with something like this—is, of course, the one tattooed on his arm. And he wins in the lottery! Then he moves to Rio de Janeiro and he buys a beautiful condo and he is happy! Happy. He doesn't know what my dirty head has in store for him.

There's one thing that bothers him though: the number tattooed on his arm. He decides to have it removed. He goes to a famous plastic surgeon (these are refinements devised by my dirty head) and undergoes surgery. But then he goes into shock and dies a slow, agonizing death. . . .

One day Mischa tells my father about the soap bars. He says he saw piles and piles of soap bars in the death camp. Do you know what the soap was made of? he asks. Human fat. Fat taken from Jews.

At night I dream about him. I'm lying naked in something resembling a bathtub, which is filled with putrid water; Mischa rubs that soap on me; he keeps rubbing it ruthlessly while shouting that he must wash the filth off my tongue and off my head, that he must wash the filth off the world.

I wake up sobbing, I wake up in the midst of great suffering. And it is this suffering that I, for lack of a better word, call the Holocaust.

Translated by Eloah F. Giacomelli

LOVE

*P*erhaps the most complex story in this volume, "Love," collected in Family Ties (1960), is to Brazilian letters what Virginia Woolf's "The Mark on the Wall" is to English literature: a meditation on feminine angst. During a tram ride, Anna, a happy housewife and mother, is thrown into existential despair when she confronts the face of a blind man chewing gum. Like the narrator of Sartre's Nausea, Lispector's protagonist is horrified by the dense fluidity of existence, which challenges the neat arrangements of domestic life as well as her reflective consciousness.

FEELING A LITTLE TIRED, WITH HER PURCHASES BULGING HER NEW STRING bag, Anna boarded the tram. She placed the bag on her lap and the tram started off. Settling back in her seat she tried to find a comfortable position, with a sigh of mild satisfaction.

Anna had nice children, she reflected with certainty and pleasure. They were growing up, bathing themselves and misbehaving; they were demanding more and more of her time. The kitchen, after all, was spacious with its old stove that made explosive noises. The heat was oppressive in the apartment, which they were paying off in installments, and the wind, playing against the curtains she had made herself, reminded her that if she wanted to she could pause to wipe her forehead, and contemplate the calm horizon. Like a farmer. She had planted the seeds she held in her hand, no others, but only those. And they were growing into trees. Her brisk conversations with the electricity man were growing, the water filling the bank was growing, her children were growing, the table was growing with food, her husband arriving with the newspapers and smiling with hunger, the irritating singing of the maids resounding through the block. Anna tranquilly put her small, strong hand, her life current to everything. Certain times of the afternoon struck her as being critical. At a certain hour of the afternoon the trees she had planted laughed at her. And when nothing more required her strength, she became anxious. Meanwhile she felt herself more solid than ever, her body become a little thicker, and it was worth seeing the manner in which she cut out blouses for the children, the large scissors snapping into the material. All her vaguely artistic aspirations had for some time been channeled into making her days fulfilled and beautiful; with time, her taste for the decorative had developed and supplanted intimate disorder. She seemed to have discovered that everything was capable of being perfected, that each thing could be given a harmonious appearance; life itself could be created by Man.

Deep down, Anna had always found it necessary to feel the firm roots of things. And this is what a home had surprisingly provided. Through tortuous paths, she had achieved a woman's destiny, with the surprise of conforming to it almost as if she had invented that destiny herself. The man whom she had married was a real man, the children she mothered were real children. Her previous youth now seemed alien to her, like one of life's illnesses. She had gradually emerged to discover that life could be lived without happiness: by abolishing it she had found a legion of persons, previously invisible, who lived as one works—with perseverance, persistence, and contentment. What had happened to Anna before possessing a home of her own stood forever beyond her reach: that disturbing exaltation she had often confused with unbearable happiness. In exchange she had created something ultimately comprehensible, the life of an adult. This was what she had wanted and chosen.

Her precautions were now reduced to alertness during the dangerous part of the afternoon, when the house was empty and she was no longer needed; when the sun reached its zenith, and each member of the family went about his separate duties. Looking at the polished furniture, she felt her heart contract a little with fear. But in her life there was no opportunity to cherish her fears—she suppressed them with that same ingenuity she had acquired from domestic struggles. Then she would go out shopping or take things to be mended, unobtrusively looking after her home and her family. When she returned it would already be late afternoon and the children back from school would absorb her attention. Until the evening descended with its quiet excitement.

In the morning she would awaken surrounded by her calm domestic duties. She would find the furniture dusty and dirty once more, as if it had returned repentant. As for herself, she mysteriously formed part of the soft, dark roots of the earth. And anonymously she nourished life. It was pleasant like this. And this was what she had wanted and chosen.

The tram swayed on its rails and turned into the main road. Suddenly the wind became more humid, announcing not only the passing of the afternoon but the end of that uncertain hour. Anna sighed with relief and a deep sense of acceptance gave her face an air of womanhood.

The tram would drag along and then suddenly jolt to a halt. As far as Humaitá she could relax. Suddenly she saw the man stationary at the tram stop. The difference between him and others was that he was really stationary. He stood with his hands out in front of him—blind.

But what else was there about him that made Anna sit up in distrust? Something disquieting was happening. Then she discovered what it was: the blind man was chewing gum . . . a blind man chewing gum. Anna still had time to reflect for a second that her brothers were coming to dinner—her heart pounding at regular intervals. Leaning forward, she studied the blind man intently, as one observes something incapable of returning our gaze. Relaxed, and with open eyes, he was chewing gum in the failing light. The facial movements of his chewing made him appear to smile then suddenly stop smiling, to smile and stop smiling. Anna stared at him as if he had insulted her. And anyone watching would have received the impression of a woman filled with hatred. She continued to stare at him, leaning more and more forward—until the tram gave a sudden jerk, throwing her unexpectedly backward. The heavy string bag toppled from her lap and landed on the floor. Anna cried out, the conductor gave the signal to stop before realizing what was happening, and the tram came to an abrupt halt. The other passengers looked on in amazement. Too paralyzed to gather up her shopping, Anna sat upright, her face suddenly pale. An expression, long since forgotten, awkwardly reappeared, unexpected and inexplicable. The Negro newsboy smiled as he handed over her bundle. The eggs had broken in their newspaper wrapping. Yellow sticky yolks dripped between the strands of the bag. The blind man had interrupted his chewing and held out his unsteady hands, trying in vain to grasp what had happened. She removed the parcel of eggs from the string accompanied by the smiles of the passengers. A second signal from the conductor and the tram moved off with another jerk.

A few moments later people were no longer staring at her. The tram was rattling on the rails and the blind man chewing gum had remained behind forever. But the damage had been done.

The string bag felt rough between her fingers, not soft and familiar as when she had knitted it. The bag had lost its meaning; to find herself on that tram was a broken thread; she did not know what to do with the purchases on her lap. Like some strange music, the world started up again around her. The damage had been done. But why? Had she forgotten that there were blind people? Compassion choked her. Anna's breathing became heavy. Even those things which had existed before the episode were now on the alert, more hostile, and even perishable. The world had once more become a nightmare. Several years fell away, the yellow yolks trickled. Exiled from her own days, it seemed to her that the people in the streets were vulnerable, that they barely maintained their equilibrium on the surface of the darkness—and for a moment they appeared to lack any sense of direction. The perception of an absence of law came so unexpectedly that Anna clutched the seat in front of her, as if she might fall off the tram, as if things might be overturned with the same calm they had possessed when order reigned.

What she called a crisis had come at last. And its sign was the intense pleasure with which she now looked at things, suffering and alarmed. The heat had become more oppressive, everything had gained new power and a stronger voice. In the Rua Voluntários da Pátria, revolution seemed imminent, the grids of the gutters were dry, the air dusty. A blind man chewing gum had plunged the world into a mysterious excitement. In every strong person there was a lack of compassion for the blind man, and their strength terrified her. Beside her sat a woman in blue with an expression which made Anna avert her gaze rapidly. On the pavement a mother shook her little boy. Two lovers held hands smiling. . . . And the blind man? Anna had lapsed into a mood of compassion which greatly distressed her.

She had skillfully pacified life; she had taken so much care to avoid up-heavals. She had cultivated an atmosphere of serene understanding, separating each person from the others. Her clothes were clearly designed to be practical, and she could choose the evening's film from the newspaper—and everything was done in such a manner that each day should smoothly succeed the previous one. And a blind man chewing gum was destroying all this. Through her compassion Anna felt that life was filled to the brim with a sickening nausea.

Only then did she realize that she had passed her stop ages ago. In her weak state everything touched her with alarm. She got off the tram, her legs shaking, and looked around her, clutching the string bag stained with egg. For a moment she was unable to get her bearings. She seemed to have plunged into the middle of the night.

It was a long road, with high yellow walls. Her heart beat with fear as she tried in vain to recognize her surroundings; while the life she had discovered continued to pulsate, a gentler, more mysterious wind caressed her face. She stood quietly observing the wall. At last she recognized it. Advancing a little further alongside a hedge, she passed through the gates of the botanical garden.

She strolled wearily up the central avenue, between the palm trees. There was no one in the garden. She put her parcels down on the ground and sat down on the bench of a side path where she remained for some time.

The wilderness seemed to calm her, the silence regulating her breathing and soothing her senses.

From afar she saw the avenue where the evening was round and clear. But the shadows of the branches covered the side path.

Around her there were tranquil noises, the scent of trees, chance encounters among the creeping plants. The entire garden fragmented by the ever more fleeting moments of the evening. From whence came the drowsiness with which she was surrounded? As if induced by the drone of birds and bees. Everything seemed strange, much too gentle, much too great.

A gentle, familiar movement startled her and she turned round rapidly. Nothing appeared to have stirred. But in the central lane there stood, immobile, an enormous cat. Its fur was soft. With another silent movement, it disappeared.

Agitated, she looked about her. The branches swayed, their shadows wavering on the ground. A sparrow foraged in the soil. And suddenly, in terror, she imagined that she had fallen into an ambush. In the garden there was a secret activity in progress which she was beginning to penetrate.

On the trees, the fruits were black and sweet as honey. On the ground there lay dry fruit stones full of circumvolutions like small rotted cerebrums. The bench was stained with purple sap. With gentle persistence the waters murmured. On the tree trunk the luxurious feelers of parasites fastened themselves. The rawness of the world was peaceful. The murder was deep. And death was not what one had imagined.

As well as being imaginary, this was a world to be devoured with one's teeth, a world of voluminous dahlias and tulips. The trunks were pervaded by leafy parasites, their embrace soft and clinging. Like the resistance that precedes surrender, it was fascinating; the woman felt disgusted, and it was fascinating.

The trees were laden, and the world was so rich that it was rotting. When Anna reflected that there were children and grown men suffering hunger, the nausea reached her throat as if she were pregnant and abandoned. The moral of the garden was something different. Now that the blind man had guided her to it, she trembled on the threshold of a dark, fascinating world where monstrous waterlilies floated. The small flowers scattered on the grass did not appear to be yellow or pink, but the color of inferior gold and scarlet. Their decay was profound, perfumed. But all these oppressive things she watched, her head surrounded by a swarm of insects, sent by some more refined life in the world. The breeze penetrated between the flowers. Anna imagined rather than felt its sweetened scent. The garden was so beautiful that she feared hell.

It was almost night now and everything seemed replete and heavy; a squirrel leapt in the darkness. Under her feet the earth was soft. Anna inhaled its odor with delight. It was both fascinating and repulsive.

But when she remembered the children, before whom she now felt guilty, she straightened up with a cry of pain. She clutched the package, advanced through the dark side path, and reached the avenue. She was almost running, and she saw the garden all around her aloof and impersonal. She shook the locked gates, and went on shaking them, gripping the rough timber. The watchman appeared, alarmed at not having seen her.

Until she reached the entrance of the building, she seemed to be on the brink of disaster. She ran with the string bag to the elevator, her heart beating in her breast—what was happening? Her compassion for the blind man was as fierce as anguish but the world seemed hers, dirty, perishable, hers. She opened the door of her flat. The room was large, square, the polished knobs were shining, the window panes were shining, the lamp shone brightly—what new land was this? And for a moment that wholesome life she had led until today seemed morally crazy. The little boy who came running up to embrace her was a creature with long legs and a face resembling her own. She pressed him firmly to her in anxiety and fear. Trembling, she protected herself. Life was vulnerable. She loved the world, she loved all things created, she loved with loathing. In the same way she had always been fascinated by oysters, with that vague sentiment of revulsion which the approach of truth provoked, admonishing her. She embraced her son, almost hurting him. Almost as if she knew of some evil—the blind man or the beautiful botanical garden—she was clinging to him, to him whom she loved above all things. She had been touched by the demon of faith.

"Life is horrible," she said to him in a low voice, as if famished. What would she do if she answered the blind man's call? She would go alone. . . . There were poor and rich places that needed her. She needed them. "I am afraid," she said. She felt the delicate ribs of the child between her arms, she heard his frightened weeping.

"Mummy," the child called. She held him away from her, she studied his face and her heart shrank.

"Don't let Mummy forget you," she said. No sooner had the child felt her embrace weaken than he escaped and ran to the door of the room, from where he watched her more safely. It was the worst look that she had ever received. The blood rose hot to her cheeks.

She sank into a chair, with her fingers still clasping the string bag. What was she ashamed of? There was no way of escaping. The very crust of the days she had forged had broken and the water was escaping. She stood before the oysters. And there was no way of averting her gaze. What was she ashamed of? Certainly it was no longer pity, it was more than pity: her heart had filled with the worst will to live.

She no longer knew if she was on the side of the blind man or of the thick plants. The man little by little had moved away, and in her torment she appeared to have passed over to the side of those who had injured his eyes. The botanical garden, tranquil and high, had been a revelation. With horror, she discovered that she belonged to the strong part of the world, and what name should she give to her fierce compassion? Would she be obliged to kiss the leper, since she would never be just a sister. "A blind man has drawn me to the worst of myself," she thought, amazed. She felt banished because no pauper would drink water from her burning hands. Ah! It was easier to be a saint than a person! Good heavens, then was it not real, that pity which had fathomed the deepest waters in her heart? But it was the compassion of a lion.

Humiliated, she knew that the blind man would prefer a poorer love. And, trembling, she also knew why. The life of the botanical garden summoned her as a werewolf is summoned by the moonlight. "Oh! but she loved the blind man," she thought with tears in her eyes. Meanwhile it was not with this sentiment that one would go to church. "I am frightened," she whispered alone in the room. She got up and went to the kitchen to help the maid prepare dinner.

But life made her shiver like the cold of winter. She heard the school bell pealing, distant and constant. The small horror of the dust gathering in threads around the bottom of the stove, where she had discovered a small spider. Lifting a vase to change the water—there was the horror of the flower submitting itself, languid and loathsome, to her hands. The same secret activity was going on here in the kitchen. Near the waste bin, she crushed an ant with her foot. The small murder of the ant. Its minute body trembled. Drops of water fell on the stagnant water in the pool.

The summer beetles. The horror of those expressionless beetles. All around there was a silent, slow, insistent life. Horror upon horror. She went from one side of the kitchen to the other, cutting the steaks, mixing the cream. Circling around her head, around the light, the flies of a warm summer's evening. A night in which compassion was as crude as false love. Sweat trickled between her breasts. Faith broke her; the heat of the oven burned in her eyes.

Then her husband arrived, followed by her brothers and their wives, and her brothers' children.

They dined with all the windows open, on the ninth floor. An airplane shuddered menacingly in the heat of the sky. Although she had used few eggs, the dinner was good. The children stayed up, playing on the carpet with their cousins. It was summer and it would be useless to force them to go to sleep. Anna was a little pale and laughed gently with the others.

After dinner, the first cool breeze finally entered the room. The family was seated around the table, tired after their day, happy in the absence of any discord, eager not to find fault. They laughed at everything, with warmth and humanity. The children grew up admirably around them. Anna took the moment like a butterfly, between her fingers before it might escape forever.

Later, when they had all left and the children were in bed, she was just a woman looking out of the window. The city was asleep and warm. Would the experience unleashed by the blind man fill her days? How many years would it take before she once more grew old? The slightest movement on her part and she would trample one of her children. But with the ill-will of a lover, she seemed to accept that the fly would emerge from the flower, and the giant water lilies would float in the darkness of the lake. The blind man was hanging among the fruits of the botanical garden.

What if that were the stove exploding with the fire spreading through the house, she thought to herself as she ran to the kitchen where she found her husband in front of the spilt coffee.

"What happened?" she cried, shaking from head to foot. He was taken aback by his wife's alarm. And suddenly understanding, he laughed.

"It was nothing," he said, "I am just a clumsy fellow." He looked tired, with dark circles under his eyes.

But, confronted by the strange expression on Anna's face, he studied her more closely. Then he drew her to him in a sudden caress.

"I don't want anything ever to happen to you!" she said.

"You can't prevent the stove from having its little explosions," he replied, smiling. She remained limp in his arms. This afternoon, something tranquil had exploded, and in the house everything struck a tragicomic note.

"It's time to go to bed," he said, "it's late." In a gesture which was not his, but which seemed natural, he held his wife's hand, taking her with him, without looking back, removing her from the danger of living.

The giddiness of compassion had spent itself. And if she had crossed love and its hell, she was now combing her hair before the mirror, without any world for the moment in her heart. Before getting into bed, as if she were snuffing a candle, she blew out that day's tiny flame.

Translated by Giovanni Ponteiro

SAMUEL RAWET

(1 9 2 9 – 1 9 8 5)

HIS MOMENT OF GLORY

"*P*rison is the infinite and the future," *says the protagonist of this multilayered meditation, an actor reflected in a mirror just before he goes on stage. In this cryptic story, the theatrical metaphor—the art of pretending to be somebody else—evokes the multiple, shifting layers of ambivalence and identity. The physical and spiritual metamorphosis of the anonymous protagonist, like the compulsive desire to humiliate oneself in front of others, can also be seen in terms of the sacrifice made by Jews who are willing to assimilate.*

◇

HE WOULD LIVE JUST THAT MOMENT. NOTHING BEFORE NOR AFTER. JUST THAT moment. For it he would pay the required price; for it he would degrade himself before others and himself. However vile was the sound of his voice, however much he affected arrogance, although in spite of this he gave himself away somewhat, he confronted with pain and anger, sufficient to make him numb to illusion, the ritual that preceded and followed the plenitude of a single instant. And it was illusion that he needed most. Seated before the mirror aged at the edges, topped by two bare lamps, his elbows on a plank that served as a table upon which they would randomly scatter the pots of cream, the tubes of makeup, the containers of Vaseline, the pencils and the rest of the materials necessary for his number, he let his smile disappear, a reflection of endless smiles, and passing from prayer he began the metamorphosis. Behind him, on some hooks driven into the wall, the clothes, and next to them the wig, and in a box at his feet, leaning on the suitcase, the shoes. The music of the quartet on the other side of the passageway, next to the dance floor, no longer bothered him. The mist of sounds filtering through the cracks, blending all the conversations from the dozen and a half tables in the hall, no longer bothered him either. Two numbers before his. He had enough time to scrutinize the emptiness between the objects and their shadows, the flaws in the wood and the water stains on the badly whitewashed wall. Between cause and effect the splinter of pain and the wall of useless, sterile, and pernicious comprehension and incomprehension. The value of the gesture implicit in the gesture itself and the chain of decay, suspended only by an interval of illusion. He gathers the courage of an aerialist to balance on this tightrope.

He would execute the act controlled by an ambivalent nature, and avenge the mortification by a collection of attitudes more than by deeds. An anticipation of undefined symbiosis would burst from the background, framed in rigid principles. As if the outpouring of pain were not unyielding, more unyielding than the act of aversion. Or of another aversion which for someone was acceptance of that which in truth he never offered. In truth he would offer nothing; he would prove nothing with false affection aside from the hatred expelled in a tireless kiss. Having rejected the thought of suicide, what other exit remained? He had eliminated still another wave of nonexistent impossibilities. He gave himself to others as an entertainer and degraded them with his mere presence. There is no path when all paths are possible and prison is the infinite and the future. Where could he run?

His face changes slowly. The plain look of his everyday features, some distinguishing mark or another which would betray him, is revealed, by means of cream and makeup, with that aura of beauty that is not exactly feminine, but which beneath the bright lights or the half-light of a stage allows one to glimpse his feminine mask par excellence, suggesting distant harmonies traced by a tremulous drawing pencil. There are grimaces, mugging and fleeting looks of frightening ugliness. And it is in his face that the subtle internal intrigue evolves, fashioned of caprice, inhibitions, hatred, enigma, debauchery, vindictiveness, and, finally, the nothingness that leads to a useless gesture, for this very reason not undesirable. Was it still necessary to explain to anyone the long painful route to arrive at the point? Was it necessary to repeat once more that there is always an irretrievable gesture, a definitively executed act, an act complete in its action and power? It was necessary to repeat the shout. Come on, turn around, turn back and forth, sprinkle the conventional fat guy's immense benevolence with imbecilic nuances and whispers, devour the favors of the naughty little exemplary heads of families, pierce the plot and weave the tortuous cloth of delirium in search of more or less firm footing, even at the cost of arrogance and humiliation. Declare your presence; it matters little that no one comprehends. And some day perhaps he himself will understand that there are limitless gestures, yet unnoticed, implicit in his act that are heavy with the burden of rebellion.

It's time for the body, for the evocations of evocations, for reminiscences of reminiscences. He adjusts his underwear with obscene grimaces awakening the degeneracy implicit in his ambivalent mien, and a strange monster observes his facial distortions in the mirror. The whole torrent of sensorial evocations billows in the grotesque repetition of an affected greeting, and with the torrent, the fears and hatred, stupidity and sarcasm, his tense body is delirious with hybrid metamorphoses. And the ill-mannered enormous guffaw before his body broken with pain, a rigid whip to flog himself, within, far from the present equilibrium, on the other side of the ambivalent border.

The ceaseless dripping water ringing in the corner washbowl conveys the construct of memories in its regular intervals, and harmoniously orchestrates the beatings, promiscuity, violence, cursing, sordid corners, nights, dreams, vast seminal delirium.

He's ready and with his back to the mirror. They've already given him his cue. His eyes shine. He places his right hand on his left collarbone and holds his elbow in the palm of his other hand. He was a man; he knew it in that instant. He turns around, looking for the dressing room door, and he glimpses a fleeting image, the beautiful reflexion of an unwanted dream. He could humiliate himself now.

Translated by Leland R. Guyer

PERU

I S A A C   G O L D E M B E R G

(b. 1 9 4 5)

THE CONVERSION

U*sed as the opening door to* Play by Play *(1984), the writer's second novel, this story narrates the physical and spiritual plight of Marquitos Karushansky, like the author half-Jew, half-native Peruvian, and "injured existentially" by the discovery, during adolescence, of his ambiguous ethnic identity. Narrated with verve, irony, and playfulness, the protagonist's identity and history are symbolized, most painfully, by his ritual circumcision.*

FIVETHOUSANDSEVENHUNDRED AND THIRTEEN YEARS OF JUDAISM HIT MAR-quitos Karushansky like a ton of bricks. At the age of eight, shortly after coming to Lima, classes in Hebrew and the history of the Jews at León Pinelo School; *bris* at the age of twelve; Bar Mitzvah at thirteen when he was a brand-new cadet at Leoncio Prado Military Academy. *Bris* was the little word taken from the Hebrew and used by the Jews in Lima to avoid saying *circumcision,* which left a bad taste in the mouth and made them bite the tip of their tongues, as if to spit it out. "Never you say *circumcision,* correct word is *bris; circumcision* is from Latin *circumcidere,* to cut around, and has no historical weight. But *bris* means covenant and is in Bible from time our father Abruhem sealed pact with Adonai." That's how Rabbi Goldstein, with his weeping willow beard, explained it to him. *Adonai,* of course, was also a word Marcos had recently picked up. Saying *God,* which seemed to have a *cholo,* half-Indian ring to it, was absolutely out of the question. And it was really something to watch him swearing, *Chai Adonai* here and *Chai Adonai* there! whip 'em in the front and whip 'em in the rear! Chahuee! Chahuaa! Pinelo, Pinelo, rah,

rah, rah! First you've got to promise not to tell. I swear to God who is my shining light! What? To God! No, that doesn't count. C'mon, do it right. Chai Adonai! You're a liar, let's see if you can swear it's true. Chai Adonai! Swear you didn't steal the ballpoint. Chai Adonai! Marcos gradually became used to the word, it was like not swearing at all, and he got a big kick out of it.

Marquitos Karushansky's circumcision, or rather his *bris*, took place on the same day as the opening of *The Ten Commandments* at the Tacna movie theater. What's more, Dr. Berkowitz's office, where the operation was done, was only half a block from the theater. Marcos was operated on in the afternoon, some time between five and seven, and the show was to start at eight. But he and his father missed the opening. The saddest part of it, old Karushansky said, was not being able to see the film together with the rest of the Jewish community of Lima. They had to see it four or five days later, sitting among Peruvians, and it wasn't the same, it wasn't the right atmosphere, what did those *cholos* know about the Bible, anyway?

It had all started when his father announced, like a patriarch in the Old Testament: "Next year you be ready for Bar Mitzvah but first is necessary you have *bris*." Marcos remembered his eyes wandering to the smudgy windowpane, and then his voice, mocking and at the same time trying to reassure him, he shouldn't worry, they had also snipped off the foreskin of Jesus the Jew.

They showed up one day in Dr. Berkowitz's office where the physician, very professional, very freckled, explained: "*Bris* is an extremely simple operation. All it amounts to is cutting off the prepuce, the end of the skin that folds over the head of the penis and covers it. Then it's much easier to keep the glans clean. No sebaceous matter collects around it and this reduces the risk of catching dangerous infections." Marcos didn't know what he was talking about and went back with his father to the doctor's office the next day. The nurse had already left and they were greeted by a silence like the Sabbath's in the homes of Orthodox Jews. Before he knew it, Marcos was stretched out on his back on the operating table. Dr. Berkowitz was standing beside it, scalpel in hand, arm poised, and his feather, sweat running down features drawn tight in pain and disgust, his father was lying across his chest, pinning his arms, papa's chunky body on top of his, would he ask him for a camphor liniment rubdown later? Every night at bedtime the ritual of the rubdown would begin and Marcos would massage him furiously, as if he wanted to tear off his skin, as if he were trying to draw blood from the heavy body with an oval head. He would pass the palm of his hand down the slope of the thick short neck, up the incline of the shoulders with their overgrowth of hair, matted like the fur on a battered old grizzly, his body stripped of every shred of nobility, letting out low grunts, soft moans of pleasure.

His penis had been put to sleep but not enough to kill the pain from the clamp holding on to his skin as if it would never let go. Then the doctor—warning him not to exaggerate, because too much anesthetic could leave him paralyzed for life—raised the needle to eye level to make sure he had the right amount in the syringe. His whole body shuddered when the needle entered his glans. His father pressed all his weight down on his chest, and on his lips and chin Marcos could feel the rough beard, soaked with sweat and tears. Now his penis was a soft mass, a spongy mushroom, an organism with a life of its own, capable of tearing free with one jerk and slipping all over his skin, looking for a way into his body, or capable of dissolving and leaving a smelly, viscous fluid on his groin. He knew his penis was already in the open and he tried to imagine its new, hoodless look. In his mind, he compared it to the image he had of his father's member, its extreme whiteness, the perfect distribution of its parts, the scarlet crest topping the head of the sleepy iguana, with its vertical blind eye. He wanted to examine his phallus, to hold it above his eyes like a flower, to fall under the spell of the rosy calyx snug around its neck, to weigh it in his hand and stroke it warmly back to the familiarity it had lost. He was conscious of the small pincers clutching his foreskin tight: they were fierce little animals with fangs, beady eyes, and metallic scales on their backs. At the same time, he felt the pressure of his father's dead weight on him as a reproach, the embodiment of all the insults he had ever had to take. He thought about how, when he went back to school, he wouldn't have to hide from his friends in the bathroom. He would be able to piss casually now, to pull out his prick, take his time shaking it out, boldly pressing hard to squeeze the last drops out and then turn around defiantly and show it to the others, to all his schoolmates at León Pinelo, proudly, now let's see who is man enough to say I'm not a Jew.

The doctor left them alone in the back office: he told them he'd return in half an hour, they'd have to wait for the anesthetic to wear off, and Marcos watched his father nodding yes. Then the old man started to pace with his hands clasped behind him. He marched up and down next to the operating table, eyes straight ahead, without bending his knees, swinging each leg sideways slowly in a semicircle, before setting his foot down on the tiles. The controlled stiffness of his body, the deliberate halt after each about-face, before he started pacing again, reflected all the misery and resignation stored up in him. But Marcos knew every detail of this tactic his father had used, over the past two years, to put a certain amount of distance between them, to make him understand that behind this temporary withdrawal, all the things he had ever silenced were crying out, louder than words, against his bad luck and his unhappiness. If he had had any hope of crossing into his father's world, he would have asked him to come over to the table, dry the sweat on his forehead, take his hand in his, and help him clear away the skein of solitude unraveling endlessly in his chest. But he was sure the old man would avoid his eyes, as he did whenever he pounded on him with his fists, only to feel sorry afterward and break down like a vulnerable Mary Magdalene.

His senses had become dulled. His father looked older now: his beard had taken on a grayish tint and a hundred wrinkles had formed around his eyes. He tried to think of his mother but he couldn't retain a solid image of her behind his eyes. He had closed them and felt himself rushing down a toboggan run, rolling over and over without being able to stop. Only his father was solid; all the objects in the room had melted into ribbons of vapor swirling around him, and only his father's presence kept him from turning into a gaseous substance too.

He didn't move a muscle when the doctor's voice burst into the room like a garble of voices and sounds, and asked him if he was feeling better. He nodded without unlocking his eyelids, and the doctor and his father helped him off the table. His eyes were still closed, he staggered as if whipped by a blizzard, and the weight of his nakedness embarrassed him. The mere brush of the doctor's gloved hands on his member, the slight pull of the threads sticking out from the skin under the glans, made him feel wretched and he had the urge to piss. He guessed the pain this rash move would bring on and stopped himself just in time; the doctor was fitting a jockstrap stuffed with wads of gauze on him and he had the sensation that he was pissing inward. His bladder was tightening up and his inward-flowing urine plunged through his ureters, was picked up by the renal tubes, flooded his kidneys like a winding current, and was pumped, bubbling and humming, into the bloodstream. He felt that he was burning up inside, explored by the fine probe of an intense blue flame. The doctor's voice jolted him back to reality. A sudden smile lit up the doctor's face as he put out his hand in an outlandishly formal way and made a big show of shaking Marcos's father's hand, saying: "Mazel tov, Señor Karushansky, congratulations, mazel tov. . . ."

The lights on Tacna Avenue woke him all the way. Walking to the corner, they passed the Tacna movie theater, its front covered with giant posters showing scenes from the movie: a beardless Charlton Heston, dressed as an Egyptian warrior, was giving a wasp-waisted princess a he-man's hug; over to the right, Charlton Heston again, beard and wig, tunic and sandals, on a promontory, arms extended like a magician's: abracadabra, let the waters divide.

As they stood on the corner trying to get a cab, Marcos thought of the late afternoon when he had arrived in Lima, four years before. Through the smoke rising steadily from a charcoal pit where some shish kebab on tiny skewers was roasting and giving off a tempting aroma, he saw his father with his hands in his pockets, coming toward the El Chasqui travel agency, where he and his mother were waiting. Then, like now, they had stopped on a corner, loaded down with bundles and suitcases, to get a cab. He looked out the side of his eye at his father, sitting cross-legged next to him; his arms were folded stiffly across his chest. Through the window on the other side of his father's aquiline profile, he watched the streetcars stretching, lumbering over the flashing tracks. Tall buildings loomed up unexpectedly, swaying like the carob trees back home, and then, with the speed of a fist coming straight at his eyes out of nowhere, the slender pyramid of the Jorge Chávez monument like an airplane full of lights—manned by a crew of graceful winged granite figures—taking off into the night.

He had seen pictures of the Plaza San Martín and the Plaza de Armas in his schoolbook and had thought of Lima as a ghost town where time had stopped without warning, freezing cars as they moved along and pedestrians as they walked. He liked to invent all kinds of stories about those unknown people suspended in midair like grotesque puppets. He had even tried to see if he could make out his father among those men in dark suits and hats. Sometimes he felt sure he had found him sitting on a bench reading a newspaper, or spotted his profile coming around a corner, and he would run to the kitchen and point him out to his mother. Without hiding her amazement at her son's fancies, she would stroke his head nervously and always tell him no, with an understanding smile. But now, sitting on his father's right, he didn't have to imagine him anymore. The city itself seemed to have come out of its sleep, happy to open the night and show him his father's world. And with all his senses set on the course of this moment so new to him, fluttering around him like a playful butterfly, he accepted that world unquestioning, wholeheartedly, as if it had always been his by right.

The taxi plunged into the warm shadows of a Salaverry Avenue studded with lights. His father was still just sitting there, his face outlined by the pale flash of the car's window, oblivious of the clusters of trees reflected in his eyes as they shot past. On the right, the Campo de Marte spread out; deserted, bleak, it disappeared for stretches at a time behind groups of houses and reappeared, somnolent and hazy. Marcos was quiet too, afraid to shift a leg that had fallen asleep and trying with his imagination to lop it off from his body and stop the swirl of bubbles climbing to his groin slowly, noisily. He let the stale air out of his lungs and sank a little into the seat, thinking That old guy is my father, I can tell by the musty odor of his clothes, he smells like dirty synagogue draperies, old velvet, damp wool, like the moth-eaten cashmere and poplin remnants he keeps in back of the store. He's probably taking the annual inventory right now, setting bolts of cloth on the counter, running his hand over them like a shepherd fondly stroking the backs of his sheep; or maybe he's repeating over and over the words he spit out at me this morning, "In a few hours you be at last one of us, at last one of us, at last one. . . ."

As the cab made a sharp turn, coming out into Mariátegui Avenue, its chassis seemed to bristle up like a cat; it went down the street chugging along unsteadily, entered Pumacahua Street and pulled up at the corner of the second block, where the houses came to a dead end, cut off by the Club Hípico's garden wall, a solid line of trees and wire. His father helped him out of the car. They walked the short distance to the project entrance and silently headed for the apartment at the rear.

In the bedroom his father helped him undress; he knelt to take off his shoes, and then took them to the foot of the valet clothes stand, dressed up in the rest of his clothes and looking like a silly scarecrow. He knelt down again to help him on with his pajama pants and then stood up with a heavy sigh seeming to come from somewhere far away; he turned down the covers, settled the boy in the center of the bed, and covered him with a rough sweep of his hand. "So if you want something, you'll call," he told him abruptly, going to the door. Marcos heard his father's footsteps fading down the hallway toward the living room and now, as he lay submerged in the warmth of the covers, the silence started winding its way through the shell of his ears, humming like the sea, and he could feel the solitude he had been longing for begin to take root in his spirit. He swept the room with his eyes, pausing carefully at each object, trying to figure out what hidden common bond there was between so many disparate things. He sensed that the suffocating mishmash of furniture, spread through the rest of the house like heavy underbrush, summed up his father's horror of empty rooms. Landscapes and scenes of Israel, torn from calendars, lined all the walls: the sea of Galilee (or Kineret, as his father knowingly called it), hemmed by a tight ring of hills; a street in Yerushalaim crammed with shops and pedestrians, exactly like Jirón de la Unión Street, right, Marcos? this is the capital of Israel, you wouldn't believe everyone in streets are Jewish, right? blond-dark-redhead and even real black children in a tiny school in Tel Aviv; also the vast wilderness of the Negev with red red sand and where are located the mines of King Shlomo, who was very wise; do you know story of two women are fighting for same son and going to King Shlomo . . .? and also many pictures of Kibbutz Givat Brenner, founded in year 'twenty-eight, I was one of founders, Marcos, see how beautiful, all people glad working in fields, look how happy everybody, and in fact his father had also worked in the kibbutz, intoning erets zavat chalav, chalav, erets zavat chalav, humming into the wind, land of milk and honey, erets zavat chalav, chalav ud'vash, and in other prints there were young patriarchs, hands twirling the udders of the goats, sinking into the labyrinthine nurseries of the bees. . . .

Marcos remembered the first time he had set foot in the house. Startled by the jungle of furniture as he stepped through the door, he stood rooted to the spot; he felt as if all his bones were giving way under a sudden deafening avalanche of rocks. Then his father took his arm and almost dragged him inside toward his room, saying Come, don't be afraid. Left standing alone in his bedroom with his suitcase beside him, he could hardly stay on his feet, a weary taste of rancid almonds in his mouth. From the back of the house his father's voice, as studied as a concierge's, reached him: "This is your room, here you will sleep. Bathroom is a few steps to your left; in front of bathroom is kitchen. You find everything there, unpack your bag, then fix yourself something to eat."

That night, as soon as his mother had gone to her room, the ritual of the bath got under way. "Am going get off all dirt from your body," his father said, rolling up his sleeves with an air of nostalgia for his ancestral past, like an old Orthodox Jew ready to wind the leather maze of phylacteries around his arm. He made Marcos climb into the tub and he let the stream of water out: it came on by fits and starts with a choking sound, then broke out in spurts till it picked up the steady murmur of an easy flow. Steam filled the bathroom with drowsiness, blurred the solid walls, and turned his father into a shadowy figure kneeling next to the tub and already beginning to soap his body with rhythmic skill, as if he were holding a newborn baby, or a body not yet born, molding its form with the nimble fingers of a Florentine goldsmith.

The scene was taking on the importance of a ceremony. The image of

VENEZUELA

E L I S A   L E R N E R
(b. 1 9 3 2)

PAPA'S FRIENDS

E*voking the world of Russian-Jewish immigrants in Caracas, this story takes place during the late 1930s and in 1940, when Leon Trotsky was assassinated in Mexico City. Told from the viewpoint of a teenage girl confronting the underside of bourgeois family life, it first appeared—ironically enough—in the slick Venezuelan magazine* Exceso *(1991).*

IN APRIL OF 1953, LYDIA WAS LOCKED UP IN THE REMOTE LAND OF A PSYCHIATric clinic, and the gentle white dawns of her uniform were never seen again in Samuel's grocery store. Berta found prosperity after years of cheerful hard work managing the restaurant she had with her husband, Bernardo. Like a versatile sofa-bed that never declines to show its hospitality, the restaurant also functioned as an inn. Freed from work, Berta began moving from one dismal house to another: you can all imagine her last home. She entertained herself buying ostentatious display cabinets for the different houses, in which she would place small, well-polished silver spoons. Now that she had money she could offer better service. But the spoons went unused, like cloistered nuns.

Señora Olinda, almost seventy years old, was obliged to close Odessa, the shoe store she had presided over for close to half a century. There were no longer customers looking for shoes with toes like pointed noses, or thin rose-stem heels. Left without the shoe store, she discovered in herself a belated religious vocation and found herself more and more at ease in the synagogue and at the jumble sales they held. Her lips (as in the younger days at the

Odessa) were, as always, covered with a throbbing scrap of a vibrant velvet red that at times obscured her smile.

As for Amelia, I heard she was stricken by an incurable disease that drove through her body like a sword watching its knight die on the battlefield. Susana got fat, as big as an ever-growing metropolis. She now lives with only her fatness for company in an apartment building in Miami where most of the tenants are rich sentimental old women—widows exiled from New York or from some town in Central or South America.

In Miami she has become addicted to vitamins. Yet she often still finds herself returning from Florida on the occasion of the weddings and Bar Mitz-vahs of her numerous relatives. These efforts, at times tiresome, to arrive on time for the family festivities have made her whine in the pharmacy for a renewed supply of her much-appreciated vitamins. "I am always on an air-plane. The day before yesterday it was Raquel's wedding in New York. In June, it's on to Caracas for Leah and Isaac's golden anniversary. Next fall I'm invited to Tel Aviv to spend the New Year with Ana Landau, she's a widow now. What a production! I don't know anyone who functions more like a well-organized Minister of Foreign Affairs than a member of a Jewish family. I'm about ready to ask for the ambassadorship. I'm just waiting for the Kafka twins' Bar Mitzvah in Rio de Janeiro."

Lydia, Amelia, Berta, Olinda, and Susana were my Papa's friends. It wasn't a conscious flirtation on their part, nor on Papa's. There never was a more tender, loving, and conciliatory husband than he. Mama was a small anxious despot, a protector. Thanks to her methodical, stubborn and proud nostalgia—above all, to the crazy collection of things she took with her on the boat—we lived in a far-off town of fiction, one that moved erratically in dark seas, ships of gigantic dimensions like massive caskets transporting entire populations.

The city that my mother founded with such care inside our house never had a real and established spot on the map. This was such an injustice when there was so much beautiful real geography that I began to suspect she was a capricious woman, of a spirit subject to sudden change. The passing of time assured me of my conviction that she is a silly woman, a scatterbrain who changes borders as if they were one-night-stands.

Papa, possessor of an educated cynicism, faced reality with distracted compassion. That was why he could not remain forever inside the rigorous region invented by Mama's mournful longings. Some Saturday mornings (if the teacher gave me good marks on the report I brought home from high school), he took me with him on the short but unconventional walks down the narrow streets in the center of town. I suspect Papa's own walk began much earlier. More than one Friday at 7 P.M., after greeting God and drinking a small glass of muscatel (his body wore the striped suit like a tablecloth ready to receive its wine glasses), nimble and content (with the jug of his heart half-full of wine), he would run to see his lovely Lydia and his needy Amelia before eight o'clock (the most melancholy time in the universe) when the stores closed.

Mama planned things like an actress in a repertory company of three-act comedies. The celebration of Hanukkah represented the first act. On the pretext of collaborating with the Israel Club, she would make a cake of honey, nuts, and raisins. The club now and then served as a house of charity, a somewhat bohemian, cordial hospice.

On Fridays, protected by the merciful music of prayer, men would appear at the door who looked as though they didn't even have a place of their own to die.

In order to do the honors to the second act, Mama put on her skirt and jacket of silk *imprimé* (that's what the pretentious employees of El Gallo de Oro called the printed material) with the firm determination of appearing, hanging on Papa's arm, at the Israel Club, to drop off the delicious cake decorated with the skill of an English assassin. She also used the argument of wanting to stretch her housewife legs (those crippled spousal extremities, sacrificed like mermaids' limbs in an ocean that prohibits voyages to worldly lands of enjoyment and pleasure) in order to arrive with dignity at the pretenses of the third act. Accompanying Papa on the short trip to his friends' shops (while he made some insignificant purchase), Mama perhaps wanted to assure herself that the visits were not just a useful excuse for a gaze or a verbal caress, performed with the enigmatic touch of love that has no homeland in bed, toward Lydia or Amelia, who, behind their safe sales counters, in the sweetness of dusk, were remote women hidden in the towers of their chaste castles.

Mama admired and at the same time despised Lydia. The variations of her indifference came in all sizes, big and small. Mama, the small domestic despot, envied Lydia her disquieting ability to sell black olives, nuts, almonds, and Maracay cheese, as she did her white uniform, that, free of marital stains, emancipated her, gave her independence.

Lydia was of short stature, a bit heavy. Her ass was the least animated part of her body, but she seemed to keep singing birds in her somewhat meddlesome belly. The hapless uniform nevertheless tried to silence the indiscreet sparrows of a troublesome digestion. Her face, the green eyes, were those of an artist of the time. A shorter and plumper Kay Francis* (the bargains she found in expensive department stores gave authority to her warm greetings), she was happy to be able to seize to her waist the liberating banner of stable and certain work.

A Kay, happy to watch life through lenses spread with foggy yellow Kupperschmidt butter. But Papa would have had to make the sacrifice of buying the necessary (as well as the unnecessary) theater seats in order for Lydia to have really been the haughty Kay Francis, to whom silver-screen husbands presented divine jewels, hidden in the lustrous silver domes of breakfast platters, in humble homage to the night before, when at the elegant party, fox skins drifted from one shoulder to the other like snow flakes swirled by the wind around the gargoyles of a palace roof.

Impassioned stars winked in Papa's eyes when he saw this domestic version of Kay Francis. Lydia, like the other Saturday morning women, didn't pay much attention to me, a pale skinny girl with braids tightly knotted like the shoelaces of shabby winter shoes, a red dress of Scotch plaid wool, and frail bones like toothpaste that called for immense bottles of calcium brimming over like a full water tank. Life was passing by. To find love one had to rush around like the race-walkers in the stadium. Papa and the women counted on those few hours a week to ignite the fires of opportunity, to try to light the logs of burning tenderness from fragile, fast-burning twigs.

I felt sorry for Lydia, something of a respectful pity. Mama cautiously mentioned (with tremendous scorn) that she was "separated." What the hell did that mean? I saw chubby Lydia flapping around in her uniform amid the comings and goings to Samuel's store, like an ocean teeming with life and topped with the whitest waves. Could it be that separation was an adult disease, different from my discouraging lack of calcium? Or is that the way she labeled it because in her house she had a Chinese folding screen which she hid behind to leisurely put in place some linen contraption supposed to reduce the vast habitation of her stomach?

This desolate operation, to tighten or to meticulously loosen the waists of a weary corset, was like that of a ship captain at the moment in which he hoists or lowers the sails that have been entrusted to him.

Papa, loaded down by his Mediterranean riches, black olives glittering

---

*A Hollywood actress—Ed.

PAPA'S FRIENDS

like the buttons on a widow's bodice, grapes like fairies' teeth, and the skinny girl at his side like some unattractive trophy of his matrimony, twenty or twenty-five minutes later would enter Amelia's store for gentlemen.

She received him with little claps of happiness and with the melodramatic gymnastics of open arms. Papa's smile was a cordial cliff of luminous teeth. I don't remember if Amelia was married then or if she did it later. It doesn't matter. In any case, her heart sheltered an extraordinary comprehension of and access to the maculine world. The sale of men's shirts and ties gave her these powers.

Sometimes it surprised me that the anxiousness of the greetings, the intimate hubbub of the encounters between Amelia and Papa, depended on a commonplace casual Saturday visit to the haberdashery. It seemed unfair that the affectionate saleswoman wasn't included at our family dinners, and that the evident happiness that Papa's arrival brought her had such a limited time frame. My girl's eyes perceived that their mutual delight was reduced to a cautious passion that could have been set in the cold snow of far-off mountains.

Amelia eagerly dressed herself up for the hours she spent in the shop. But the pale mauve or blue blouses, the gray wool skirts, seemed to age rapidly on her body. She looked lovely, however, when she wore her Romanian white silk camisole, covered with pleats and done up in a profusion of multicolored sashes. How beautiful it would have been, her entrance into the house for an innocent domestic meal, dressed in the Romanian camisole and with the fire of her eyes burning in golden affection. Then perhaps Amelia's love wouldn't have been limited to the embrace that stung by its similarity to farewells from a train en route to distant lands. In the ecstasy of being in such close proximity to Papa (different from the stolen and wounding hour that, on his quick visits to the store, he offered her every Saturday), perhaps Amelia would have let him pull up the multicolored sashes of her adornment, as if they were the backdrop or house curtain of a small and illicit theater.

Berta had set up her restaurant in a long thin building a block up from Amelia's store. The tables were at the back, in a raised area that meant climbing three or four bare steps unprotected by the decorations of the rest of the scene. But for me, to arrive at this upper section of the house was like being installed on the gently sloping hill of a theater house.

There was always something frustrating about these visits to Berta. Papa and I would arrive just as the preparations for the noonday meal were taking place. At the table they would have already placed large platters overflowing

145

with salads of potato, beet, onion, and tomato. The chunks of lettuce were veritable gardens.

When Papa said goodbye to Berta I knew we were going to miss the show, the real entertainment: the predictable actions of the actors, the customers' unexpected moments. "It's time to go." Papa watched life through the jealous mirrors of haste. Mama's tyranny awaited us in the dining room at 12:30 precisely, with the Venetian blind up, the sun shining on a fountain of chopped egg, potato, and onion salad. That's why I was never able to see any of Berta's customers. Not once did I eat at her place of business. A restaurant was a prohibited adventure, a swelling of high waves. In order to get near such proud waters, it was necessary to make a crossing that would take an entire childhood.

The lower part of the house held the bedrooms where taciturn guests took their lodging. Berta had a slender, good-natured husband with the body of a dancer who used it only to call the actors to their places: light taps on the doors to offer aspirins, front-door keys, correspondence from remote areas, vague messages. He spent the rest of the time in a corner, the chair balanced awkwardly against the wall behind the stairs that led to the tables, watchfully idle (carrying on the shoulders of his thin body the insomnia that flourishes in boarding houses, and also in theaters).

Sometimes he would let the newspaper drop from his hands onto the stairs as he murmured in a faltering voice: "Ay, Leybele! Leybele!* Good God, the only one of us who got this far and they wouldn't rest until they tracked him down in the last corner of the world to kill him."

Papa would hold me tight, tenderly taking my hand, trying to soothe with his smile the misfortune of the world. But a sad haze clouded the proud granite of his teeth.

I remember that Bernardo, Berta's husband, would take a napkin from one of the tables, and it wasn't sweat he wiped off his face. They were small and fragile tears. His Adam's apple would swell up disjointedly, as if he had already served himself salad without waiting for the customers. As if the spines of an evil accursed fish had lodged itself in his throat.

In this restaurant, suspended as in a dream of some high tower, the tables were covered by a type of cheap oilcloth generally reserved for the kitchen. I was enchanted by the innocent little animals and the rough-drawn dahlias printed on the cloth.

---

*He is referring to Leon Trotsky by the Yiddish diminutive—Ed.

PAPA'S FRIENDS

The petty maternal despot had never seen such crude material on a table. Now I understand: for her, to omit the white starched tablecloths would have been like renouncing the snow of her native city.

On the occasions that they laid out white tablecloths in Berta's restaurant, criminal fingerprints and blood (Del Monte ketchup spilled by negligent diners) ended up staining them. Anyway, the owner of the establishment would never have had the patience to thumb through fashion magazines for ideas about interior decorating.

And it was Berta who triumphed. She jumped over the tables like a thoroughbred horse going over a fence. She didn't bother herself with haughty refinement. A malady such as that would have shrouded Mama early in her pure white tablecloths of nostalgia.

Berta tended toward stockiness, and the gestures of a sharp and fierce worldliness peeked out from her face. Her eyes were spirited and vivacious. It was impossible for those pupils to fall victim to myopia or any other visual ailment. The abundance in her ebony gaze would have smashed to smithereens the glass of any lens. Those imperial violets! Her hair was all boisterous curls, like that of "Imperio Argentina" or some other torch singer, a joyful celebration of black ringlets.

A peaceful garbanzo bean of a mole, cooked over a slow fire on her skin and placed between the nose and the upper lip, gave belligerent notice of a large and brutal mouth, one that let loose virile laughs and cheerful curses in the way of greetings.

Sometimes the musical laughs, the insolent sarcasm, seemed to abandon her body that was so occupied with changes in the menu and conversations with unattractive guests whose smiles revealed teeth like rusted grilles. And, indeed, the fighting and the celebrating in her grandiloquent voice migrated to a freer part of the body: straight to her arms. Berta's mischievousness traversed her upper arms until it arrived at her hands, folded in a gesture of prayer (of embrace) toward Papa. But on a moment's notice she would have to go back to the kitchen for more platters of food, for soon the diners would arrive and the oil and vinegar would be scattered around the tables like incense at a church. And Papa had the officious tyranny of home waiting for him.

Perhaps because I was visiting a restaurant without being interested in any of the men who came for the platters of food, I began to dream about a customer who, in the middle of noon's torrential heat, would make his majestic entrance, suited in a black tuxedo and wearing soft patent leather shoes. A man with massive shoulders and gallant manners, with a moustache and graying temples like the actor Arturo de Córdoba.

He would snap his fingers in command and say to Berta and her husband, "Do you see my beautiful suit? Take my order. What dish do you recommend today? I want wine for everyone. But, for the love of God, no more potato salad with beets. I have triumphed. From sunrise on it's a constant party. For Leybele, our unfortunate brother, as well. In his memory. After all, Berta, what are we, anyway? Commerce and memory. One last favor: bring me some shoeshine boys from the corner to shine my shoes. That way they'll realize I don't crawl in the gutters and the streets anymore. I would like everyone to notice that my shoes are made of patent leather, fit for a ballroom."

Berta and Bernardo would appear, surrounded by waiters in starched uniforms like members of an army. In homage to the courteous diner, my fantasy transplanted itself to the great hall of the *Paris* restaurant with its vast cemetery of dining room. The elegant diner chose a filet mignon.

Olinda in the shoe store Odessa was always on her feet, a party hostess with no parties, attending to the door and maneuvering the cash register. Her hair was a fuzzy, fat gold cloud. She reigned over the store with a petulant and virtuous grace, dressed in a silk blouse adorned with exquisite designs of delicate lace and pleated Scotch plaid skirts. But in her white complexion, in her mouth painted a surprisingly shameless red, she was a woman of daring. Capable of taking on the whole night as if it were a big house, something unknown, with thick curtains of velvet surrounded by gilded railings. A mansion where it was necessary to break down all resistance, something that had to be possessed in full youth and vigor, when strength for the attack and the decision still remained.

The rotund housebound despot would snivel with spite when she saw her little one arrive with a bag containing shoes bought at Odessa. She also sobbed bitterly on seeing Papa enter with packages of olives and mortadella, purchased in the shop where Lydia worked, or with socks bought in haste at Amelia's bazaar. But for Mama the visits to Odessa were the most mortifying.

Olinda, the manager of the store, was a woman sufficiently audacious to have embarked alone for America. Customers at the store (especially on the days when prices were raised) would whisper: in Havana she stood up her boyfriend who, it was said, had purchased the ticket for her long voyage. While she was there she had spent all her time dancing the rumba and, between dances, she had met the Russian shoemaker who now crafted his wares at Odessa.

But to go to Olinda's shop was like becoming attached to an expensive lover. That was why some Saturdays Papa took me to Susana's shoe store, a less pretentious one next to the market.

Susana was voluminous and large. But the emphasis of her nose offered certain inroads into her character. She herself, without calling for one of the employees (all of melancholy faces and dressed in dark clothes, as if celebrating a burial), sat on a small stool to try the shoes on me. She was generous, complacent, and clever. Her knees, like juicy oranges recently brought in from the field, brushed up innocently against Papa's legs while concealing the arduous struggle with my shoe.

But I think he preferred Olinda, high-priced Olinda, along with the doves who found treasures beneath the bow of a silk blouse. Those doves that the Havana night sent off to hover over the body of the Russian artisan.

Over the years, it seems I have become Lydia, Berta, Olinda, and Susana. In moments of vain coquetry, I am Amelia. The fugitive illusions of the Saturdays of their youth are my longings today.

An affable and timid man runs in brief and affectionate spells from his frigid marriage to my house; he pops up by chance, like the playing card that a blind man chooses. And then from my comfortable home back to the cold and imposing marble of his conjugal domicile where, at the cocktail hour, they feed on shriveled peanuts.

The comings and goings of my lover are so rapid and so forced, so that he can return exactly on time to the gloomy castle of his marriage, that last spring he tripped and for months wore his right arm in a sling. Another time, in the winter, he tore his Achilles tendon. The plaster cast, enemy of action and adventure (mountains of snow in the garden, the neighboring park, illicit paths), has him waylaid in the failed throne of a wheelchair.

I adore in my lover the exquisiteness of his manners, the sublime freshness of his body sprinkled with Loewe cologne. As for the rest of it, these fractures have become part of the custom of our passionate love.

He will return next spring on crutches (his suitcases of disability), ready to lose one leg or another as if in some ancient war. Because he will never stop running between his matrimony of solitary eiderdown and the love that we— Lydia, Amelia, Berta, Olinda, Susana, and I—offer him.

Translated by Amy Prince

gUATEMALA

KINDERGARTEN

W*hen* Rites: A Guatemalan Boyhood *first appeared, in 1986, critics immediately celebrated its engaging lyricism and touching honesty. This story from that collection, originally written in English, is reminiscent of Isaac Babel's "The Story of My Dovecot." The autobiographical narrator describes in an openly unsentimental fashion a child's first encounter with anti-Semitism. The plot involves two apparently unconnected murders: that of Jesus Christ and another of the narrator's favorite maid.*

MY EARLIEST IMAGES ARE GEOMETRICAL: THE NARROW BARS OF THE BEDSTEAD that I amazed everyone by squeezing through one windy night when I was frightened by a sheet flapping on a clothesline and wanted my mother; the perfect rectangle of Parque Central, with its octagonal tiled benches, encircled fountains, chequered flagstones. And across the way the twin towers of the cathedral, housing a dark mystery of candles and painted idols that would forever be barred to me.

In my pedal-car I explored the limits of my universe, always certain that beyond our doorstep and the park's four borders lay unnamed terrors. I was especially fond of a wooded labyrinth in the park's northern end, a dark, sinuous place where I could act out my heroic reveries unseen by Chata, the Indian girl with long braids and sweet-smelling skirts who looked after me. To my five-year-old's eyes Chata seemed a rare beauty; she dressed in the vivid, handwoven *huipil* blouse and skirt of her region, and had unusually fine olive skin. Chata was a spirited and mischievous young woman who let me eat forbidden sweets from street vendors and who would gently tease me into fondling her firm round breasts under the thin blouse.

I made friends in Parque Central, the year before my second branding. The first I can recall was Jorge, an idiot boy with gray drooping eyes that did not disguise his sunny nature. I liked Jorge because he was affectionate—indeed, he was little else—and disarmed my budding defenses by hugging me uninhibitedly and stroking my face. Jorge taught me to touch another without shame or ulterior motive, and for this I am forever indebted to him. I grew to love Jorge and had begun to interpret his grunts and noises into a modest vocabulary when he stopped coming to the park. Chata found out from his *china* that Jorge had been placed in a home.

That year I acquired my first heroes, the platoon of uniformed guards who marched past every afternoon on their way to the Palacio. I would follow them the length of the park, beating my hands to the beat of the drum, pumping my legs as high as I could to their stride. At the curb I would stop and mark time until they turned the corner and disappeared.

Chata had an admirer, a tall Indian laborer named Ramiro who courted her in the afternoons and on weekends, when Chata would take me to the park. Ramiro wore a straw hat and leather shoes, and used to flash a gold tooth when he smiled or smirked. Chata kept Ramiro on tenterhooks, encouraging his advances and then rebuffing him with a toss of her head, or mocking his confusion with a whinnying giggle that appeared to goad and arouse him. He looked at her at times with a cold, hungering menace that I recognized even then as lust. I disliked and feared Ramiro, but I never dared to intrude on their lovers' play or their frequent spats in the park. Instead, I would retaliate by making Chata admit, when she tucked me into bed at night, that I was her favorite.

I was some weeks short of five, and small for my age, the first time Chata took me to school and abandoned me in the hands of a tall, gaunt woman with hard eyes and a pursed mouth. Her name was Miss Hale, and I detected from her accent that she was foreign.

"Aren't we a little small to be starting school?" she said, in slow, badly slurred Spanish. I understood this to be a taunt, which, on top of my desertion by Chata, brought tears to my eyes. I feared and distrusted Miss Hale all the more when I realized this was the exact reaction she wanted, and my tears had placated her.

The room she led me into was musty and dim. I was presented to my classmates, most of whom seemed strange to me, and very large. Even their names, Octavio, Gunter, Michel, Loretta, had a foreign ring. From my earliest consciousness I had known I was a foreigner in this strange place, Guatemala. Now, in the kindergarten room of the English-American School, I felt an alien among aliens.

"My mother says you are a Jew." It was Arturo, a dark, thickset boy with hooded eyes and hairy legs below his short trousers. Within a week he and Gunter, a tall blond boy with smudged knees who made in his pants, established themselves as the class bullies. We were at recess, which meant I could play with my new friends, plump-cheeked Grace Samayoa and Michel Montcrassi, who was French, and wore sandals on his stockinged feet and a round blue cap. There was a fountain in the patio with goldfish in it, and a rising nymph with mossy green feet who poured water from her pitcher. In each corner of the patio (Mother said it had once been a convent) was a large red flowerpot, with pink and white geraniums. I sensed the question was critical and I must reply with care.

"Yes," I said.

"My mother says the Jews killed Christ."

Now this was a trickier question. Who was Christ? "They did not," I said, but all I could be certain of was that I, at least, had not killed Christ— whoever he was—because I had never killed anyone, at least not knowingly. Then I remembered stepping on a cockroach once, and stomping on ants in the kitchen. Maybe I had killed Christ by accident.

"Prove it," Octavio said.

I told him I would ask Father about it and give him a reply the next day.

That night I asked Father why I was a Jew. He hoisted me up by the armpits, sat me on his knee, and told me a long and complicated story about God, the Bible, and a Jew named Moses. When I asked if it was true that the Jews had killed Christ he frowned and said the Romans had done it. He said I should pay no attention to Arturo.

When Arturo approached me next day Father's story had gone clear out of my head. All I remembered was that the Romans had done it.

"The Romans killed Christ," I said.

"Who are the Romans?" Arturo asked.

I said I wasn't sure, but would ask Father and let him know.

When I asked Father in the evening he was reading a newspaper. He said the Romans did it and that was that, and I was to pay no heed to Arturo.

Father was not in a talkative mood, and I did not press the matter. But I was confused, and feared my next encounter with Arturo.

Several days passed, and Arturo did not mention the Jews and Christ. I dared hope the whole subject had been forgotten. In the meantime my friendship with Michel grew. He let me call him "Coco," which was his nickname, because his head was round and hard like a coconut; even his curly blond hair resembled a coconut husk. Coco was as much a foreigner in the school as I was. He was Protestant, and the bigger boys mocked his French accent and played catch with his cap.

Grace Samayoa was a little shy of me, although she liked me to tell her stories I'd made up in the labyrinth. Now and again she gave me an approving smile when I answered Miss Hale's questions correctly—and once she let me stroke her hair. Grace Samayoa was the most attractive female I knew next to Chata and my mother. But Grace was also my own size, which made her a challenge. I longed to hug her.

One afternoon Chata failed to pick me up at school. That morning Ramiro had followed us to school, as usual, although they had quarreled in the park the day before when he caught her flirting with a young chauffeur.

"He's following us. Don't turn around," I recall Chata saying, glancing behind her without turning her head. They were the last words of Chata's I would ever hear.

It had grown dark outside and my knees were cold when Father finally came for me, after closing the store.

"Chata has gone away," was all he would say. "We will get you another *china*."

After dinner I went into the kitchen and I wormed the truth out of Clara, the cook. She said Chata and I had been followed by Ramiro. After she deposited me at the school he waylaid Chata a block away and gave her "*siete puñaladas en el mero corazón*" (seven knife stabs in the very heart). I accepted Clara's story on faith, not at all concerned that her description matched word for word the title of a popular song. I stamped about the house, pumping my legs high like the palace guards and chanting the song title aloud: "*Sie-te Puña-ladas en El Mero Corazón. Sie-te Puña-ladas en El Mero Corazón.*" The resonance of the phrase, its hard metric beat, gave Chata's disappearance a finality I could comprehend.

The fuller import of Chata's death did not dawn on me until the following day, when I was taken to school by her older sister, Elvira, whose braids were neither as long nor as glossy as Chata's, and whose skirts did not smell half as good.

In the days that followed, Chata's violent death and Arturo's hard questions got mixed together in my dreams, and my apprehension grew that Chata had been murdered because of me, and because I was a Jew.

Unlike her younger sister, Elvira was a practicing Catholic, and one Sunday afternoon she sneaked me into the Cathedral across from the park.

"You must pray to our Lord," she whispered, pointing to the pale naked statue, with bloodied ribs and thorns on his head, that hung with arms outstretched from the front wall, in the same place where the Ark would stand in our synagogue; only this place was a lot bigger and scarier.

When I balked at reciting the Pater Noster she had taught me, Elvira rebuked me, "You must pray to our Lord to be forgiven for your ancestors' sins against him. That way you can go to Heaven, even if you're not Catholic."

Choking back tears, I mumbled the Pater Noster, not for myself so much but for Chata, who Elvira said had been punished for her sins.

During recess one noon Arturo again brought up the Jews and Christ. This time Gunter was with him, and there was something in his face I had not seen there before. Gunter's blue eyes never looked right at yours.

"My mother says all Jews have tails and horns," Arturo said, with an accusing look. Now this I knew was absurd, because I had seen myself in the mirror.

"They do not," I said.

"Jews have bald-headed pigeons," Gunter said, with a smirk.

I flushed, because this was true—at least I did, Father did and Uncle Mair, and Mr. Halevi at the Turkish baths, but not Señor Gonzales and the others there that day—their pigeons weren't bald. . . . But then—what business was it of Gunter's anyway?

"It's none of your business," I said. My face was hot.

"My mother says Jews are the devil," Arturo said, and gave me a shove.

Gunter called the other boys over and said, "Look at the Jew who killed Christ." Then they all gathered behind him and Arturo and stared at me.

"Leave him alone," called a thin, furry voice from the back. "He's not the devil." It was Coco.

"You keep still, dirty Frenchy," Gunter said.

"Dirty Frenchy, dirty Frenchy," chorused the other boys. Someone snatched the beret from Coco's head and they all stomped on it, one by one.

"Let's look at his bald-headed pigeon," Gunter said, turning toward me, without looking in my eyes.

I was growing frightened now, but not of Gunter, whom I suspected to be the instigator of all this. I feared the mob.

"He killed Christ," Gunter said, in a rising voice, and the group behind him grew tighter. Arturo shoved me again, harder. Torn between fear and anger, I wanted to punch Gunter in the face. But Gunter was a head taller than I, and out of reach.

I stretched to my full height. "At least I don't make in my pants," I said, and looked Gunter straight in the eye.

He made a grab for my suspenders and I swung at his face. But Arturo held me fast and then all the other boys fell on top of me. I kicked and scratched and defended myself, but they were too many. When they had stripped off all my clothes—except my shoes and socks—they stepped back to look at me.

"He lost his tail," Arturo said, almost in relief.

"But he has a bald-headed pigeon," Gunter said. A giggle came out of his face that was unlike any sound I had ever heard from a boy, or anyone else.

I turned toward the wall. My chest ached from the effort to hold back tears. Several of the boys had drifted away, as if they wished to distance themselves from the two leaders.

Silence, except for the trickle of the fountain and the heaving of my chest. Coco came forward and offered me his crushed beret so I could cover myself.

More boys moved away and I saw that the girls had all gathered at the far end of the patio, behind the fountain—all except Grace Samayoa. She sat on the rim of the fountain, and stared at me.

"Don't look," I said to Grace Samayoa, and turned to one side. But she kept on looking.

Then Grace Samayoa said, "I hate you," and walked toward the girls at the far end of the patio.

I covered myself with Coco's cap, and I cried. I cried at the top of my lungs until Miss Hale came. She cleared everyone from the patio and told me to get dressed.

The following year I was left back in kindergarten. Miss Hale and my parents agreed I was underage for the first grade.

A L C I N A L U B I T C H D O M E C Q
(b. 1 9 5 3)

BOTTLES

Alberto Manguel, the celebrated Argentinian-born Canadian translator and editor, once divided writers into two categories: those who perceive a single corner of the world as their entire universe, and those who wander everywhere in the universe looking for a place called home—the particularists and the universalists. This novelist and storyteller unquestionably belongs to the first group. Her novel The Mirror's Mirror: or, The Noble Smile of the Dog *(1983) established her as a postmodernist in the tradition of Italo Calvino and Jorge Luis Borges; and* Intoxicated *(1988), her memorable collection of tales from which "Bottles" is taken, immediately elevated her to the level of master of the short-story genre. A surrealist examination of motherhood, this tale has as protagonist a woman alienated from herself, a robotlike creature trapped in her own corner of the universe.*

MOM WAS TAKEN AWAY, I DON'T KNOW EXACTLY WHERE. DAD SAYS SHE IS IN A nice place where they take good care of her. I miss her . . . although I understand. Dad says she suffered from a sickening love for bottles. First she started to buy them in the supermarket. All sorts of bottles—plastic and crystal, small and big. Everything had to be packed in a bottle—noodle soup, lemon juice, bathroom soap, pencils. She just wouldn't buy something that wasn't in one. Dad complained. Sometimes that was the reason we wouldn't have toilet paper, or there wouldn't be any salt. And Mom used to kiss the bottles all day long. She polished them with great affection, talked to them, and at times I remember her saying she was going to eat one. You could open a kitchen cabinet and find a million bottles. A million. I hated them, and so did my sister. I mean, why store the dirty linen in a huge bottle the size of a garbage can? Dad says Mom didn't know anything about logic. I remember one night, after dinner, when Mom apologized and left in a hurry. An hour later she returned with a box full of wine bottles. Dad asked her what had got into her. She said she had been at the liquor store, and immediately started to empty every single bottle into the toilet. All the wine was dumped. She just needed the bottles. Dad and I and my sister just sat there, on the living-room couch, watching Mom wash and kiss those ugly wine bottles. I think my sister began to cry. But Mom didn't care. Then Dad called the police but they didn't do a thing. Weeks later, we pretended to have forgotten everything. It was then that Mom began screaming that she was pregnant, like when my sister was born. She was shouting that a tiny plastic bottle was living inside her stomach. She said she was having pain. She was vomiting and pale. She cried a lot. Dad called an ambulance and Mom was taken to the hospital. There the doctors made X-rays and checked her all over. Nothing was wrong. They just couldn't find the tiny plastic bottle. But for days she kept insisting that it was living inside her, growing; that's what she used to say to me and my sister. Not to Dad anymore, because he wouldn't listen to her, he just wouldn't listen. I miss Mom. . . . She was taken away a month later, after the event with the statue in the living room. You see, one afternoon she decided that the tiny bottle wasn't in her stomach anymore. Now she felt bad because something was going to happen to her. Like a prophecy. She was feeling that something was coming upon her. And next morning, before my sister and I left for school, we found Mom near the couch, standing in the living room. She was vertical, standing straight. She couldn't walk around. Like in a cell. I asked her why she wouldn't move, why she wouldn't go to the kitchen or to my room. Mom answered that she couldn't because she was trapped in a bottle, a gigantic one. We could see her and she could see us too, but according to Mom, nobody could touch her body because there was glass surrounding it. Actually, I touched her and I never felt any glass. Neither did Dad or my sister. But Mom insisted that she couldn't feel us. For days she stayed in that position, and after some time I was able to picture the big bottle. Mom was like a spider you catch in the back yard and suffocate in Tupperware. That's when the ambulance came for the second time. I wasn't home, but Dad was. He was there when they took her away. I was at school, although I knew what was happening. That same day we threw away all the bottles in a nearby dump. The neighbors were staring at us but we didn't care. It felt good, very good.

Translated by Ilan Stavans

D A V I D   U N G E R
(*b. 1 9 5 0*)

CANILLAS DE LECHE

*his tale of curiosity and violence, originally written in English
and published here for the first time, moves around two adolescent
brothers from the United States who are spending their summer
vacation with their grandparents, Sephardic Jews living in Guatemala City. The anti-Americanism and class conflict they encounter
should not be confused with anti-Semitism: what makes the protagonists a target of local animosity is not their religion but their
clothing, skin color, and good manners.*

SOFIA ROLLED A SIX AND A FIVE, A GOOD THROW, BUT SHE STILL HAD FOUR
pieces to bear off the backgammon board.

"Double six, Don Samuel."

Glaring down at the dice, he only saw a blur. He looked back up at his
wife, his chrome-colored eyes bulging, and cursed in Arabic: "Yin'al dinak!"

"Same to you," Sofia answered, picking up the last four red pieces and
depositing them in a side chute of the gameboard. "I won again."

Don Samuel turned to us—silent witnesses perched beside them—and
asked: "Is Doña Sofia telling the truth? Don't lie to me."

We glanced at our grandmother. A slightly lame woman not even five
feet tall, she stoically bore the demands and curses of an old, increasingly
selfish husband. She bit down on her lower lip and nodded.

"Dushesh" we chorused in Turkish.

Don Samuel threw his dice down on the backgammon board, slammed the wooden halves shut. "Three doubles in a row. I should have won this game easily, but I can't compete with your luck. Forty years of *Tavla* and you still don't know how to play. You have to cheat me to win!"

Doña Sofia shrugged. She had learned to relish each of her victories. This was now her fourth straight triumph.

Don Samuel pushed up on the arms of his blue velvet chair and cleared his throat, as if about to spit: the phlegm held. He then pulled his pocket watch out of his vest, opened the gold case, and extended it toward his wife. "What's the time, Doña Sofia?"

"One-thirty, Don Samuel."

He put his watch away, felt around the oval table for his cigarettes. He straightened the skull cap on his smooth head. "Come, let's take our nap," he said to our grandmother. And then turning to us, added: "We'll be up at three. Not a word from you and no going out alone. Guatemala streets are full of thieves now."

Henry looked at me and frowned.

Our grandmother struggled up, linked one arm through her husband's. "Play some *Tavla*. Read some books. Write your parents a letter. They must be so lonely in Miami without you. When we wake up, we'll take a ride to the zoo and buy some *atol de elote* and *enchiladas*."

"Promise?"

"Only if you behave," bellowed Don Samuel. He tugged on his wife's arm and they shuffled out of the living room, down the corridor, to their darkened bedroom.

We played backgammon, Henry winning three of five games, underneath the stare of our grandmother's parents, long dead in Egypt. They were humorless portraits—severe, religious faces—blending in perfectly with the yellow walls. The afternoon stretched out before us, long and lifeless.

"Let's go see what Nico is doing," I said.

"Probably plucking a chicken," answered Henry. "Half the time she's covered with feathers. And then she saves the beaks and the feet for a soup she forces us to eat."

"You love her soups."

"Yeah, right!"

We walked down the open corridor that skirted the patio and the other rooms of the house. We peered into the kitchen; Nico wasn't there. Next door was her bedroom. Pine needles covered the tile floor; copal was burning in little brown ceramic dishes. Nico was on her knees, praying to the crucifix of her homemade altar. Her tar-black hair, braided with a red silk cloth, hung down to her rump; it brushed the floor like a horse's tail each time she moved.

"What do you want?" she asked, as she crossed herself without looking at us. She stood up, flattening the full-length blue and gold threaded Indian dress she was wearing. Her puckered face shone like obsidian.

"Grandma said you would take us to the park," said Henry.

"Can't you see I'm busy?"

"What are you doing?"

"I'm praying to God the Father and to his martyred Son." She opened her right fist and revealed an amethyst-and-gold rosary coiled in her palm.

"Can we pray with you?" I asked, dizzied by the incense that had turned the air gray.

Nico's eyes darted about the room. "Your grandparents wouldn't like it."

"Please?"

Nico pulled us over, forcing us to our knees at her sides. She put a hand over each of our heads, and began mumbling in Quiché. The Indian syllables passed by unintelligibly except for the occasional *Jesucristo* and *Santa María*. She prayed, eyes closed, and every few minutes she would shake her fist at the crucifix and then kiss it. For a second I saw old Haham Musan davening, *tallit** over his head, in front of the Ark, and felt my grandfather's erect body swaying rhythmically next to me. I was quietly flipping coins inside my pants pockets. My mind wandered to the Aurora Zoo: I saw the carousel, the photographer who used a big black box to take pictures, the elephants gulping down bananas—

"You can get up now," said Nico, rising.

"What did you do?" I asked.

"You're protected from the devil and the wandering skeleton for the next seven days. But you have to behave, otherwise you'll lose the protection and a snake will swallow you up."

"That's creepy," I said.

Henry whispered to me: "Don't believe that mumbo-jumbo. Last week she said I'd get eaten by a toad with leopard spots. She's just trying to scare us." And then he said to Nico: "What about the park?"

"I can't go now. Your grandmother left me a canasta of clothes to wash in the *pila*. Then I have to cook *kibbes* for dinner." She patted our heads. "Why don't you play *Tavla*?"

---

*Prayer shawl—Ed.

"We just finished playing five games," Henry complained.

"So play cards, read. You're lucky you can read. I have to memorize everything." Nico shooed us out of her room, went to her bureau where she picked up a wooden barrette to knot her braid into a bun.

We walked back to our room where we slept surrounded by foot-pedal Singers, cones of white thread, and stacks of folded cloth. As we passed our grandparents' room, Henry asked: "What do you think grandpa would do if he knew we had prayed with Nico?"

"He'd curse us, then force us to go to Hebrew classes twice a week! I couldn't take that!"

"Do you think Nico's a witch?"

The thought had crossed my mind. "If she is, she's a good witch. I've never heard her curse anyone but the walking skeleton."

"Yeah," sighed Henry. "I'd hate to wake up dead one day just because I kicked one of her lousy chickens!"

In our room, I wrote a letter to our parents, while Henry read through a Superman comic in English we had found in a book store in El Portal. When he had finished the comic, he passed it to me and added a note to my letter.

"What now?" asked Henry, giving me back the letter.

"We can play catch in the patio."

"Are you kidding? That'd wake up our grandparents, and we'd get a real frying. Let's go buy some *canillas de leche* at the corner store."

I sat up on my mattress. "Grandpa said no going out."

"He'd never know. We'll leave the door open and go out for just a minute."

"I know your minutes, Henry. Then you'll want to go to the park and climb the jungle gym or go hunting for new comics."

"Danny, sometimes you're a real pussy."

"You're nuts," I answered, not knowing exactly what he meant. It was something dirty, but I imagined a kitten licking his milk paws.

"Well, I'm no pussy, and I'm going out!" He jumped off his bed and dug fifty cents out of his pocket. "I've got the money Uncle Aaron gave me last week."

"Didn't you spend yours?"

"Not all of it."

My mouth began to water for the creamy, rich *canillas de leche*. "Alright. But only to the corner!"

Henry slapped my shoulder. "Let's get out of here before Nico comes looking for us."

The way out of the house was through the carport. Henry pulled up the latch and held the heavy green door for me to pass. Outside, it had begun drizzling, earlier than on most summer days in Guatemala.

"We'll get soaked," I said, still hoping to turn back.

Henry shoved me through the lintel and gave the door a push. I ran back, but it was too late. The door had closed. "Damn you, Henry, it's locked. You should've wedged a piece of wood to hold it open. Now we'll have to ring to get back in!"

Henry shrugged. "I wasn't about to leave the door open so that one of the drunk Indians living in the park could come in with a machete and cut out all our hearts!"

"What'll we tell them?"

"We were sitting here on the curb, talking, when the wind blew the door shut. Grandma'll believe us . . . Come on! Last one to the corner is a rotten egg."

The store on the corner sold everything. Soap, bananas, batteries, firecrackers. It was filled with Indian maids, buying food and staples. We waited patiently on wooden chairs, eyeing the big candy jars that lined the counter. When it was our turn, Henry ordered two six-cent Cokes and four *canillas de leche*. His sudden generosity made me think he had filched the money from our grandfather's dresser. I wasn't in the mood to question him.

Next door was a shoeshine parlor with four thronelike chairs. Through a double door marked *privado*, there were two slot machines, cracked and rickety as if salvaged from a casino fire. We generally lost, but once Henry scored three plums and won fourteen nickels. He was sure that the next coin would bring him the jackpot: fifteen dollars, enough money to go through the summer in style. He now loaded each machine and pulled down on the arms simultaneously, whispering his own mumbo-jumbo as the wheels spun and clicked. Nothing. He put more coins in the machines and, once more, came up empty-handed. He gave the machines kicks and said: "These slots are rigged. Let's go to the park!"

"You promised, Henry—"

"Promised nothing. You can go back if you want, baby, but that's where I'm going."

I could do nothing but follow. Momentarily it had stopped drizzling, but the dirt in the park had turned muddy. Above the huge eucalyptus trees, the thick gray sky threatened to explode. We played on the swings, swooping higher and higher, till the frame vibrated. Then we clambered up the jungle gym onto a nearby tree. We zigzagged branch by branch to the top, until we were perched forty feet from the ground. Here the tops of the trees swayed in the steady breeze, and the wind blew cold. We could see the roof and water tower of my grandparents' house, the turrets of the blue National Palace six blocks away, and even the top of the hundred-foot imitation Eiffel Tower that stood on Reforma Boulevard nearly two miles away.

"I'm freezing, Henry," I said, shuddering.

"Yeah, we better get down. I'll go first."

Henry hopped from branch to branch like a Capuchin monkey, and I followed. Below us a crowd of kids, yelling and waving, cheered us on. When we reached the jungle gym, we jumped the last four feet to the ground and were immediately surrounded by six boys, all barefoot and with their shoeshine kits off to the side. Their pants rode up to their knees, and their stained shirts were either too big or several sizes too small.

Their leader was a boy, a head taller than us, whose dull black eyes were like burned paper. Few teeth were left in his mouth and his right hand was twisted up toward his elbow. "Hey gringos, shoeshine?" He taunted, in English.

"No, thanks, maybe later," I answered, looking down at my scuffed leather Buster Browns.

A boy that looked like the leader's younger brother added: "Ten centavos. Cheap."

"No way," said Henry. "I can get a seat and a shine for a nickel at the parlor in El Portal."

Henry tried to walk away, but the leader grabbed him tight with his injured paw. "Relax," he said, smiling.

"What'll we do?" I asked Henry, in English.

Henry smiled. "Just keep smiling like me. When I say 'three,' run like hell. We'll meet back at the house."

"Paco," said a boy, perhaps my age. "Look at their clothes. They must be twins."

The leader grabbed my shirt with his polish-stained hands. The shirt was dandyish: cream-colored long sleeves with wooden buttons and French cuffs. Henry's shirt matched mine, as did his blue woolen pants. I suddenly realized, for the first time, that we always dressed like twins.

"You better leave us alone, or we'll yell for the *chontes*," threatened Henry, using the Indian word for "police."

My legs danced, as they usually did when a classmate in Miami called me a "dirty Jew." Saltiness flooded my mouth, recalling how I always felt on a mission as I put down my books to defend five thousand years of Jewish history. But these were six street-wise boys. Dirty, hungry. I tried to think of a way out, but drew a blank.

"Give me your money!" Paco ordered.

"Three!" Henry screamed and off he went, shooting through two of the boys who then chased him. The other four boys closed in around me. Turning, I tried to go up the jungle gym, but was easily pulled down.

"Let me check your pockets—"

"I have no money, see—" I emptied my pockets in front of them, fighting back my tears.

"Give me your shirt!" Paco's hands were on me again; suddenly I started swinging at him. My punches landed wildly, mostly in the air, but I kept them coming like a pitching machine. I must have hit Paco in the mouth because there was blood on my fist and the knuckles on my left hand were hurting. A boy grabbed me from behind; his body smelled like rancid cheese. Then someone pulled off my glasses, and I could barely see: trees, swings, ground spun about me. Closing my eyes, I had a vision of death: endless tumbling, no way to stop it. Suddenly my face was wet, but it felt sticky, and I realized that the Indian boys were spitting on me. I fell to the ground, on my back, covered my head with my arms, and started kicking. The spit kept raining down: I heard whistles, screams, and then the boys' voices vanishing.

Sitting up, I saw a blurred figure in front of me. "Henry?" I asked.

"No," a throaty voice answered in Spanish. "Are these yours?"

Squinting, I stretched my hand out and grabbed the two flattened wings of my glasses. I bent one back into shape, but the other broke off. I put them on. Before me stood a man in a three-piece brown suit holding a matching cane. He sported a thin mustache; otherwise, he was clean-shaven.

"Come, my boy," he said, putting his arm out to me.

"My hand hurts," I whimpered.

"Yes, and they also tore off the sleeves of your shirt," said the man, touching my bare arms.

"Oh, no," I cried, also noticing that my pants were streaked with mud and that I had lost a shoe.

"Why don't you come with me? I can get you some clothes."

"No, thanks," I said, sucking the blood off my fist. "I live right around the corner. My grandfather'll kill me."

"Did the bullies hurt you? You have such nice arms."

Still dizzy, confused, I looked at the man's face. His mouth was slightly ajar, almost trembling. Something didn't feel right. Suddenly I bolted as if I had finally heard Henry scream his one-two-three.

"Come back, come back, I can help you."

The lightning flashes seemed to crack open the sky. It began raining hard. I ran through the park, then crossed the street. Small hailstones were pinging off the tin roofs of the surrounding buildings; the water ran in streams down the streets to the open gutters. I raced around the shoeshine parlor and the corner store. As I approached the house, I saw Henry waving me away; then my grandfather stepped out through the green door and strode blindly and angrily down the street. I ducked into the tailor shop next door, hid behind some plastic manikins bunched near the entrance. The tailor in back had called out when I had run in, but getting no response, he had returned to his sewing.

My grandfather turned into the store, screaming: "Daniel, where are you? Don't you dare hide from me!"

I crouched down, nuzzling my face against the wall. As soon as my grandfather had passed, I scurried out of the tailor shop. Henry was still by the carport door, now waving me in, as if I were a runner racing toward the finish line.

"The buzzer woke him up. He was so angry he almost pulled my ears off. Hey, what happened to you?"

My tears were mixing with the rain. "They ganged up on me—after you left!"

"I told you to run, stupid!"

"You could've come back to help me."

"What, and get socked? No way! As it is, my ears are about to fall off," he said rubbing them. "Quick, here he comes. Better hide inside till he cools off."

Down the street I saw my grandfather approaching. I noticed he was still in slippers, his dressing gown over his cotton underclothes. I scampered into the house, past my grandmother who was looking out the living room window, and hurried till I reached my grandparents' bedroom. With the shades still pulled down, the room was dark as night. I went over to my grandmother's armoire, fiddled with the key, opened the lock, and climbed in. I buried myself behind the dresses and the neat row of open-toed shoes on the armoire floor.

I was trying to still my breathing when I heard grandpa's slippers shuffling on the wooden floor, and grandma's halting limp trailing after him. The movements stopped in front of their bedroom.

"Come out, Daniel. Don't think you can hide from a blind man! I know where you are!"

"Don Samuel, stop it. The boy's still a child."

"I told them not to go out. Now this one's defying me."

The air was hot in the armoire. The naphthalene odor of mothballs wedged into my nostrils. I muffled a sneeze in one of grandma's dresses.

"Daniel, come here," my grandfather said. "Sofia, put on the lights!"

"No, I won't let you hit the child."

I could hear grandpa groping around for the light string, and not finding it. Then he was feeling around the room for me: in the corners, with a broomstick under the bed. The footsteps came closer. Where was Superman now? I clutched a shoe; it had velvety uppers and a small, worn-down heel.

The armoire door opened. I pressed the back of my head into a corner and saw dozens of tentacles reaching toward me through the dresses. A hand clasped my throat and pulled me out. Grandpa's face was blanched in the sharp light. I dropped the shoe as he pulled me toward him.

In the doorway, Henry and my grandmother stood, inert.

"You won't do this ever again!" screamed my grandfather. He began whacking my rear with one hand and softly stroking my face with the other. The flesh of my behind stung sharply, before losing all feeling. Then, suddenly, I felt myself turned around and my face driven into Don Samuel's stubbled cheeks. The familiar scent of his 47–11 cologne engulfed me. My grandfather was sobbing.

MEXICO

MARGO GLANTZ
(b. 1 9 3 0)

GENEALOGIES

*Two favorite immigrant genres, memoir and autobiography,
allow for an intimate exploration of the triumphs and obstacles of
the new milieu. Genealogies (1981), Glantz's best-known work,
is precisely that: a family album complete with photos and vignettes of the writer's family past and present, a narrative of how
Mexico has at once welcomed and rejected the Jewish population
that emigrated from Russia and Eastern Europe, and how the
immigrants responded to their exotic new environment. This ex-
cerpt, ambitiously framed between 1920 and 1982, views the experience of Glantz's father during the Bolshevik Revolution and
his journey across the Atlantic as part of the communal history of
the Jews of Mexico. The straightforward prose incorporates techniques from journalism and storytelling.*

"A TALL COSSACK AND A SHORT ONE PASSED BY OUR HOUSE, WITH THEIR HANDS
covered in blood, and my mother, crying her eyes out, washed their hands in
a bowl." My father's mother wore those broad skirts that we all know now,
after reading or seeing *The Tin Drum*: she hid my two aunts, Jane and Myra,
girls of sixteen and seventeen, under them.

"I was almost out of my mind, I walked (I was only a boy), I ran from
one place to another and crossed the town over the little bridge that led to the

baths and I tried to find shelter in my Uncle Kalmen's house, he was my father's brother. It was 1917. I went into my uncle's house and I almost went mad, my uncle had a long curly red beard, all crimson with blood, and he was sitting with the blood pouring down and his eyes open. The fear of death still hadn't left him, perhaps he was still even breathing! Beside him, wrapped in a sheet were all the household utensils, everything made of silver or copper, the Sabbath candlesticks, the samovar. I was scared stiff, I had no idea what to do, I just ran out of the village like a madman. The pogrom lasted several days, I went out into the country and I found an abandoned well, deep, but with no water in it, and I clung to the rungs and spent several days down there. When I heard that everything had calmed down, I came out. Before that, I could hear the terrible cries of the girls and children."

It all happened so fast that one pogrom piled up on top of another.

"In those troubled times different groups were chasing one another and as they went through towns and villages they sacked everything in their path."

It all sounds so familiar. It's like those revolts that our nineteenth-century novelists wrote about and like what you read in novels about the Mexican Revolution, the revolts and the levies, the confusion, the sacking of towns and villages, the deaths.

"The Bolsheviks came back and we had some of the short rifles left by the bandits and some of the horses too; only the reservists who'd been in the World War knew how to defend themselves, the rest of us were saved by a miracle. Many of the bandits were peasants who knew us, and as they were stealing they preferred to kill so that they couldn't be denounced."

Yasha hid in the house of a muzhik, a friend of his grandfather's, Sasha Ribak "with an enormous moustache, like the poet Sevshenko" (the great popular poet of the Ukraine). My father stayed hiding in a corncrib, breathing through a hole, even when bandits stuck their bayonets into it. Ribak took him food and water and let him out when things calmed down a little. As soon as things started up again, back my father went to his hideout.

"General Budiony's Bolshevik cossacks arrived. When things were a bit calmer, I came out. When it was dangerous I went back into hiding again. I remember Sasha well; he was very good. I wrote a poem about all that, in 1920, in Russia."

"And what about your mother and your sisters, how were they saved?"

"We survived by chance, by luck. My mother and my sisters hid in the top of the house, where there was a loft used as a storeroom, in the space under the rafter. As the groups were all chasing each other, they hardly had time to look, and they sacked and killed everything they found in their way. My mother was saved that first time because she washed the cossacks' hands."

My grandmother and two aunts were given permission to leave Russia around 1923 to rejoin their family in *America, America* (the title of the famous film by Elia Kazan). My father was doing his military service and had to stay in the Soviet Union.

"Your mother was afraid that I'd get lost in the revolution. I was very impulsive, it was a dangerous situation and the revolution didn't tolerate people who were impulsive. What the revolution demanded was total commitment from each individual, and those who tried to see things their own way were put on the list of counter-revolutionaries. Well, I was pretty well done for, as you can imagine, being a gabby Jew. And later on they arrested me."

"Why did they arrest you?"

"They arrested me for . . . you see, I was marked down in the revolution as a man with nationalist deviationist tendencies."

My grandmother and my aunts stayed on in Russia for another year after being granted permission to leave, because my grandmother was afraid she might never see her son again. But in the end they travelled to Turkey and then they couldn't go any further because the North Americans had restricted their immigration quotas and only the mother was eligible to enter the United States. However, my father was also granted permission to leave, though afterwards he went to a protest meeting about unfair practices that prevented people from obtaining work. One of the men who had been refused work threw himself out of a fourth floor window as a protest, then the police arrived and put most of the protesters in jail, including my father.

At this point in the story a friend of the family turns up, a pro-Soviet Jew who had left Russia round 1924 and immigrated to Cuba in 1928, from where he had been chased out by Machado's henchmen because of his militancy. He has brought some Soviet journals sent him from New York, worth 123.50 pesos.

"They used to reach me quickly direct from Moscow. They only cost 17.50 pesos then, but you have to pay a full year's subscription."

"When did you leave Russia?"

"My family left first. My father went to the United States in 1912. He left my mother in Russia with the children. In 1914 he sent us tickets and we were due to leave on the 19th of August and the First World War broke out on the 29th. My father went back to Russia in 1922, but he couldn't settle, because he was a businessman and they accused him of being a bourgeois, so in 1923 he went to New York with his other two brothers. I went to Cuba in 1924, but then they brought in new regulations about immigration quotas so I couldn't go on to the United States."

"That's what happened to us too," says Yankl.

"I went on to Mexico later, because otherwise I'd have ended up drowned in the bay at Havana sooner or later."

His friend leaves, and my father comments:

"He stayed you know, he's one of the very few who stayed on the left."

He insists on recalling that meeting where a worker threw himself down from the fourth floor. I remember something similar in one of Wajda's films.

"Then the riot started," interrupts Mother. "The police were there and they started taking workers away. They took your father along with a friend of his, a journalist who was about forty. Your father didn't turn up and I was worried and I started looking for him round the police stations. I asked different policemen about him and nobody knew anything. I said to one of them, you've got your people all over the place, don't you know or can't you tell me? He told me he couldn't say anything. It was a Thursday. On Saturday a lady came to see me. I was playing the piano and she asked me if I was Glantz's fiancée. I was surprised, but I said yes. 'I've brought you a message from your fiancé that my husband gave me, because both of them have been arrested.'"

"I travelled third class, that is, your father and I did. And I couldn't eat anything, because the food was so awful, even though there were times when we went hungry. There was a very bright woman who got on well with the zeil meister and she used to give us herring with vinegar and onions, and that was a real treat. I sold everything in Moscow because I was going to Cuba and Russian clothes wouldn't be any use over there. I had some very smart gray suede shoes which were open down the front and a pair of stockings that I had to darn every day. In Holland we got some money from Uncle Ellis and I bought two dresses, a black crepe one which was very smart and one in lovely soft green wool."

It's raining, San Miguel Regla is really beautiful, with its gentle countryside and all the trees, the house with its slender columns, that huge, friendly hacienda which I almost like better than Marienbad, a place I've only ever seen on film, except that I'm a bit of a snob and it seems rather more exotic to me, as the mother of my Colombian friend said, when we were in Paris and she was talking about American clothes:

"They're so nice, they look so foreign!"

Mother goes on talking: "Your father wasn't worried, in the daytime we stayed under cover and at night we slept in our cabin." (And to think that so much love can actually wear itself out!)

"There was a very interesting man travelling with us, a very strange man, he spoke Russian but I think he was born in Poland. We called him Miloshka, which means 'favorite.' He disappeared when we got here," she sighs, then continues: "You know, when we came to Mexico I didn't know how to use earthenware pots, so at first I boiled milk in a pan a lot, and now I can't stand blenders, I prefer to mash things in an old Mexican earthenware bowl. You can get used to anything, that's for sure. Though I still don't know where I really am."

"What do you mean?"

"I still don't know if I'm on my own or what. I don't want to send your father's books because it'll make the place seem so empty."

"You should send his books, and his papers so they can be put in order and catalogued. I think it's the right thing to do; they'll be very useful for people who are trying to write the history of the Mexican Jewish community."

The ground is wet. We have been sitting in a little garden, surrounded by cloistered arches, on antique style leather chairs, like the rest of the hacienda, like the bedrooms. Later we sit around the fireplace. The cleaning woman says softly, "there's a bit of watery sunshine." Everything is so peaceful, so lovely, so melancholy. I've eaten so much I can hardly move. I go out for a long walk, through the trees, past the pools, the remains of the old metal smelting furnace, and memories flood back with every step, memories of the former owner, the Marquis of Guadalupe, Count of Regla, my mother's memories.

"That's how I learned to make strudel."

"When did you learn that? Did you learn it at home? Did your mother teach you?"

"Yes, I learned quite a lot from her in Russia. In Tacuba Street, number 15, there was a restaurant and there was a Russian man who had immigrated there recently and he was chief cook, and I don't know how it came about, but I think I said to him that you could make strudel in the little coal-burning ovens, the portable ones, with two chimney vents and two openings, and they were making strudels and I made one and he liked it a lot. . . ."

We go in because it is starting to rain.

"He said to me: 'Such a lovely young woman with all sorts of talents and she's interested in strudel.' And I just got on and made it, and I don't even remember how much he paid me. We used to go to the club in the evenings. . . ."

"You and strudel man?"

"No, me and your father. We used to see Mr. Perkis there, and Dr. King and Katzenelson. Everybody changed their names. First they were living in the United States and then when the First World War broke out they went to Mexico to start again, and they founded the Young Men's Hebrew Association."

"With an English name?"

"Yes, English because they'd just come from the United States, you see, they looked after us, in a way. Dr. King used to give your father dental products, I've told you that already. And your father used to teach Hebrew at first to some of the children, our friends' children when they were preparing for their bar mitzvahs. Some people were very kind, and we were very grateful to people too. Horacio Minich's father, for example, taught natural sciences in the Yiddish school, but since I didn't know any Yiddish I couldn't even teach things I knew about."

"So what did you know about?"

"Lots of things, I was always learning, I never seemed to stop. Playing the piano, science, art, even singing. But I ended up having to make strudel. That's the way it is. We brought lots of books instead of clothing, we had a basket of books that weighed 60 kilos. They were very important books and important people used to ask to borrow them and most of them we never set eyes on again. That's the way it is."

"Do you still have any of those books?"

"Oh yes, there are a few left but I'm going to send them to Israel. There was a group of non-Jewish Russians here too, some very nice people, they were quite old, well, at least they seemed quite old to me."

"How old were they?"

"I don't know, but they were a lot older than we were. They lived in Xochimilco, which was a big place in those days, very beautiful with a lot of flowers everywhere and boats covered with greenery. They had a herb garden, they were typical Russians, very refined, honest, special people. There were some others who were former nobility. What were their names? How could I forget? Oh, yes, they were called Sokolov."

"Who were? The ones with the herb garden or the others?"

"No, the other ones, the nobility, were much younger. I don't remember what the others were called, but they had a little house in Xochimilco, it wasn't much more than a hut. They made us a typical Russian meal, they were so pleased to be able to speak Russian with someone."

"Anything else, Mother?"

"Oh, Margo, it all happened fifty years ago. Every night we used to go to the club, it didn't matter if you were on the right or the left, nobody bothered. Then Abrams came, and he was an anarchist, a real leftist. It didn't matter what we did during the daytime to earn a living, because in the evenings we all went to the club."

"Why didn't it matter what you did in the daytime?"

"Well, we sold bread, or I don't know, some people were peddlers, street traders during the daytime, but in the evening we all came together for something better. There were all sorts of people, some as young as 14 or 15. You never knew them, maybe you did or maybe you didn't, but we all had to use Yiddish because we couldn't manage any other way. Some of them had come from Poland and some from Russia and some came from tiny little villages where they spoke a sort of Yiddish, and some even came from the United States and goodness knows what sort of English they could speak. So we all had to learn Yiddish, and when I started I couldn't understand anything because there were so many dialects, from Warsaw and Lithuania and Romania and Estonia and little Polish villages. I couldn't understand a word and then I started to learn gradually. Your father used to read to me, he was in bed a lot because he had trouble with his lungs and sometimes he used to cough up blood, and then he had to lie down because that frightened him. Your father used to read me Yiddish books, he used to translate them into Russian and that's how I learned. I knew the alphabet because when I was a little girl I'd been taught that before I went on to high school."

"Didn't your mother speak Yiddish?"

"Of course she did, but she spoke a Ukrainian dialect, which was completely different. Later on all sorts of very well educated young people used to come to our house. . . ."

"Later on when?"

"In Russia. Before I went to high school. They used to come to Odessa from their little villages to study and take important exams. I remember before the First World War there was one of those students living in our house, a Zionist, who knew Hebrew perfectly. We put him up and fed him and he used to give us Hebrew lessons. He gave lessons to Uncle Volodya, but I don't remember if Ilusha and I did any. That's how I learned the alphabet. He went to Israel later. Your uncle Volodya told me he went on to become Minister of Finance."

"In Israel?"

"Yes, in Israel. Uncle Volodya could remember his name, but I can't. I learned the alphabet and when I learned some Yiddish I wrote a letter to my parents once, just a few words. My mother wrote back in a terrible state because I'd suddenly written to her in Yiddish and she didn't think it could be me, she thought I must be dead, so then I wrote back again to her in Russian and calmed things down. That's what it's like when your children leave home. . . ."

I come back to where I once was. I go through the park, past the pools, and everything is damp, mildewed. It is slippery underfoot. There are flowers everywhere. I go over to a prickly-pear tree and try to pluck some fruit. The pear defends itself and sticks its spikes in me. I go back to my room to try and pull out the prickles with a pair of tweezers from my arms, my cheeks, and the side of my mouth, my hands, and my fingers. My father died, early in the morning of January 2, 1982.

Living with someone probably means losing part of your own identity. Living with someone contaminates; my father alters my mother's childhood and she loses her patience listening to some accounts of my father's childhood. Once we had all gone to the cemetery on the first anniversary of my uncle's death and Lucia recalled the attempted pogrom that my father had experienced. So I asked him to tell me what had happened to him:

"I was working in the Jewish Charity Association at 21 Gante Street, on the corner of Venustiano Carranza that used to be called Capuchinas, and your mother had her shop called Lisette on 16th September Street, number 29, selling ladies' bags and gloves. I came out of the charity place and there was a big meeting underway (it was in January 1939). I was on my way to the shop when I met a young man called Salas, he knew who I was, he'd been a student in Germany and spoke very good German. He came toward me with two other lads and he yelled 'Death to the Jews. Jews out of Mexico!' and I had a willow stick with me, and I broke it over his head and it split into three. He grabbed it out of my hand and tried to push me in front of a tram, but I held onto a lamp-post and wouldn't let go. I don't know how I managed to break free and run to the shop, which was shut, though the steel door still wasn't down.

"The police came right away, I don't remember how many there were, there could have been fifty or a hundred, and Siqueiros' brother; if he hadn't been there I'd have been killed. He said to me: 'They'll have to get me before they get you, Jacobo,' and he stretched both arms out wide. He was a giant of a man. They had a truck outside full of stones and they were throwing them at the shop and they smashed the shop window and took everything they could get. I don't know how I got out of there."

"Where was mother?"

"She'd got out with the assistant. There were stones flying all over the place. I didn't know where to hide, because everywhere I went there were more stones. I thought I'd never get out of there, I thought I was done for, there was nothing I could do. There were so many people outside and so many stones and I was covered in blood. There was a man called Osorio outside, a Cuban whom I knew quite well, and he stood up on a platform and made a Hitler-type speech, and even though he knew me he spoke against me and against Jews in general. When they ran out of stones, they went to San Juan de Letran where your uncle Mendel had his drinks stand and they came back with great chunks of ice which they started throwing at me, and a massive lump of ice hit me on the head and that was a sign from God, because the ice saved me. I was bleeding heavily, because I'd been hit on the head, but that ice was a sign from God, I wouldn't have survived without the ice."

"Where were we?"

"You were all very little, I don't think you ever saw any of that. General Montes appeared later and he put his cloak round me and said, 'Don't cry Jew, I'm here to save you.'"

Translated by Susan Bassnett

E S T H E R   S E L I G S O N

(b. 1 9 4 1)

THE INVISIBLE HOUR

F*irst published in* Indicios y quimeras *(1988), this story can be read as a study of Bergsonian time or as a surrealist vision of eternity. Seligson manages to deal with several layers of time: clock time, calendar time, psychological time, and metaphysical time, thus the quote: "Time is either an invention or nothing at all." The anonymous narrator, the owner of a broken quartz watch, takes it to be fixed at a store unlike any other. What follows is an examination of life in and beyond time—a journey through a metaphysical universe in which the experience of time itself is abstracted.*

Blindness is a weapon against time and space. Our existence is nothing more than an immense and unique blindness, with the exception of those tiny bits transmitted to us by our miserly senses. The dominant principle within the cosmos is blindness. . . . Time, which is a continuum, can only be escaped by a single means: to avoid observing it from time to time. Thus can we reduce it to those fragments we can recognize.
—Elias Canetti, *Auto-da-fé*

"WELL, YES, SIR, WE'LL HAVE TO KEEP IT FOR OBSERVATION."
"But, how come? The only problem was that the glass fell off."

"We are a serious company, Sir. We are specialists. Our obligation is to return it to You in perfect condition."

"There's nothing wrong with it."

"The hands appear to be a little loose, and the face is somewhat dusty. It's only logical, since it had been exposed for a while."

"And how long will you keep it for observation?"

"Come back in ten days, please. Here You have your receipt. You can claim it with this piece of paper. You mustn't lose it, under any circumstances."

And that is how he saw it disappear, in a dainty red velvet case, withdrawn by a pair of mysterious gloved hands coming from behind a narrow window with thin bars in front of it. Then, one of those so-called gravelike silences befell the place. Where could his watch have wound up?

"This crystal is not for measuring time, but rather for awakening in one's everyday memory the flash of other instants which need to be urgently freed from their temporary prison." That is what she said while giving it to him, that singular afternoon: a flat sphere, extremely white, the numbers barely marked by silver droplets. There was no need to wind it up, nor to touch or move it: it would tirelessly mark the time, without the slightest slowing down, with the merriment of mercury sliding through the fingers to reach the palm of the hand, lightweight, twinkling, and absolutely silent. The thin hands, silvery too, together with the second hand, would progress in little jumps that looked to him like the back of his Siamese cat when she was petted and the hair on her back would rise and then settle again, trembling slightly. Where could it be now, below the vaults of that old building with brown-grained marble staircases and high walls with straw-colored ornaments on the architraves and bondstone arches? Yes, an old edifice with enormous windows curling around metal volutes, through which the opaline daylight filtered with a milky luminousness. The receptionist would reply with the same chant to any client who approached the counter, "We are a serious company, Sir. Our obligation is to return it to You in perfect condition."

She was stiff, without moving a single facial muscle, as if she were a perfect piece of clockwork. And the clients would exit through the revolving doors with the feeling that they had been dispossessed, defeated by an unknown force which could not be at all opposed: in there, one's hours, minutes, and seconds would be sifted through until they were denuded of time. But, doubtlessly, there would be clients who would stay there to wait; otherwise, what were those soft, tawny leather couches with ocher-colored buttons for? Long brownish counters flanked the walls of the room and at the back wall there was a wide staircase, morosely carpeted in the same red color of the cases in which the watches would leave for an unknown destination. And it occurred to him that upstairs, behind the finely sanded mahogany doors in the upper corridor that could be seen through the convoluted metalwork of the bannister, one found the death chambers, the conservatories, the incubators, the urns, the capsules where the time-catching quartzes would be buried, embalmed, or simply allowed their recovering sleep; and, in the midst of all of that, his own would be there, that marvelous box into which he had deposited his consciousness of the fleeting, the days, weeks, and months that had slowly oozed along. What would he do in the meantime? How could he follow the pulse of his thoughts, that pendular sway which he had tied to the bursts of light given by those sparkles which it was his task to rescue from the unlimited dullness of the everyday grind? Memories in the shape of an Argand lamp without oil or wick lay languishing in the empty recesses of his mind, left between one oscillation and the other. His work had been interrupted, an unavoidable setback in his mindful task; and only now had he begun to decipher the path along the labyrinth of gears through which he had to enter, a network of minute pins, of small wheels and pivots, crowns, springs, and anchors!

His body shook with a shiver. He covered the whole room with his gaze. A doorman bid the clients farewell with a slight bowing of the head. Two sales clerks behind the counters stood erect as mannequins. A janitor cleaned with an enormous white feather-duster the pier-glasses on the walls and the large pendulum clocks attached to them. Full of resolve, he straightened his back. Taking his portfolio under his arm, he walked directly to the staircase, like a person with an inevitable appointment upstairs. Nobody stopped him or paid attention. *Trespassing Prohibited, Personnel Only,* read the signs on door after door. Not a single sound outside. Perhaps only the slight shuffle of his shoes on the thick carpet and a creaking of the wood here and there, as if it were breathing behind the doorways. Some bell was ringing, muffled, solitary. Inside, on the contrary, everything was beating: a multiplicity of living organisms, coming apart and fertilizing each other, a multitude of time-giving terms, little seeds of endurance, which a giant-gloved hand pretended to remove and return to the dust of the uncreated, to the chaos that came before temporality, to exile, to alienation. With extreme care, he turned the shiny knob on one of the doors. He was greeted by a thick darkness that began to dissipate as his eyes got accustomed to it and could distinguish the streaks of neon light from the street lights, filtering through the windows, due to the wrinkled curtains, without fully shining. An endless gallery opened up before him, with an incessant ticking, an interminable collection of bell-jars casting their shadows on the mirrored tables where they rested; and inside these, the watches, mechanisms of uniform movement and completely regular cadence—wind-up barrel, main wheel, second wheel, instant wheel, fly wheel, compensating balance, hand shaft, rhomboid wheel, hour wheel, crown wheel and rod—quartz crystals, chime clocks, cuckoo clocks, repeating watches, watch chains, stopwatches, water clocks, vibrations, oscillations, pulses, synchronizations; all subject to change, nonetheless having a before and an after, a beginning and an end, all subject to error, it being impossible to eliminate the imperfection between that beginning and that end, not the eternal returning but the cycle, what is advent because it is awaited, and it is awaited even if it is not announced, a wait which suddenly erupts even if expected, the succession of discernible units in a continuum prolonged toward infinity, an infinity which can be measured, however, regularly, rhythmically, one-two, one-two, the abolition of what is discontinuous no matter how much the sense of each day is dependent on the possibility of reducing that to its everyday context subject to office hours and a job that devalues it by turning it monotonous, tick-tock. But sometimes he manages to capture some white butterflies and rescue them from the smoke in the garden where he plants roses and forget-me-nots. For he is a scrupulous gardener, and there is not a corner left without a lovingly watered and trimmed plant, supervised from its tenderest sprouting, growing, thickening, blooming, feeding on the future, on successions of light and air, chlorophyll and oxygen; slow tropisms, those that search for the sun and those that withdraw from the sun, those that open up during the day and close up at night, the ever thirsty, the ones with adventitious roots, the creepers, the ones with straight stems, those that bloom and those that only have leaves, those with tendrils and those with verticillate leaves. He too, like other children, had arranged them, album plate after plate, to acquaint himself with their shape, knife-shaped, palmate, lanceolate, arrowhead, penninervate. . . .

He closed the door cautiously behind him. A slight smell of alcohol and rusted metal tickled the inside of the nose. Where could he begin? And what if his wondrous crystal had not even arrived there yet? How could he make it out, so small among such gigantic secret-keepers? He stepped on the fossilized roots of a carboniferous forest as he entered. Breath transpiring, was it his, or that of those bodies and assembly-joints? As he descended, he was immersed in a subtle gas vapor: a liquid could be felt circulating through his veins, something thinner and lighter than blood, his ears were buzzing. He perspired. An avalanche came down, and, in the nursery, the hours began to burst out inside their vials: everything was transformed into an onslaught of thousands of seconds flying around the gallery, crazed fireflies. Everything: time and memory, memory and remembrance, remembrance and continuity, continuity and atemporality. Everything: what he had always postponed, the moments that had not been lived, the distracted hours, the grayish days, the truncated weeks, the severed months like dried-up branches, and some of the years, purulent years molding away in neglect. Neglect? Not entirely. There were also the gems, rubies, sapphires and spinels, garnets, beryl crystals, and of course, quartz—that crystal of shiny crystals, margarites, citrines, amethyst, with its iridescent transparency and its contents of moss, speckled agates forming their arborization with the remembrance of their body, fingers of singular afternoons plucking their deepest strings, those whose sound escaped, precisely, the tick-tock and the calendar, those that palpitated awake—a name, a face, its laughter—in the marl of his daily perambulations: the invisible hour. He descended. Minute fish scales, slight flakes of endurance would hit upon the membranes that stretched out in his mind like a wide spiderweb: strung in there, innumerable superimposed images would pivot, swirling and stumbling, a vertigo of cells filled up with a mellifluous vapor where the tick-tock seemed to suckle, avid bumble-bee, on his most distant memories, far away, very far away, spore, sperm, atom, nebula, light particle, energy flow, wave, 186,000 miles per second, ion. He ascended, blowing, helix, spiral, shedding its leaves backward, enveloping itself, forging itself, suturing itself, pod opened to the wind thus recovering its tightly circular coherence, tenderly follicled berry, still a promise, not yet fruit, present, only a present being created in a progressive manner, genesis, continuous elaboration of the totally new, growth of the unforeseen—"time is either an invention or nothing at all." In his throat, then, the shout exploded like a beam, the frightful abyss. And the crystals began to shatter, but toward the inside, as if being soldered to their own interior revolving around that point, that voice which was his, not the everyday voice however, but another one, a first one, pristine tick-tock, dust storm of recovered instants in the clay of the original man, in the simultaneity of the grain and the flower, the sowing and the reaping: unequivocal signs of time, its language of signs, its language of doors opened toward infinity. He ascended in successive commotions, in successive vibrations, slashing the foliage at right and left, inventing his own path, liberating it from silence to turn it into word, articulation of names to give the objects and rescue them from their movable lime, white dew that burst out spraying a multitude of letters, intermittent points like lanterns banging the mouth in their fight to spring out vowels, consonants, syllables, onomatopoeias, rivers of voices in swelling elasticity, rapid and burning vibration that opens its way to his eyes and lips from a depth growing upward to the alike and contiguous in successive stages. Voices and visions of the instruments and artifacts accumulated there danced their shadows before him and inside him without his being able to distinguish, in that simultaneity, where the outer and the inner were. He felt the tired sickle of time reaping the center of the circles which coincided with the center of other circles, and something escaped the measurable and visible to get lost in the transfinite. A chamber clock gave the signal: the space turned over, coextensive and concomitant, the gears came off their flying axles and pivots. His human presence and curiosity had awakened them from their rhythmic and cadencelike sleep to the chaos of the unspoken, of the potentially lived; and, like in nightmares, they spun in place, full of rancor, and with the evident intention of taking on a body and transforming themselves from mere desires, from simple movement, into concrete facts and acts. The arms linked to the clock hands, the legs of the pendulums, the cavity of the faces, the tongues of the springs and flexors, the molars of the crowns and discs, came apart in a merry and threatening clamor. Fire spurted from a solar quadrant which he carelessly approached, fascinated by that dance of stellar incandescences—something told him that, this mirage of proximity notwithstanding, Alpha Centauri was over four light years away—inside that circumference resembling an empty water clock whose border formed a flaming fringe. He wanted to look inside. But time is also a reflection of shadows. Therefore, the daring man who attempts to decipher it, spell it out, look at it in the light, can be blinded by its brightness. For time is also blindness, a fragment of life wrapped inside a blind layer until occluded. His eardrums and pupils overwhelmed, he began to crash against the mirrors and crystals, attempting to defend himself with a metal rod from the phantasmagoric round assaulting him, cordless marionettes that pulled him by the hair and skin with parsimonious animosity, tick-tock tick-tock, fine-edged rubies stabbing his retina and shredding his ear, sectioning his vocal cords into the thinnest slices. Thirsting for sharp luminous corpuscles, tick tock tick tock, time turned out its irreversible drunkenness, like a ritual flaying, until touching, blood and chlorophyll, the *yod* of all births. . . .

Promptly, ten days later, at the invisible hour before the sunset, he picked up his quartz watch, returned in perfect condition. Months later, however, he lost it. . . .

Translated by Iván Zatz

ANGELINA
MUÑIZ - HUBERMAN
(b. 1 9 3 7)

IN THE NAME OF HIS NAME

An audacious interpreter of mystical texts, this Mexican novelist and critic, of Sephardic ancestry, has made a career of telling allegorical tales. This one, from her award-winning collection Enclosed Garden *(1985), is a tribute to Sephardic culture, especially kabbalistic imagery, but also to Mendele Mokher Sforim, particularly his novel* The Travels of Benjamin the Third, *and Rabbi Nahman of Bratslav's story "The Rabbi's Son." The river the protagonist dreams of crossing, which supposedly ceases its flow on the Sabbath, is taken from Jewish folklore. Compared to Seligson's "The Invisible Hour," this tale has a clear-cut symbolic code.*

ABRAHAM OF TALAMANCA PONDERED LONG UPON THE WORD OF GOD BEFORE making his decision. He had studied the signs and portents of the world. He had read and reread the Great Book and sought its revelation. Somewhere he would find the divine word. He felt a profound anxiety, though he did not know why; he knew only that the answer was there somewhere and he could not find it. Not that the world was mute, but that he could not understand its language. Not that God was silent, but that he could not hear Him. He continued to search and time continued to pass. To be possessed by a certainty which cannot be explained, a truth which cannot be proven. A sound that has no time. A color that cannot be painted. A word that cannot be deciphered. A thought that cannot be expressed. What then does he possess? How can one live by doubt, divination, foreshadowing?

Abraham of Talamanca senses his ideas spinning round and round in the confined and infinite chaos of his mind. Arrows fly in his head and at times he supports his head in his hands, so heavy it seems to him. And then comes the pain. It begins with his eyes which, as a source of enlightenment, embrace much and suffer much. He who does not see does not weep. He who does not weep does not ache. A sword-stroke at the center of his skull. Pain which makes a fiefdom of his arteries, a whip of his nerves and a torment of his muscles. Abraham, who loves light, flees into darkness; he searches for the word and flees into silence. Pain imprisons half of his head, while the other half struggles for lucidity. But the battle is never won; pain triumphs, and with his hands Abraham covers his eyes: no light, no word. Thus he loses days which turn to nights, nights of the soul which become darker and darker.

But the answer does not appear. After thirty days of constant pain in which the unafflicted side of his head rested no more than the afflicted, he made his decision. He would go in search of the Sambatio, the distant river of the Promised Land, the river which flows six days a week and ceases on the Sabbath, or perhaps instead flows on the day of the Sabbath and ceases on the other six. The frightful roar of the rushing river which carries rocks, not water, and sand, and which on the seventh day, shrouded in clouds, keeps total silence. The river protects, for him who crosses it, the paradise inhabited by the Ten Lost Tribes. If he should manage to reach it, Abraham the Talamantine, and if he should manage to cross it.

He would leave behind his books, his studies, his prayers, his meditation. He would try the paths and byways of pilgrims and wanderers, soldiers and vagabonds, merchants and adventurers. Tranquility and wisdom would be lost along the way. He would go unrecognized, and lose himself among the rest. To be lost and alone, and so to find himself more deeply. And with the cool of the dawns and the dust of distant places, he would forget that search for the unknowable. He would breathe deeply the air of mountain and sea. He would belong to nothing, to no one. The absolute freedom of one who has only himself. He would try for once to be God. Impossible to be integral; always dual; always the divine presence. I speak to myself and He answers me, spark of eternity. Can't one be alone? Absolute solitude? No, no, no. He always appears, God, the One without a name, the One sought after, desired, never found, He who requires perfection. So we wander, with Abraham of Talamanca, in search of the unsearchable.

Abraham prepares his departure, taking few possessions, fulfilled in himself. The pain has disappeared. Now he knows what he seeks; he seeks the name of God and he knows that it will appear when he crosses the final river at the end of the long journey. He seeks the meaning of the word, that which is beyond asking. He cannot accept the imperfection of the sign. The difficult connection between things and their name. The attempt to enclose in the space of a word the idea of perfection, of unity, of infinity, of creation, of plenitude, of supreme good. God is a conventional sign. How can one find its true essence? *Baruch ha-shem.* Blessed be His Name.

To approach immensity little by little. Slowly twining the links of the chain. More slowly still ascending the steps toward illumination. Losing ourselves in the partial and fragmented reflection of a thousand facing mirrors. And still aspiring to rise higher and higher. That longing to fly which is only achieved in dreams. To climb the mountain. To arrive at the summit of pure air and blue sky. Below, seas and rivers and lakes.

Through open fields and enclosed gardens, along paths and byways, up and down, the road unwinds before Abraham the wanderer. And when the land runs out and sand borders the water, he furrows the water and creates light foam and soft waves which, uncreating, erase his vain steps. The sun is ensconced in an immense blue cradle, and the four phases of the moon as well. When at length the sea loses its freedom and the high rocks force it to recede and close upon itself, the foot of the wanderer again falls upon the worn sand, so often trod, so often shifted and displaced.

The Holy Land he touched not only with his feet but also with his hands, raising the fine dust to his lips, kissing it. Only then did he begin the pilgrimage. Eyes, feet, hands, lips, eager. Whether the ancient tomb, the golden rock, the stones of the desert. And then, northward, in search of the Sambatio. In search of the revealed word. But the river is a mirage. It appears and disappears. It recedes and overflows. It sings and is silent. It approaches and withdraws forever. For years, hope detains Abraham. Then certitude detains him. Meanwhile, the word has sounded, he knows that it is there, that it circulates within him: like the blood which flows through his body, it fills him to overflowing. It encourages him, nourishes him, gives him life. It has no form but that given to it by the vessel that contains it. It moves freely, flawlessly, smoothly. It has no equal.

Abraham no longer speaks. He no longer writes. The Word has eliminated words. The Name is. The Revelation cannot be communicated. Silence fills everything, finding its proper form.

Abraham has stopped searching for the Sambatio. The name of His Name flows in his veins.

Translated by Lois Parkinson Zamora

I L A N   S T A V A N S
(b.   1 9 6 1)

THE DEATH OF YANKOS

In the tradition of "fantastic" literature practiced in South America by Felisberto Hernández and Julio Cortázar, this story, from La pianista manca (1992), is a meditation on fate and chance—what Diderot saw as the essential distinction between his characters Jacques the Fatalist and his Maître: one sees the universe as spontaneous, the other as predetermined.

GULP!—I REMEMBER THIS SOUND AS IF IT JUST HAPPENED. IT WAS A STRANGE sound, the consummation of the bizarre journey that ended in Yankos's sad and peculiar death.

Yankos was a close friend of mine. We met in high school and since those early days of our relationship I can't forget his constant sneezing. Everybody in school thought he was allergic to flowers, newspapers, certain foods, or something. But it wasn't the case. Teachers always granted him permission to go to doctors every other week, but his disease was so rare that no diagnosis could be made. In the end, it was assumed that he suffered from the metaphysical distortion of measurement. Exactly what that is I still don't know, but nobody, as far as I am concerned, ever suffered from something similar.

I have tried to recount this story elsewhere, more than once. I failed because I never understood it entirely. The "metaphysical distortion of measurement" is by itself ridiculous. But Yankos's story was true; it happened in time and space, and it is disrespectful to assume otherwise. That is why I am now giving my telephone number—at the same time to honor my friend and to explain things further, if needed: 537-3342. If anyone is skeptical after reading my account, please call me. I may not give convincing answers. I remain skeptical myself, but we can join forces.

About a month before Yankos passed away, I saw him walking on the sidewalk of Avenida Pinocchio. He was thin, pale, and nervous. His eyes were red. It was the first time we met after seven or eight years. After graduation, although living in the same city, Caracas, we decided to split. I became an accountant and he wanted to apply to medical school. He couldn't because of the constant impediments the disease inflicted upon him. I remembered him somehow short, and seeing him again was an opportunity to verify my recollection: now he seemed even shorter. If standing in a crowd, Yankos could easily be stepped on. Never was he so short—and this was evidently another symptom of his fatal disease. When greeting him, I had to reach far down to touch his hand.

That same day he told me his father, a scholar in medieval art, had died a few months earlier, of cancer, and that he was deeply saddened. He felt apathetic, so when I asked him to come and have supper together with me and Alison, my future wife, he refused. It's not that he was rejecting my invitation. His feelings, Yankos assured me, forced him to evade social reunions.

The conversation took less than three minutes. Close to the end, I realized that Yankos's nose was somehow flat, but I didn't pay much attention to the peculiarity. After a short while we said goodbye and departed.

Two days later, as I was watching television, mindless, the phone suddenly rang: 537-3342. I answered and it was Yankos's voice. "I've been looking for you everywhere, Noam," he said. "I need you desperately. If only you will help me. That day we met on Avenida Pinocchio, do you remember? Well, after I shook your hand I knew that only you I could trust. I've chosen you, Noam, because I want you to be my last and final confessor." I didn't understand what was going on. "What happened, Yankos?" I said. His answer was direct: "Quickly, come to my house. Come as fast as you can! I think I'm dying." Before saying goodbye he dictated his address.

Still today I don't know why he selected me to witness his decay. He lived approximately seven miles away in a small, ugly, one-bedroom apartment located in the Bellavista neighborhood, near an old bridge. An old carpet, a table and three chairs were the only furniture.

Before going any further in describing what happened next, I must say I never leave my place without my precious die. It's a small, blue die, with points in black, a present from my grandfather. I generally have it in my right-hand pocket, but it can happen that I find it in the left-hand one. I play with it between my fingers nervously. It's therapy: it helps me to keep calm on difficult occasions.

I wanted to take a taxi to Yankos but I couldn't find one. So I walked. As I entered his apartment, I saw him lying on the floor, completely horizontal. He looked at me with surprise. His face was white and I could swear he had shortened several inches. He was constantly sneezing. "What is wrong?" I asked. "Can't you see?" he responded. "Look, the ceiling is descending."

"What?"

"My ceiling is descending," he corrected. "Not yours but mine. Look up! If you think the ceiling keeps an architectural proportion with the rest of the room, you're wrong!"

"I don't get it," I replied while playing anxiously with my die.

"Look up, Noam. Yesterday the ceiling was one inch higher. Can you believe it? It has been descending one inch every day. I feel trapped. I can't breathe. I just realized this morning: in a few days I'll be the content of a sandwich made between the floor and the stupid ceiling."

I couldn't but laugh. How can the ceiling descend? I looked around. Everything in the apartment seemed normal. The walls were in their proper places. The objects in the room kept their normal proportions. Either Yankos was joking or he was losing his mind.

"Frankly, I don't understand," I said. He sneezed again. While lying horizontal, Yankos seemed tense, his body incapable of movement. I realized once more that his nose was flat, even more than when I saw him in Avenida Pinocchio. Flat, as if compressed by some external force. My die was dancing rapidly.

"The distance between our eyes and the ceiling," Yankos continued, "although uniform for all, is different. My father said it as he was dying. . . . The sky is always the limit and everybody keeps a different proximity with the limit."

"Yankos, there's nothing strange here."

"The sky is the limit, Noam. The sky is the limit." He repeated that sentence ten or more times. Then he sneezed again.

"Why don't you stand up?" I said. "I can't," Yankos replied. "There is no space in this room for me to stand. Can't you see my nose, Noam? It's flat."

"That I know. So go to the doctor. Perhaps a doctor could help you. He could give you medicine. An anti-depressive pill or something. You may be depressed because of your father's death. Your flattened nose could be a symptom of . . . Everything will be all right, Yankos. Have some confidence."

"I can't, Noam."

What could I do? I gave him an aspirin, that's all. We talked a bit more about his miserable state. He stubbornly believed the ceiling was descending. Even as I was leaving Yankos never stood up.

Two weeks later the same situation: 537-3342. The phone rang while I was watching television. The conversation had the same tone—"I need you, Noam. . . . Please, come soon. . . ." I took my gabardine out (I thought it was raining), put my die in my right-hand pocket, and went to Yankos.

When I arrived at the Bellavista neighborhood, he was lying on his floor again, this time more tense. "Look," Yankos said. "The ceiling is lower. It has descended half the way. I am worried, Noam. What am I going to do?"

"Did you see the doctor?" I interrupted.

"Yes."

"And?"

"The doctor laughed. He spoke for ten minutes. He gave me a prescription. Eye-drops. Eye-drops. This isn't a sight problem. I told him that my nose hurts but he didn't know what else to say. It's horrible: the ceiling will end up killing me and nobody can do a thing."

I looked up at the ceiling. No change. "You are crazy, Yankos," I said. "How am I standing?"

His nose was a disaster, almost one-dimensional. I wanted to understand but I couldn't. With *my* die I was trying to overcome the absurdity of the scene.

"I can't stand, Noam. Altitude is individual. We are on one planet but in multiple worlds."

"Go to hell!" I joked.

"Don't get me wrong, friend!" he replied.

"Go to the doctor again."

"What for?" And Yankos sneezed again, this time even stronger.

I am no psychologist. It must be clear by now. Why should I be one? Every person has to deal with his individual problems. Why should I get mixed up in somebody else's life? Individuality was created so that men would understand their limits. Individuality is a challenge, and I wasn't going to involve myself in Yankos's life. He may have felt angry with me. I am sorry! I couldn't understand and there is nothing I could have done at the moment. So this time I left without goodbye.

THE DEATH OF YANKOS

537-3342. Two weeks later I went there a third time. I had received the telephone call as always, when watching television. I put on my gabardine (once more I thought it was raining) and decided to take a bus. While standing at the bus station, I saw two identical children standing close to their mother. They were smiling, as if happy for being who they were. The expression on their two faces, fresh, joyful, made me understand their inner lives, both together and each separately. They were twins. The same genetic heritage, same blood, but two bodies. One of the children was shorter. To listen to his mother, he needed to incline twice as far as his taller brother. Yankos's existential paradox surprisingly became evident to me. He could be right: the sky is located as far as each of us can reach, and also the ceiling. Never before did I realize it and now, after this epiphany, I slightly understood my friend's sickness. "Mmm. . . ." Yankos is getting shorter, farther from the limit. To a certain point, each of us has his own sky. To a certain degree, each of us lives in his own three-dimensional universe. "What an insight!" I said to myself. "Mmm. . . . Insights are a product of pure chance."

Yankos, again, lay horizontal in his apartment. It was obvious in his nose that he was dying. He was even shorter. He looked like a dwarf. The dimensions of his universe didn't allow him to live any longer. The ceiling was so close, and yet so far. "Everybody's sky is everybody's limit," I repeated for my own. "Is there a reasonable explanation for Yankos's fatal disease?"

We started talking about diverse subjects, metaphysics among them. I wanted to tell Yankos about my epiphany. I was willing to acknowledge that now I understood a little more, that Yankos's sickness was somehow less obscure to me. But I couldn't. Evading the subject, he talked about his late father, about our years in school, about his nose, and other "stupid" (this was Yankos's own adjective) things. My die was dancing in my pocket as never before. "You must fight, Yankos. Nobody can be flattened by the ceiling. Nobody can die of a metaphysical distortion of measurement."

It was now that he unexpectedly sneezed. He hadn't sneezed before during this, our final encounter, and as he did so, the volume of his body was instantaneously lost. Rapidly my friend became part of that morbid environment. He, on the old carpet, became the carpet. He, in that apartment, became the apartment. Just one second and his life became a sandwich between ceiling and floor. The phenomenon was astonishing. He had been three-dimensional . . . and, then, Yankos was completely flat, a piece of paper. Yankos's shadow and himself were one.

By reflex, I saw my gabardine on one of the chairs. I had placed it there

Appendix
*t*HE MYTHICAL JEW

Stories of Jorge Luis Borges

EMMA ZUNZ

First published in September 1948 in the Buenos Aires magazine Sur, *later part of* The Aleph and Other Stories *(1949; included in its English translation in* Labyrinths, *1962), this story constantly surprises with its secret messages. Like Isidoro Blaisten's "Uncle Facundo," it is a tale of revenge and theodicy where the protagonist challenges the code of ethics by taking the law into her own hands. While the word* Jew *and its synonyms never appear, the historic and linguistic context leave no doubt as to the ethnic setting. The selection of the character's first name, Emma, is not arbitrary: its heroine is passionate and rebellious—like Jane Austen's Emma Woodhouse and Flaubert's Emma Bovary.*

RETURNING HOME FROM THE TARBUCH AND LOEWENTHAL TEXTILE MILLS ON the 14th of January, 1922, Emma Zunz discovered in the rear of the entrance hall a letter, posted in Brazil, which informed her that her father had died. The stamp and the envelope deceived her at first; then the unfamiliar handwriting made her uneasy. Nine or ten lines tried to fill up the page; Emma read that Mr. Maier had taken by mistake a large dose of veronal and had died on the third of the month in the hospital of Bagé. A boarding-house friend of her father had signed the letter, some Fein or Fain from Río Grande, with no way of knowing that he was addressing the deceased's daughter.

Emma dropped the paper. Her first impression was of a weak feeling in her stomach and in her knees; then of blind guilt, of unreality, of coldness, of fear;

then she wished that it were already the next day. Immediately afterward she realized that that wish was futile because the death of her father was the only thing that had happened in the world, and it would go on happening endlessly. She picked up the piece of paper and went to her room. Furtively, she hid it in a drawer, as if somehow she already knew the ulterior facts. She had already begun to suspect them, perhaps; she had already become the person she would be.

In the growing darkness, Emma wept until the end of that day for the suicide of Manuel Maier, who in the old happy days was Emmanuel Zunz. She remembered summer vacations at a little farm near Gualeguay, she remembered (tried to remember) her mother, she remembered the little house at Lanús which had been auctioned off, she remembered the yellow lozenges of a window, she remembered the warrant for arrest, the ignominy, she remembered the poison-pen letters with the newspaper's account of "the cashier's embezzlement," she remembered (but this she never forgot) that her father, on the last night, had sworn to her that the thief was Loewenthal. Loewenthal, Aaron Loewenthal, formerly the manager of the factory and now one of the owners. Since 1916 Emma had guarded the secret. She had revealed it to no one, not even to her best friend, Elsa Urstein. Perhaps she was shunning profane incredulity; perhaps she believed that the secret was a link between herself and the absent parent. Loewenthal did not know that she knew; Emma Zunz derived from this slight fact a feeling of power.

She did not sleep that night and when the first light of dawn defined the rectangle of the window, her plan was already perfected. She tried to make the day, which seemed interminable to her, like any other. At the factory there were rumors of a strike. Emma declared herself, as usual, against all violence. At six o'clock, with work over, she went with Elsa to a women's club that had a gymnasium and a swimming pool. They signed their names; she had to repeat and spell out her first and her last name, she had to respond to the vulgar jokes that accompanied the medical examination. With Elsa and with the youngest of the Kronfuss girls she discussed what movie they would go to Sunday afternoon. Then they talked about boyfriends and no one expected Emma to speak. In April she would be nineteen years old, but men inspired in her, still, an almost pathological fear. . . . Having returned home, she prepared a tapioca soup and a few vegetables, ate early, went to bed and forced herself to sleep. In this way, laborious and trivial, Friday the fifteenth, the day before, elapsed.

Impatience awoke her on Saturday. Impatience it was, not uneasiness, and the special relief of it being that day at last. No longer did she have to plan and imagine; within a few hours the simplicity of the facts would suffice.

She read in *La Prensa* that the *Nordstjärnan*, out of Malmö, would sail that evening from Pier 3. She phoned Loewenthal, insinuated that she wanted to confide in him, without the other girls knowing, something pertaining to the strike; and she promised to stop by at his office at nightfall. Her voice trembled; the tremor was suitable to an informer. Nothing else of note happened that morning. Emma worked until twelve o'clock and then settled with Elsa and Perla Kronfuss the details of their Sunday stroll. She lay down after lunch and reviewed, with her eyes closed, the plan she had devised. She thought that the final step would be less horrible than the first and that it would doubtlessly afford her the taste of victory and justice. Suddenly, alarmed, she got up and ran to the dresser drawer. She opened it; beneath the picture of Milton Sills, where she had left it the night before, was Fain's letter. No one could have seen it; she began to read it and tore it up.

To relate with some reality the events of that afternoon would be difficult and perhaps unrighteous. One attribute of a hellish experience is unreality, an attribute that seems to allay its terrors and which aggravates them perhaps. How could one make credible an action which was scarcely believed in by the person who executed it, how to recover that brief chaos which today the memory of Emma Zunz repudiates and confuses? Emma lived in Almagro, on Liniers Street: we are certain that in the afternoon she went down to the waterfront. Perhaps on the infamous Paseo de Julio she saw herself multiplied in mirrors, revealed by lights and denuded by hungry eyes, but it is more reasonable to suppose that at first she wandered, unnoticed, through the indifferent portico. . . . She entered two or three bars, noted the routine or technique of the other women. Finally she came across men from the *Nordstjärnan*. One of them, very young, she feared might inspire some tenderness in her and she chose instead another, perhaps shorter than she and coarse, in order that the purity of the horror might not be mitigated. The man led her to a door, then to a murky entrance hall and afterwards to a narrow stairway and then a vestibule (in which there was a window with lozenges identical to those in the house at Lanús) and then to a passageway and then to a door which was closed behind her. The arduous events are outside of time, either because the immediate past is as if disconnected from the future, or because the parts which form these events do not seem to be consecutive.

During that time outside of time, in that perplexing disorder of disconnected and atrocious sensations, did Emma Zunz think *once* about the dead man who motivated the sacrifice? It is my belief that she did think once, and in that moment she endangered her desperate undertaking. She thought (she was unable not to think) that her father had done to her mother the hideous thing that was being done to her now. She thought of it with weak amazement and took refuge, quickly, in vertigo. The man, a Swede or Finn, did not speak Spanish. He was a tool for Emma, as she was for him, but she served him for pleasure whereas he served her for justice.

When she was alone, Emma did not open her eyes immediately. On the little night table was the money that the man had left: Emma sat up and tore it to pieces as before she had torn the letter. Tearing money is an impiety, like throwing away bread; Emma repented the moment after she did it. An act of pride and on that day. . . . Her fear was lost in the grief of her body, in her disgust. The grief and the nausea were chaining her, but Emma got up slowly and proceeded to dress herself. In the room there were no longer any bright colors; the last light of dusk was weakening. Emma was able to leave without anyone seeing her; at the corner she got on a Lacroze streetcar heading west. She selected, in keeping with her plan, the seat farthest toward the front, so that her face would not be seen. Perhaps it comforted her to verify in the insipid movement along the streets that what had happened had not contaminated things. She rode through the diminishing opaque suburbs, seeing them and forgetting them at the same instant, and got off on one of the side streets of Warnes. Paradoxically her fatigue was turning out to be a strength, since it obligated her to concentrate on the details of the adventure and concealed from her the background and the objective.

Aaron Loewenthal was to all persons a serious man, to his intimate friends a miser. He lived above the factory, alone. Situated in the barren outskirts of the town, he feared thieves; in the patio of the factory there was a large dog and in the drawer of his desk, everyone knew, a revolver. He had mourned with gravity, the year before, the unexpected death of his wife—a Gauss who had brought him a fine dowry—but money was his real passion. With intimate embarrassment, he knew himself to be less apt at earning it than at saving it. He was very religious; he believed he had a secret pact with God which exempted him from doing good in exchange for prayers and piety. Bald, fat, wearing the band of mourning, with smoked glasses and blond beard, he was standing next to the window awaiting the confidential report of worker Zunz.

He saw her push the iron gate (which he had left open for her) and cross the gloomy patio. He saw her make a little detour when the chained dog barked. Emma's lips were moving rapidly, like those of someone praying in a low voice; weary, they were repeating the sentence which Mr. Loewenthal would hear before dying.

Things did not happen as Emma Zunz had anticipated. Ever since the morning before she had imagined herself wielding the firm revolver, forcing the wretched creature to confess his wretched guilt and exposing the daring stratagem which would permit the Justice of God to triumph over human justice. (Not out of fear but because of being an instrument of Justice she did not want to be punished.) Then, one single shot in the center of his chest would seal Loewenthal's fate. But things did not happen that way.

In Aaron Loewenthal's presence, more than the urgency of avenging her father, Emma felt the need of inflicting punishment for the outrage she had suffered. She was unable not to kill him after that thorough dishonor. Nor did she have time for theatrics. Seated, timid, she made excuses to Loewenthal, she invoked (as a privilege of the informer) the obligation of loyalty, uttered a few names, inferred others and broke off as if fear had conquered her. She managed to have Loewenthal leave to get of glass of water for her. When the former, unconvinced by such a fuss but indulgent, returned from the dining room, Emma had already taken the heavy revolver out of the drawer. She squeezed the trigger twice. The large body collapsed as if the reports and the smoke had shattered it, the glass of water smashed, the face looked at her with amazement and anger, the mouth of the face swore at her in Spanish and Yiddish. The evil words did not slacken; Emma had to fire again. In the patio the chained dog broke out barking, and a gush of rude blood flowed from the obscene lips and soiled the beard and the clothing. Emma began the accusation she had prepared ("I have avenged my father and they will not be able to punish me . . ."), but she did not finish it, because Mr. Loewenthal had already died. She never knew if he managed to understand.

The straining barks reminded her that she could not, yet, rest. She disarranged the divan, unbuttoned the dead man's jacket, took off the bespattered glasses and left them on the filing cabinet. Then she picked up the telephone and repeated what she would repeat so many times again, with these and with other words: *Something incredible has happened . . . Mr. Loewenthal had me come over on the pretext of the strike . . . He abused me, I killed him. . . .*

Actually, the story *was* incredible, but it impressed everyone because substantially it was true. True was Emma Zunz' tone, true was her shame, true was her hate. True also was the outrage she had suffered: only the circumstances were false, the time, and one or two proper names.

Translated by Donald A. Yates

DEATH AND
THE COMPASS

Included in Ficciones *(1944) and translated into English in* Labyrinths *(1962), this masterful detective story constructed with esoteric symbols is a homage to Edgar Allan Poe's "The Murders in
the Rue Morgue." The unnamed metropolis in which it is set could
be Amsterdam, where an important group of* converso *families,
including that of Baruch Spinoza, lived in the seventeenth century.
And indeed, the unraveling of the mysterious death of three Jews
in three different cardinal points of the city is based on the idea
that geometry is a tool for achieving knowledge of God, a theory
proposed in the* Ethics.

OF THE MANY PROBLEMS WHICH EXERCISED THE RECKLESS DISCERNMENT OF
Lönnrot, none was so strange—so rigorously strange, shall we say—as the
periodic series of bloody events which culminated at the villa of Triste-le-Roy,
amid the ceaseless aroma of the eucalypti. It is true that Erik Lönnrot failed
to prevent the last murder, but that he foresaw it is indisputable. Neither did
he guess the identity of Yarmolinsky's luckless assassin, but he did succeed
in divining the secret morphology behind the fiendish series as well as the
participation of Red Scharlach, whose other nickname is Scharlach the Dandy.
That criminal (as countless others) had sworn on his honor to kill Lönnrot,
but the latter could never be intimidated. Lönnrot believed himself a pure

reasoner, an Auguste Dupin, but there was something of the adventurer in him, and even a little of the gambler.

The first murder occurred in the Hôtel du Nord—that tall prism which dominates the estuary whose waters are the color of the desert. To that tower (which quite glaringly unites the hateful whiteness of a hospital, the numbered divisibility of a jail, and the general appearance of a bordello) there came on the third day of December the delegate from Podolsk to the Third Talmudic Congress, Doctor Marcel Yarmolinsky, a gray-bearded man with gray eyes. We shall never know whether the Hôtel du Nord pleased him; he accepted it with the ancient resignation which had allowed him to endure three years of war in the Carpathians and three thousand years of oppression and pogroms. He was given a room on Floor R, across from the suite which was occupied— not without splendor—by the Tetrarch of Galilee. Yarmolinsky supped, postponed until the following day an inspection of the unknown city, arranged in a *placard* his many books and few personal possessions, and before midnight extinguished his light. (Thus declared the Tetrarch's chauffeur who slept in the adjoining room.) On the fourth, at 11:03 A.M., the editor of the *Yidische Zaitung* put in a call to him; Doctor Yarmolinsky did not answer. He was found in his room, his face already a little dark, nearly nude beneath a large, anachronistic cape. He was lying not far from the door which opened on the hall; a deep knife wound had split his breast. A few hours later, in the same room amid journalists, photographers and policemen, Inspector Treviranus and Lönnrot were calmly discussing the problem.

"No need to look for a three-legged cat here," Treviranus was saying as he brandished an imperious cigar. "We all know that the Tetrarch of Galilee owns the finest sapphires in the world. Someone, intending to steal them, must have broken in here by mistake. Yarmolinsky got up; the robber had to kill him. How does it sound to you?"

"Possible, but not interesting," Lönnrot answered. "You'll reply that reality hasn't the least obligation to be interesting. And I'll answer you that reality may avoid that obligation but that hypotheses may not. In the hypothesis that you propose, chance intervenes copiously. Here we have a dead rabbi; I would prefer a purely rabbinical explanation, not the imaginary mischances of an imaginary robber."

Treviranus replied ill-humoredly:

"I'm not interested in rabbinical explanations. I am interested in capturing the man who stabbed this unknown person."

"Not so unknown," corrected Lönnrot. "Here are his complete works."

He indicated in the wall-cupboard a row of tall books: a *Vindication of the Kabbalah; An Examination of the Philosophy of Robert Fludd;* a literal translation of the *Sepher Yezirah; a Biography of the Baal Shem; a History of the Hasidic Sect;* a monograph (in German) on the Tetragrammaton; another, on the divine nomenclature of the Pentateuch. The inspector regarded them with dread, almost with repulsion. Then he began to laugh.

"I'm a poor Christian," he said. "Carry off those musty volumes if you want; I don't have any time to waste on Jewish superstitions."

"Maybe the crime belongs to the history of Jewish superstitions," murmured Lönnrot.

"Like Christianity," the editor of the *Yidische Zaitung* ventured to add. He was myopic, an atheist and very shy.

No one answered him. One of the agents had found in the small typewriter a piece of paper on which was written the following unfinished sentence:

The first letter of the Name has been uttered

Lönnrot abstained from smiling. Suddenly become a bibliophile or Hebraist, he ordered a package made of the dead man's books and carried them off to his apartment. Indifferent to the police investigation, he dedicated himself to studying them. One large octavo volume revealed to him the teachings of Israel Baal Shem Tobh, founder of the sect of the Pious; another, the virtues and terrors of the Tetragrammaton, which is the unutterable name of God; another, the thesis that God has a secret name, in which is epitomized (as in the crystal sphere which the Persians ascribe to Alexander of Macedonia) his ninth attribute, eternity—that is to say, the immediate knowledge of all things that will be, which are and which have been in the universe. Tradition numbers ninety-nine names of God; the Hebraists attribute that imperfect number to magical fear of even numbers; the Hasidim reason that that hiatus indicates a hundredth name—the Absolute Name.

From this erudition Lönnrot was distracted, a few days later, by the appearance of the editor of the *Yidische Zaitung.* The latter wanted to talk about the murder; Lönnrot preferred to discuss the diverse names of God; the journalist declared, in three columns, that the investigator, Erik Lönnrot, had dedicated himself to studying the names of God in order to come across the name of the murderer. Lönnrot, accustomed to the simplifications of journalism, did not become indignant. One of those enterprising shopkeepers who have discovered that any given man is resigned to buying any given book published a popular edition of the *History of the Hasidic Sect*.

The second murder occurred on the evening of the third of January, in the most deserted and empty corner of the capital's western suburbs. Towards dawn, one of the gendarmes who patrol those solitudes on horseback saw a man in a poncho, lying prone in the shadow of an old paint shop. The harsh features seemed to be masked in blood; a deep knife wound had split his breast. On the wall, across the yellow and red diamonds, were some words written in chalk. The gendarme spelled them out. . . . That afternoon, Treviranus and Lönnrot headed for the remote scene of the crime. To the left and right of the automobile the city disintegrated; the firmament grew and houses were of less importance than a brick kiln or a poplar tree. They arrived at their miserable destination: an alley's end, with rose-colored walls which somehow seemed to reflect the extravagant sunset. The dead man had already been identified. He was Daniel Simon Azevedo, an individual of some fame in the old northern suburbs, who had risen from wagon driver to political tough, then degenerated to a thief and even an informer. (The singular style of his death seemed appropriate to them: Azevedo was the last representative of a generation of bandits who knew how to manipulate a dagger, but not a revolver.) The words in chalk were the following:

The second letter of the Name has been uttered

The third murder occurred on the night of the third of February. A little before one o'clock, the telephone in Inspector Treviranus's office rang. In avid secretiveness, a man with a guttural voice spoke; he said his name was Ginzberg (or Ginsburg) and that he was prepared to communicate, for reasonable remuneration, the events surrounding the two sacrifices of Azevedo and Yarmolinsky. A discordant sound of whistles and horns drowned out the informer's voice. Then, the connection was broken off. Without yet rejecting the possibility of a hoax (after all, it was carnival time), Treviranus found out that he had been called from the Liverpool House, a tavern on the rue de Toulon, that dingy street where side by side exist the cosmorama and the coffee shop, the bawdy house and the bible sellers. Treviranus spoke with the owner. The latter (Black Finnegan, an old Irish criminal who was immersed in, almost overcome by, respectability) told him that the last person to use the phone was a lodger, a certain Gryphius, who had just left with some friends. Treviranus went immediately to Liverpool House. The owner related the following. Eight days ago Gryphius had rented a room above the tavern. He was a sharp-featured man with a nebulous gray beard, and was shabbily dressed in black; Finnegan (who used the room for a purpose which Treviranus guessed) demanded a rent which was undoubtedly excessive; Gryphius paid the stipulated sum without hesitation. He almost never went out; he dined and lunched in his room; his face was scarcely known in the bar. On the night in question, he came downstairs to make a phone call from Finnegan's office. A closed cab stopped in front of the tavern. The driver didn't move from his seat; several patrons recalled that he was wearing a bear's mask. Two harlequins got out of the cab; they were of short stature and no one failed to observe that they were very drunk. With a tooting of horns, they burst into Finnegan's office; they embraced Gryphius, who appeared to recognize them but responded coldly; they exchanged a few words in Yiddish—he in a low, guttural voice, they in high-pitched, false voices—and then went up to the room. Within a quarter hour the three descended, very happy. Gryphius, staggering, seemed as drunk as the others. He walked—tall and dizzy—in the middle, between the masked harlequins. (One of the women at the bar remembered the yellow, red and green diamonds.) Twice he stumbled; twice he was caught and held by the harlequins. Moving off toward the inner harbor which enclosed a rectangular body of water, the three got into the cab and disappeared. From the footboard of the cab, the last of the harlequins scrawled an obscene figure and a sentence on one of the slates of the pier shed.

Treviranus saw the sentence. It was virtually predictable. It said:

The last of the letters of the Name has been uttered

Afterwards, he examined the small room of Gryphius-Ginzberg. On the floor there was a brusque star of blood; in the corners, traces of cigarettes of a Hungarian brand; in a cabinet, a book in Latin—the *Philologus Hebraeo-Graecus* (1739) of Leusden—with several manuscript notes. Treviranus looked it over with indignation and had Lönnrot located. The latter, without removing his hat, began to read while the inspector was interrogating the contradictory witnesses to the possible kidnapping. At four o'clock they left. Out on the twisted rue de Toulon, as they were treading on the dead serpentines of the dawn, Treviranus said:

"And what if all this business tonight were just a mock rehearsal?"

Erik Lönnrot smiled and, with all gravity, read a passage (which was underlined) from the thirty-third dissertation of the *Philologus: Dies Juda-corum incipit ad solis occasu usque ad solis occasum diei sequentis.*

"This means," he added, "'The Hebrew day begins at sundown and lasts until the following sundown.'"

The inspector attempted an irony.

"Is that fact the most valuable one you've come across tonight?"

"No. Even more valuable was a word that Ginzberg used."

The afternoon papers did not overlook the periodic disappearances. *La Cruz de la Espada* contrasted them with the admirable discipline and order of the last Hermetical Congress; Ernst Palast, in *El Mártir*, criticized "the intolerable delays in this clandestine and frugal pogrom, which has taken three months to murder three Jews"; the *Yidische Zaitung* rejected the horrible hypothesis of an anti-Semitic plot, "even though many penetrating intellects admit no other solution to the triple mystery"; the most illustrious gunman of the south, Dandy Red Scharlach, swore that in his district similar crimes could never occur, and he accused Inspector Franz Treviranus of culpable negligence.

On the night of March first, the inspector received an impressive-looking sealed envelope. He opened it; the envelope contained a letter signed "Baruch Spinoza" and a detailed plan of the city, obviously torn from a Baedeker. The letter prophesied that on the third of March there would not be a fourth murder, since the paint shop in the west, the tavern on the rue de Toulon, and the Hôtel du Nord were "the perfect vertices of a mystic equilateral triangle"; the map demonstrated in red ink the regularity of the triangle. Treviranus read the *more geometrico* argument with resignation, and sent the letter and the map to Lönnrot—who, unquestionably, was deserving of such madnesses.

Erik Lönnrot studied them. The three locations were in fact equidistant. Symmetry in time (the third of December, the third of January, the third of February); symmetry in space as well. . . . Suddenly, he felt as if he were on the point of solving the mystery. A set of calipers and a compass completed his quick intuition. He smiled, pronounced the word Tetragrammaton (of recent acquisition) and phoned the inspector. He said:

"Thank you for the equilateral triangle you sent me last night. It has enabled me to solve the problem. This Friday the criminals will be in jail, we may rest assured."

"Then they're not planning a fourth murder?"

"Precisely because they *are* planning a fourth murder we can rest assured."

Lönnrot hung up. One hour later he was traveling on one of the Southern Railway's trains, in the direction of the abandoned villa of Triste-le-Roy. To the south of the city of our story flows a blind little river of muddy water, defamed by refuse and garbage. On the far side is an industrial suburb where, under the protection of a political boss from Barcelona, gunmen thrive. Lönnrot smiled at the thought that the most celebrated gunman of all—Red Scharlach—would have given a great deal to know of his clandestine visit. Azevedo had been an associate of Scharlach; Lönnrot considered the remote possibility that the fourth victim might be Scharlach himself. Then he rejected the idea. . . . He had very nearly deciphered the problem; mere circumstances, reality (names, prison records, faces, judicial and penal proceedings) hardly interested him now. He wanted to travel a bit, he wanted to rest from three months of sedentary investigation. He reflected that the explanation of the murders was in an anonymous triangle and a dusty Greek word. The mystery appeared almost crystalline to him now; he was mortified to have dedicated a hundred days to it.

The train stopped at a silent loading station. Lönnrot got off. It was one of those deserted afternoons that seem like dawns. The air of the turbid, puddled plain was damp and cold. Lönnrot began walking along the countryside. He saw dogs, he saw a car on a siding, he saw the horizon, he saw a silver-colored horse drinking the crapulous water of a puddle. It was growing dark when he saw the rectangular belvedere of the villa of Triste-le-Roy, almost as tall as the black eucalypti which surrounded it. He thought that scarcely one dawning and one nightfall (an ancient splendor in the east and another in the west) separated him from the moment long desired by the seekers of the Name.

A rusty wrought-iron fence defined the irregular perimeter of the villa. The main gate was closed. Lönnrot, without much hope of getting in, circled the area. Once again before the insurmountable gate, he placed his hand between the bars almost mechanically and encountered the bolt. The creaking of the iron surprised him. With a laborious passivity the whole gate swung back.

Lönnrot advanced among the eucalypti treading on confused generations of rigid, broken leaves. Viewed from anear, the house of the villa of Triste-le-Roy abounded in pointless symmetries and in maniacal repetitions: to one Diana in a murky niche corresponded a second Diana in another niche; one balcony was reflected in another balcony; double stairways led to double balustrades. A two-faced Hermes projected a monstrous shadow. Lönnrot circled the house as he had the villa. He examined everything; beneath the level of the terrace he saw a narrow Venetian blind.

He pushed it; a few marble steps descended to a vault. Lönnrot, who had now perceived the architect's preferences, guessed that at the opposite wall there would be another stairway. He found it, ascended, raised his hands and opened the trap door.

A brilliant light led him to a window. He opened it: a yellow, rounded moon defined two silent fountains in the melancholy garden. Lönnrot explored the house. Through anterooms and galleries he passed to duplicate patios, and time after time to the same patio. He ascended the dusty stairs to circular antechambers; he was multiplied infinitely in opposing mirrors; he grew tired of opening or half-opening windows which revealed outside the same desolate garden from various heights and various angles; inside, only pieces of furniture wrapped in yellow dust sheets and chandeliers bound up in tarlatan. A bedroom detained him; in that bedroom, one single flower in a porcelain vase; at the first touch the ancient petals fell apart. On the second floor, on the top floor, the house seemed infinite and expanding. *The house is not this large*, he thought. *Other things are making it seem larger: the dim light, the symmetry, the mirrors, so many years, my unfamiliarity, the loneliness.*

By way of a spiral staircase he arrived at the oriel. The early evening moon shone through the diamonds of the window; they were yellow, red and green. An astonishing, dizzying recollection struck him.

Two men of short stature, robust and ferocious, threw themselves on him and disarmed him; another, very tall, saluted him gravely and said:

"You are very kind. You have saved us a night and a day."

It was Red Scharlach. The men handcuffed Lönnrot. The latter at length recovered his voice.

"Scharlach, are you looking for the Secret Name?"

Scharlach remained standing, indifferent. He had not participated in the brief struggle, and he scarcely extended his hand to receive Lönnrot's revolver. He spoke; Lönnrot noted in his voice a fatigued triumph, a hatred the size of the universe, a sadness not less than that hatred.

"No," said Scharlach. "I am seeking something more ephemeral and perishable, I am seeking Erik Lönnrot. Three years ago, in a gambling house on the rue de Toulon, you arrested my brother and had him sent to jail. My men slipped me away in a coupé from the gun battle with a policeman's bullet in my stomach. Nine days and nine nights I lay in agony in this desolate, symmetrical villa; fever was demolishing me, and the odious two-faced Janus who watches the twilights and the dawns lent horror to my dreams and to my waking. I came to abominate my body, I came to sense that two eyes, two hands, two lungs are as monstrous as two faces. An Irishman tried to convert me to the faith of Jesus; he repeated to me the phrase of the *goyim:* All roads lead to Rome. At night my delirium nurtured itself on that metaphor; I felt that the world was a labyrinth, from which it was impossible to flee, for all roads, though they pretend to lead to the north or south, actually lead to Rome, which was also the quadrilateral jail where my brother was dying and the villa of Triste-le-Roy. On those nights I swore by the God who sees with two faces and by all the gods of fever and of the mirrors to weave a labyrinth around the man who had imprisoned my brother. I have woven it and it is firm: the ingredients are a dead heresiologist, a compass, an eighteenth-century sect, a Greek word, a dagger, the diamonds of a paint shop.

"The first term of the sequence was given to me by chance. I had planned with a few colleagues—among them Daniel Azevedo—the robbery of the Tetrarch's sapphires. Azevedo betrayed us: he got drunk with the money that we had advanced him and he undertook the job a day early. He got lost in the vastness of the hotel; around two in the morning he stumbled into Yarmolinsky's room. The latter, harassed by insomnia, had started to write. He was working on some notes, apparently, for an article on the Name of God; he had already written the words: *The first letter of the Name has been uttered.* Azevedo warned him to be silent; Yarmolinsky reached out his hand for the bell which would awaken the hotel's forces; Azevedo countered with a single stab in the chest. It was almost a reflex action; half a century of violence had taught him that the easiest and surest thing is to kill. . . . Ten days later I learned through the *Yidische Zaitung* that you were seeking in Yarmolinsky's writings the key to his death. I read the *History of the Hasidic Sect;* I learned that the reverent fear of uttering the Name of God had given rise to the doctrine that that Name is all powerful and recondite. I discovered that some Hasidim, in search of that secret Name, had gone so far as to perform human sacrifices. . . . I knew that you would make the conjecture that the Hasidim had sacrificed the rabbi; I set myself the task of justifying that conjecture.

"Marcel Yarmolinsky died on the night of December third; for the second 'sacrifice' I selected the night of January third. He died in the north; for the second 'sacrifice' a place in the west was suitable. Daniel Azevedo was the necessary victim. He deserved death; he was impulsive, a traitor; his apprehension could destroy the entire plan. One of us stabbed him; in order to link his corpse to the other one I wrote on the paint shop diamonds: *The second letter of the Name has been uttered.*

"The third murder was produced on the third of February. It was, as Treviranus guessed, a mere sham. I am Gryphius-Ginzberg-Ginsburg; I endured an interminable week (supplemented by a tenuous fake beard) in the perverse cubicle on the rue de Toulon, until my friends abducted me. From the footboard of the cab, one of them wrote on a post: *The last of the letters of the Name has been uttered.* That sentence revealed that the series of murders was *triple.* Thus the public understood it; I, nevertheless, interspersed repeated signs that would allow you, Erik Lönnrot, the reasoner, to understand that the series was quadruple. A portent in the north, others in the east and west, demand a fourth portent in the south; the Tetragrammaton—the name of God, JHVH—is made up of *four* letters; the harlequins and the paint shop sign suggested *four* points. In the manual of Leusden I underlined a certain passage: that passage manifests that Hebrews compute the day from sunset to sunset; that passage makes known that the deaths occurred on the *fourth* of each month. I sent the equilateral triangle to Treviranus. I foresaw that you would add the missing point. The point which would form a perfect rhomb, the point which fixes in advance where a punctual death awaits you. I have premeditated everything, Erik Lönnrot, in order to attract you to the solitudes of Triste-le-Roy."

Lönnrot avoided Scharlach's eyes. He looked at the trees and the sky subdivided into diamonds of turbid yellow, green and red. He felt faintly cold, and he felt, too, an impersonal—almost anonymous—sadness. It was already night; from the dusty garden came the futile cry of a bird. For the last time, Lönnrot considered the problem of the symmetrical and periodic deaths.

"In your labyrinth there are three lines too many," he said at last. "I know of one Greek labyrinth which is a single straight line. Along that line so many philosophers have lost themselves that a mere detective might well do so, too. Scharlach, when in some other incarnation you hunt me, pretend to commit (or do commit) a crime at A, then a second crime at B, eight kilometers from A, then a third crime at C, four kilometers from A and B, half-way between the two. Wait for me afterwards at D, two kilometers from A and C, again halfway between both. Kill me at D, as you are now going to kill me at Triste-le-Roy."

"The next time I kill you," replied Scharlach, "I promise you that labyrinth, consisting of a single line which is invisible and unceasing."

He moved back a few steps. Then, very carefully, he fired.

For Mandie Molina Vedia

Translated by Donald A. Yates

THE SECRET MIRACLE

This tale, also from Ficciones (1944; included in its English translation in Labyrinths 1962), recalls Ambrose Bierce's "An Occurrence at Owl Creek Bridge," which takes place during the American Civil War. Suspending the paste of Nature, the two are dazzling visions of death in which the protagonists are allowed to return to their past sub specie aeternitatis. But a religious element is added here: Jaromir Hladik, Czech playwright and translator of kabbalistic literature imprisoned by the Nazis in Prague, whose intellectual plight recalls that of Kafka, asks God, before dying, for enough time to finish a drama he has begun. Borges's ending is troublesome: Can a miracle, in the biblical sense, be truly secret? Other possible conclusions have been suggested, including one in which the manuscript of Hladik's The Enemies is found in a rare book room of a New York City library.

> And God had him die for a hundred years and then
> revived him and said:
>> "How long have you been here?"
>> "A day or a part of a day," he answered.
>> Koran, II, 261

THE NIGHT OF MARCH 14, 1943, IN AN APARTMENT IN THE ZELTNERGASSE OF Prague, Jaromir Hladik, the author of the unfinished drama entitled *The Enemies,* of *Vindication of Eternity,* and of a study of the indirect Jewish sources of Jakob Böhme, had a dream of a long game of chess. The players were not two persons, but two illustrious families; the game had been going on for centuries. Nobody could remember what the stakes were, but it was rumored that they were enormous, perhaps infinite; the chessmen and the board were in a secret tower. Jaromir (in his dream) was the first-born of one of the contending families. The clock struck the hour for the game, which could not be postponed. The dreamer raced over the sands of a rainy desert, and was unable to recall either the pieces of the rules of chess. At that moment he awoke. The clangor of the rain and of the terrible clocks ceased. A rhythmic, unanimous noise, punctuated by shouts of command, arose from the Zeltnergasse. It was dawn, and the armored vanguard of the Third Reich was entering Prague.

On the nineteenth the authorities received a denunciation; that same nineteenth, toward evening, Jaromir Hladik was arrested. He was taken to an aseptic, white barracks on the opposite bank of the Moldau. He was unable to refute a single one of the Gestapo's charges; his mother's family name was Jaroslavski, he was of Jewish blood, his study on Böhme had a marked Jewish emphasis, his signature had been one more on the protest against the *Anschluss.* In 1928 he had translated the *Sepher Yezirah* for the publishing house of Hermann Barsdorf. The fulsome catalogue of the firm had exaggerated, for publicity purposes, the translator's reputation, and the catalogue had been examined by Julius Rothe, one of the officials who held Hladik's fate in his hands. There is not a person who, except in the field of his own specialization, is not credulous; two or three adjectives in Gothic type were enough to persuade Julius Rothe of Hladik's importance, and he ordered him sentenced to death *pour encourager les autres.* The execution was set for March 29th, at 9:00 A.M. This delay (whose importance the reader will grasp later) was owing to the desire on the authorities' part to proceed impersonally and slowly, after the manner of vegetables and plants.

Hladik's first reaction was mere terror. He felt he would not have shrunk from the gallows, the block, or the knife, but that death by a firing squad was unbearable. In vain he tried to convince himself that the plain, unvarnished fact of dying was the fearsome thing, not the attendant circumstances. He never wearied of conjuring up these circumstances, senselessly trying to exhaust all their possible variations. He infinitely anticipated the process of his

dying, from the sleepless dawn to the mysterious volley. Before the day set
by Julius Rothe he died hundreds of deaths in courtyards whose forms and
angles strained geometrical probabilities, machine-gunned by variable soldiers
in changing numbers, who at times killed him from a distance, at others from
close by. He faced these imaginary executions with real terror (perhaps with
real bravery); each simulacrum lasted a few seconds. When the circle was
closed, Jaromir returned once more and interminably to the tremulous vespers
of his death. Then he reflected that reality does not usually coincide with our
anticipation of it; with a logic of his own he inferred that to foresee a circum-
stantial detail is to prevent its happening. Trusting in this weak magic, he
invented, *so that they would not happen,* the most gruesome details. Finally,
as was natural, he came to fear that they were prophetic. Miserable in the
night, he endeavored to find some way to hold fast to the fleeting substance
of time. He knew that it was rushing headlong toward the dawn of the twenty-
ninth. He reasoned aloud: "I am now in the night of the twenty-second; while
this night lasts (and for six nights more), I am invulnerable, immortal." The
nights of sleep seemed to him deep, dark pools in which he could submerge
himself. There were moments when he longed impatiently for the final burst
of fire that would free him, for better or for worse, from the vain compulsion
of his imaginings. On the twenty-eighth, as the last sunset was reverberating
from the high barred windows, the thought of his drama, *The Enemies,* de-
flected him from these abject considerations.

Hladik had rounded forty. Aside from a few friendships and many habits,
the problematic exercise of literature constituted his life. Like all writers, he
measured the achievements of others by what they had accomplished, asking
of them that they measure him by what he envisaged or planned. All the books
he had published had left him with a complex feeling of repentance. His studies
of the work of Böhme, of Ibn Ezra, and of Fludd had been characterized
essentially by mere application; his translation of the *Sepher Yezirah,* by care-
lessness, fatigue, and conjecture. *Vindication of Eternity* perhaps had fewer
shortcomings. The first volume gave a history of man's various concepts of
eternity, from the immutable Being of Parmenides to the modifiable Past of
Hinton. The second denied (with Francis Bradley) that all the events of the
universe make up a temporal series, arguing that the number of man's possible
experiences is not infinite, and that a single "repetition" suffices to prove that
time is a fallacy. . . . Unfortunately, the arguments that demonstrate this fallacy are equally fallacious. Hladik was in the habit of going over them with a
kind of contemptuous perplexity. He had also composed a series of Expres-

sionist poems; to the poet's chagrin they had been included in an anthology published in 1924, and no subsequent anthology inherited them. From all this equivocal, uninspired past Hladik had hoped to redeem himself with his drama in verse, *The Enemies.* (Hladik felt the verse form to be essential because it makes it impossible for the spectators to lose sight of irreality, one of art's requisites.)

The drama observed the unities of time, place, and action. The scene was laid in Hradčany, in the library of Baron von Roemerstadt, on one of the last afternoons of the nineteenth century. In the first scene of the first act a strange man visits Roemerstadt. (A clock was striking seven, the vehemence of the setting sun's rays glorified the windows, a passionate, familiar Hungarian music floated in the air.) This visit is followed by others; Roemerstadt does not know the people who are importuning him, but he has the uncomfortable feeling that he has seen them somewhere, perhaps in a dream. They all fawn upon him, but it is apparent—first to the audience and then to the Baron— that they are secret enemies, in league to ruin him. Roemerstadt succeeds in checking or evading their involved schemings. In the dialogue mention is made of his sweetheart, Julia von Weidenau, and a certain Jaroslav Kubin, who at one time pressed his attentions on her. Kubin has now lost his mind, and believes himself to be Roemerstadt. The dangers increase; Roemerstadt, at the end of the second act, is forced to kill one of the conspirators. The third and final act opens. The incoherencies gradually increase; actors who had seemed out of the play reappear; the man Roemerstadt killed returns for a moment. Someone points out that evening has not fallen; the clock strikes seven, the high windows reverberate in the western sun, the air carries an impassioned Hungarian melody. The first actor comes on and repeats the lines he had spoken in the first scene of the first act. Roemerstadt speaks to him without surprise; the audience understands that Roemerstadt is the miserable Jaroslav Kubin. The drama has never taken place; it is the circular delirium that Kubin lives and relives endlessly.

Hladik had never asked himself whether this tragicomedy of errors was preposterous or admirable, well thought out or slipshod. He felt that the plot I have just sketched was best contrived to cover up his defects and point up his abilities and held the possibility of allowing him to redeem (symbolically) the meaning of his life. He had finished the first act and one or two scenes of the third; the metrical nature of the work made it possible for him to keep working it over, changing the hexameters, without the manuscript in front of him. He thought how he still had two acts to do, and that he was going to die very soon. He spoke with God in the darkness: "If in some fashion I exist, if I am not one of Your repetitions and mistakes, I exist as the author of *The Enemies*. To finish this drama, which can justify me and justify You, I need another year. Grant me these days, You to whom the centuries and time belong." This was the last night, the most dreadful of all, but ten minutes later sleep flooded over him like a dark water.

Toward dawn he dreamed that he had concealed himself in one of the naves of the Clementine Library. A librarian wearing dark glasses asked him: "What are you looking for?" Hladik answered: "I am looking for God." The librarian said to him: "God is in one of the letters on one of the pages of one of the four hundred thousand volumes of the Clementine. My fathers and the fathers of my fathers have searched for this letter; I have grown blind seeking it." He removed his glasses, and Hladik saw his eyes, which were dead. A reader came in to return an atlas. "This atlas is worthless," he said, and handed it to Hladik, who opened it at random. He saw a map of India as in a daze. Suddenly sure of himself, he touched one of the tiniest letters. A ubiquitous voice said to him: "The time of your labor has been granted." At this point Hladik awoke.

He remembered that men's dreams belong to God, and that Maimonides had written that the words heard in a dream are divine when they are distinct and clear and the person uttering them cannot be seen. He dressed: two soldiers came into the cell and ordered him to follow them.

From behind the door, Hladik had envisaged a labyrinth of passageways, stairs, and separate buildings. The reality was less spectacular; they descended to an inner court by a narrow iron stairway. Several soldiers—some with uniform unbuttoned—were examining a motorcycle and discussing it. The sergeant looked at the clock; it was 8:44. They had to wait until it struck nine. Hladik, more insignificant than pitiable, sat down on a pile of wood. He noticed that the soldiers' eyes avoided his. To ease his wait, the sergeant handed him a cigarette. Hladik did not smoke; he accepted it out of politeness or humility. As he lighted it, he noticed that his hands were shaking. The day was clouding over; the soldiers spoke in a low voice as though he were already dead. Vainly he tried to recall the woman of whom Julia von Weidenau was the symbol.

The squad formed and stood at attention. Hladik, standing against the barracks wall, waited for the volley. Someone pointed out that the wall was going to be stained with blood; the victim was ordered to step forward a few paces. Incongruously, this reminded Hladik of the fumbling preparations of photographers. A big drop of rain struck one of Hladik's temples and rolled slowly down his cheek; the sergeant shouted the final order.

The physical universe came to a halt.

The guns converged on Hladik, but the men who were to kill him stood motionless. The sergeant's arm eternized an unfinished gesture. On a paving stone of the courtyard a bee cast an unchanging shadow. The wind had ceased, as in a picture. Hladik attempted a cry, a word, a movement of the hand. He realized that he was paralyzed. Not a sound reached him from the halted world. He thought: "I am in hell, I am dead." He thought: "I am mad." He thought: "Time has stopped." Then he reflected that if that was the case, his mind would have stopped too. He wanted to test this; he repeated (without moving his lips) Vergil's mysterious fourth Eclogue. He imagined that the now remote soldiers must be sharing his anxiety; he longed to be able to communicate with them. It astonished him not to feel the least fatigue, not even the numbness of his protracted immobility. After an indeterminate time he fell asleep. When he awoke the world continued motionless and mute. The drop of water still clung to his cheek, the shadow of the bee to the stone. The smoke from the cigarette he had thrown away had not dispersed. Another "day" went by before Hladik understood.

He had asked God for a whole year to finish his work; His omnipotence had granted it. God had worked a secret miracle for him; German lead would kill him at the set hour, but in his mind a year would go by between the order and its execution. From perplexity he passed to stupor, from stupor to resignation, from resignation to sudden gratitude.

He had no document but his memory; the training he had acquired with each added hexameter gave him a discipline unsuspected by those who set down and forget temporary, incomplete paragraphs. He was not working for posterity or even for God, whose literary tastes were unknown to him. Meticulously, motionlessly, secretly, he wrought in time his lofty, invisible labyrinth. He worked the third act over twice. He eliminated certain symbols as over-obvious, such as the repeated striking of the clock, the music. Nothing hurried him. He omitted, he condensed, he amplified. In certain instances he came back to the original version. He came to feel an affection for the court-yard, the barracks; one of the faces before him modified his conception of Roemerstadt's character. He discovered that the wearying cacophonies that bothered Flaubert so much are mere visual superstitions, weakness and limitation of the written word, not the spoken. . . . He concluded his drama. He had only the problem of a single phrase. He found it. The drop of water slid down his cheek. He opened his mouth in a maddened cry, moved his face, dropped under the quadruple blast.

Jaromir Hladik died on March 29, at 9:02 A.M.

Translated by Harriet de Onís

B I B L I O G R A P H Y

The following list of titles provides a source for further reading and research. Section 1, including the most authoritative works in the field (a number of which I cited in the Introduction), serves as historical, sociological, and literary context; Section 2 is devoted to the work of each writer and includes the outstanding critical essays on his or her work; Section 3 refers to works by Jewish–Latin American writers not included in this book.

1

Aizenberg, Edna. "Sephardim and Neo-Sephardim in Latin American Literature." *Sephardic Scholar Series* 4 (1979–1982):125–32.

AMIA [Asociación Mutual Israelita Argentina]. *Pluralismo e identidad*. Buenos Aires: Milá, 1984.

Avni, Haim. *Argentina y la historia de la inmigración judía (1810–1950)*. Buenos Aires: AMIA/Comunidad Judía de Buenos Aires/Hebrew University of Jerusalem, 1983.

Beller, Jacob. *Jews in Latin America*. New York: Jonathan David, 1969.

Cohen, J. X. *Jewish Life in South America: A Survey Study for the American Jewish Congress*. New York: Bloch, 1941.

Cohen, Martin A., ed. *The Jewish Experience in Latin America: Selected Studies from the Publications of the American Jewish Historical Society*. 2 vols. Waltham, Mass.: American Jewish Publication Society/KTAV, 1971.

DiAntonio, Robert F. *Brazilian Fiction: Aspects and Evolution of the Contemporary Narrative*. Fayetteville: University of Arkansas Press, 1989.

———. "Redemption and Rebirth on a Safe Shore: The Holocaust in Contemporary Brazilian Fiction." *Hispania* 74, 4 (December 1991):876–80.

———. *Tradition and Innovation. Reflections on Jewish-Latin American Writing*. Edited with Nora Glickman. Albany: State University of New York Press, 1993.

Gardiol, Rita M. *Argentine Jewish Short Story Writers*. Muncie, Ind.: Ball State University Monographs no. 32, 1986.

———. "Jewish Writers: An Emerging Force in Contemporary Argentina." *Hispanófila* 91 (1987):65–76.

Gojman, Alicia. *Los conversos en la Nueva España*. Mexico: UNAM [Universidad Nacional Autónoma de México], 1984.

Elkin, Judith Laikin. "Goodnight, Sweet Gaucho: A Revisionist View of the Jewish Agricultural Experiment in Argentina." *American Jewish Historical Society* 67 (1978):208–23.

———. *Jews of the Latin American Republics*. Chapel Hill: University of North Carolina Press, 1980.

———. "A Gallery of Former Jews." *Commentary* 92, 6 (December 1991):23–28.

Elkin, Judith Laikin, and Gilbert W. Merkx, eds. *The Jewish Presence in Latin America*. Boston and London: Allen and Unwin, 1982.

Feierstein, Ricardo. *Cien años de narrativa judeoargentina: 1889–1989*. Buenos Aires: Milá, 1989.

———. *Cuentos judíos latinoamericanos*. Buenos Aires: AMIA, 1990.

Kaufman, Edy, with Yoram Shapira and Joel Barroni. *Israeli-Latin American Relations*. New Brunswick, N.J.: Transaction Books, 1979.

Lieberman, Seymour B. *Los judíos en México y América Central (Fé, llamas e Inquisición)*. Mexico: Siglo XXI, 1971.

———. "Argentine Jews and Their Institutions." *Jewish Social Studies* 43 (1981):311–38.

———. *The Inquisitors and the Jews in the New World*. Coral Gables, Fla.: University of Miami Press, 1974.

Lindstrom, Naomi. *Jewish Issues in Argentine Literature: From Gerchunoff to Szichman*. Columbia, Mo.: University of Missouri Press, 1989.

———. "Problems and Possibilities in the Analysis of Jewish Argentine Literary Works." *Latin American Literary Review* 18, 1 (1983):118–26.

Lipp, Solomon. "Israel and the Holocaust in Contemporary Spanish-American Poetry." *Hispania* 64 (1982):536–43.

Martin, Gerald. *Journeys Through the Labyrinth: Latin American Fiction in the Twentieth Century*. London and New York: Verso, 1989.

Muñiz-Huberman, Angelina, ed. *La lengua florida. Antología sefaradí*. Mexico: Fondo de Cultura Económica-UNAM, 1989.

Nesbit, Lewis. "The Jewish Contribution to Argentine Literature." *Hispania* 33 (1950):313–20.

Orgambide, Pedro. "¿Existe el escritor judeoargentino?" *Nueva Presencia* (Buenos Aires) 441 (13 December 1985):1–2.

Sable, Martin H. *Latin American Jewry: A Research Guide*. Cincinnati: Hebrew Union College Press, 1978.

Schwartz, Kessel. "Antisemitism in Modern Argentine Fiction." *Jewish Social Studies* 40 (1978):131–40.

———. "The Jew in Twentieth-Century Argentine Literature." *The American Hispanist* 3, 19 (1977):9–12.

Senkman, Leonardo. "Between Revolution and Reaction." *Jewish Frontier* (March 1981):10–13.

———. *La identidad judía en la literatura argentina*. Buenos Aires: Pardés, 1983.

Senkman, Leonardo, Ricardo Feierstein, Isidoro Niborski, and Sara Itzigson, eds. *Integración y marginalidad: Historia de vidas de inmigrantes judíos a la Argentina*. Buenos Aires: Milá, 1985.

Sofer, Eugene. *From Pale to Pampa: The Jewish Immigrant Experience in Buenos Aires*. New York: Holmes & Meier, 1982.

Sosnowski, Saul. *La orilla inminente. Escritores judíos argentinos*. Buenos Aires: Legasa, 1987.

———. "Contemporary Jewish-Argentine Writers: Tradition and Politics." *Latin American Literary Review* 6, 12 (1978):1–14.

———. "Latin American Jewish Authors: A Bridge Toward History." *Prooftexts* 4 (1984):71–92.

Stavans, Ilan. "América Latina y su pluma judía." *Revista Hispánica Moderna* XLIII, 1 (June 1990):114–17.

———. "Perfil del judío en *La cabeza de la hidra* de Carlos Fuentes," *La historia de la literatura iberoamericana*, Raquel Chang-Rodríguez and Gabriella de Beer, eds. Hanover, N.H.: Ediciones del Norte, 1989, 235–41.

Toro, Alfonso. *La familia Carvajal*. 2 vols. Mexico: Editorial Patria, 1944.

Vieira, Nelson H. "Judaic Fiction in Brazil: To Be or Not to Be Jewish." *Latin American Literary Review* 14, 28 (July–December 1986):31–45.

——. "Hitler and Mengele in Brazil: The Testimony of Roberto Drummond." *Modern Fiction Studies* 32, 3 (Autumn 1986):427–38.

——. "Post-Holocaust Literature in Brazil: Jewish Resistance and Resurgence as Literary Metaphors for Brazilian Society and Politics." *Modern Language Studies* 16, 1 (Winter 1986):62–70.

Weisbrot, Robert. *The Jews of Argentina: From the Inquisition to Perón.* Philadelphia: Jewish Publication Society, 1979.

Winsberg, Morton. *Colonia Barón Hirsch: A Jewish Agricultural Colony in Argentina.* Gainesville: University Presses of Florida, 1964.

Winter, Calvert J. "Some Jewish Writers of the Argentine." *Hispania* 19 (1936):431–36.

2

ISIDORO BLAISTEN (b. 1933)

El mago. Buenos Aires: Ediciones del Sol, 1974.

Dublin al sur. Buenos Aires: Sudamericana, 1980.

Cerrado por melancolía. Buenos Aires: Editorial de Belgrano, 1981.

Cuentos anteriores. Buenos Aires: Editorial de Belgrano, 1982.

Anti-conferencias. Buenos Aires: Emecé, 1983.

A mí nunca me dejan hablar. Buenos Aires: Sudamericana, 1985.

Carroza y reina. Buenos Aires: Emecé, 1986.

JORGE LUIS BORGES (1899–1986)

Labyrinths. Selected Stories and Other Writings, ed. and trans. Donald Yates, J. E. Irby, *et al.* New York: New Directions, 1962.

Historia universal de la infamia, 1935. *A Universal History of Infamy,* trans. Norman Thomas di Giovanni. New York: E. P. Dutton, 1972.

Ficciones, 1944. *Fictions,* trans. Anthony Kerrigan, Alastair Reid, *et al.* New York: Grove, 1962.

El Aleph, 1948. *The Aleph and Other Stories 1933–1969,* trans. Norman Thomas di Giovanni. New York: E. P. Dutton, 1970.

Otras inquisiciones, 1952. *Other Inquisitions,* trans. Ruth L. C. Simms. Austin: University of Texas Press, 1964.

El hacedor, 1960. *Dreamtigers,* trans. Mildred Boyer and Harold Morland. Austin: University of Texas Press, 1964.

El informe de Brodie, 1970. *Dr. Brodie's Report,* trans. Norman Thomas di Giovanni. New York: E. P. Dutton, 1972.

El libro de arena, 1975. *The Book of Sand,* trans. Norman Thomas di Giovanni. New York: E. P. Dutton, 1977.

Criticism

Aizenberg, Edna. *The Aleph Weaver. Biblical, Kabbalistic, and Judaic Elements in Borges.* Potomac, Md.: Scripta Humanistica, 1985.

——. *Borges and His Successors.* Columbia: University of Missouri Press, 1990.

Alazraki, Jaime. *Borges and the Kabbalah, and Other Essays on His Fiction and Poetry.* New York: Cambridge University Press, 1988.

——. *Critical Essays on Jorge Luis Borges.* Boston: G. K. Hall & Co., 1987.

Bloom, Harold, ed. *Jorge Luis Borges.* New York: Chelsea House, 1986.

Lindstrom, Naomi. *Jorge Luis Borges: A Study of the Short Fiction*. New York: Twayne, 1990.

Rodríguez Monegal, Emir. *Jorge Luis Borges: A Literary Biography*. New York: E. P. Dutton, 1978.

Solotorevsky, Myrna. "The Model of Midrash and Borges's Interpretative Tales and Essays," *Midrash and Literature*, Geoffrey H. Hartman and Sanford Budick, eds. New Haven and London: Yale University Press, 1986, 253–64.

Sosnowski, Saul. *Borges y la cábala*. Buenos Aires: Hispamérica, 1976.

Stavans, Ilan. "Emma Zunz: The Jewish Theodicy of Jorge Luis Borges." *Modern Fiction Studies* 32, 3 (Autumn 1986):469–75.

———. "Borges and the Jews [review of *The Aleph Weaver*]." *Prooftexts* 7, 1 (January 1987):96–105.

AÍDA BORTNIK (b. 1942)

Guiones cinematográficos. Buenos Aires: Centro Editor de América Latina, 1981.

La historia oficial (with Luis Puenzo). Buenos Aires: Ediciones de la Urraca, 1985.

ALBERTO GERCHUNOFF (1884–1950)

Los gauchos judíos, 1910. *The Jewish Gauchos of the Pampas*, trans. Prudencio de Pereda. New York: Abelard-Schuman, 1955.

Cuentos de ayer. Buenos Aires: Ediciones América, 1919.

La jofaina maravillosa: Agenda cervantina. Buenos Aires: Biblioteca Argentina de Buenas Ediciones Literarias, 1922.

La asamblea de la bohardilla. Buenos Aires: Manuel Gleizer, 1925.

Historia y proezas de amor. Buenos Aires: Manuel Gleizer, 1926.

El hombre que habló en la Sorbona. Buenos Aires: Manuel Gleizer, 1926.

Pequeñas prosas. Buenos Aires: Manuel Gleizer, 1926.

Heine, poeta de nuestra intimidad. Buenos Aires: BABEL, 1927.

Los amores de Baruj Spinoza. Buenos Aires: BABEL, 1932.

El hombre importante. Montevideo/Buenos Aires: Sociedad Amigos del Libro Rioplatense, 1934.

La clínica del Dr. Mefistófeles: Moderna milagrería en diez jornadas. Santiago de Chile: Ercilla, 1937.

Entre Ríos, mi país. Buenos Aires: Futuro, 1950.

Retorno de Don Quixote. Prologue by Jorge Luis Borges. Buenos Aires: Sudamericana, 1951.

El pino y la palmera. Buenos Aires: Sociedad Hebráica Argentina, 1952.

Argentina, país de advenimiento. Buenos Aires: Losada, 1952.

Criticism

Aizenberg, Edna. "Parricide on the Pampas: Deconstructing Gerchunoff and His Jewish Gauchos." *Folio* 17 (1987):24–39.

Borges, Jorge Luis. "Prologue" to *Retorno de Don Quixote*. Buenos Aires: Sudamericana, 1951, 7–11.

Dujovne, León. "Introduction" to *The Jewish Gauchos of the Pampas*, trans. Prudencio de Pereda. New York: Abelard-Schuman, 1955, iii–xiv.

Glickman, Nora. "Biografía como auto-reflexión." *Folio* 17 (1987):23–41.

Jaroslawsky de Lowy, Sara. *Alberto Gerchunoff: Vida y obra: Bibliografía: Antología*. New York: Columbia University/Hispanic Institute of the United States, 1957.

Liacho, Lázaro [Lázaro Liachovitsky]. *Alberto Gerchunoff.* Buenos Aires: Colombo, 1975.

Lindstrom, Naomi. "*Los gauchos judíos:* The Rhapsodic Evocation of a Jewish New World." *Romance Quarterly* 33, 2 (May 1986):231–35.

Mujica Laínez, Manuel. "Gerchunoff." *La Nación* (31 December 1983):25.

Stavans, Ilan. "Alberto Gerchunoff and the Jewish Writer in Argentina [review of *La identidad judía en la literatura argentina* and *La orilla inminente*]." *Prooftexts* 9, 2 (May 1989):184–94.

MARGO GLANTZ (b. 1930)

Onda y escritura en México. México: Siglo XXI, 1971.

Repeticiones. Ensayos sobre literatura mexicana. Xalapa: Universidad Veracruzana, 1979.

Intervención y pretexto. Mexico: UNAM, 1980.

Las genealogías. Mexico: Martín Casillas, 1981; *Genealogies,* trans. Susan Bassnett. London: Serpent's Tail, 1990.

Erosiones. Toluca: Universidad Autónoma del Estado de México, 1984.

NORA GLICKMAN (b. 1942)

Uno de sus Juanes. Buenos Aires: Ediciones de la Flor, 1983.

"Introduction" to *Regeneración* [A play in Yiddish by Leib Malach], trans. into Spanish by Rosalía Rosembuj. Buenos Aires: Pardés, 1984.

Mujeres, memorias, malogros. Buenos Aires: Milá, 1991.

ISAAC GOLDEMBERG (b. 1945)

De Chepén a La Habana (with José Kozer). New York: Editorial Bayú-Menoráh, 1973.

La vida a plazos de Don Jacobo Lerner, 1980. *The Fragmented Life of Don Jacobo Lerner,* trans. Roberto S. Picciotto. New York: Persea, 1976.

Hombre de paso/Just Passing Through, trans. David Unger and Isaac Goldemberg. Hanover, N.H.: Point of Contact/Ediciones del Norte, 1981.

Tiempo al tiempo, 1984. *Play by Play,* trans. Hardie St. Martin. Hanover, N.H.: Ediciones del Norte, 1983.

"On Being a Writer in Peru and Other Places," *Lives on the Line,* ed. and introd. Doris Meyer, trans. David Unger. Berkeley and Los Angeles: University of California Press, 1988, 300–305.

La vida al contado. Hanover, N.H.: Ediciones del Norte, 1992.

Criticism

Gazarian Gautier, Marie-Lise. "Isaac Goldemberg." *Interviews with Latin American Writers.* Lisle, Ill.: The Dalkey Archive Press, 1989.

Friedman, Edward. "Marginal Narrative: Levels of Discourse in *La vida a plazos de dos Jacobo Lerner*." *Modern Fiction Studies* 5, 4 (1984):74–81.

Morgenroth Schneider, Judith. "Cultural Meanings in Isaac Goldemberg's Fiction." *Folio* 17 (1987):128–40.

Rosser, Harry L. "Being and Time in *La vida a plazos de don Jacobo Lerner*." *Chasqui: Revista de Literatura Latinoamericana* 17, 1 (May 1988):43–49.

Stavans, Ilan. "Judaísmo y letras latinoamericanas: Una entrevista con Isaac Goldemberg." *Folio* 17 (1987):141–50.

Tittler, Jonathan. *"The Fragmented Life of Don Jacobo Lerner:* The Esthetics of Fragmentation," *Narrative Irony in the Contemporary Spanish American Novel.* Ithaca, N.Y.: Cornell University Press, 1984.

Roses, Lorraine E. "El lector como jurado: El monólogo interior en *La vida a plazos de don Jacobo Lerner." Discurso Literario* 2, 1 (1984):225–32.

GERARDO MARIO GOLOBOFF (b. 1939)

Entre la diáspora y octubre Buenos Aires: Stilcograf, 1966.

Caballos por el fondo de los ojos. Barcelona: Planeta, 1976.

Leer Borges. Buenos Aires: Huemul, 1978.

Criador de palomas. Buenos Aires: Bruguera, 1984.

La luna que cae. Barcelona: Muchnik, 1989.

Genio y figura de Roberto Arlt. Buenos Aires: Editorial Universitaria, 1989.

El soñador de Smith. Barcelona: Muchnik, 1990.

Criticism

Edna Aizenberg. "The Writing of the Disaster: Gerardo Mario Goloboff's *Criador de Palomas." Inti: Revista de Literatura Hispánica* 28 (Fall 1988):67–73.

Leonardo Senkman. "Entrevista con Gerardo Mario Goloboff." *Noah: Revista Literaria* 1, 1 (August 1987):75.

ELISA LERNER (b. 1932)

Vida con mamá. Caracas: Monteávila, 1975.

Una sonrisa detrás de la metáfora. Caracas: Monteávila, 1977.

Yo amo a Columbo. Caracas: Monteávila, 1979.

CLARICE LISPECTOR (1925–1977)

Perto do coração salvagem, 1944. *Near to the Wild Heart,* trans. Giovanni Pontiero. New York: New Directions, 1990.

Laços de família, 1960. *Family Ties,* trans. Giovanni Pontiero. Austin: University of Texas Press, 1972.

A maçã no escuro, 1961. *The Apple in the Dark,* trans. Gregory Rabassa. New York: Alfred A. Knopf, 1967.

A legião estrangeira, 1964. *The Foreign Legion,* trans. Giovanni Pontiero. New York: New Directions, 1992.

A paixão segundo G.H., 1964. *The Passion According to G.H.,* trans. Ronald W. Souza. Minneapolis: University of Minnesota Press, 1988.

Uma aprendizagem ou O Livro dos Prazeres, 1969. *An Apprenticeship, or The Book of Delights,* trans. Richard A. Mazarra and Lorri A. Parris. Austin: Texas University Press, 1986.

A hora da estrêla, 1977. *The Hour of the Star,* trans. Giovanni Pontiero. New York, New Directions, 1991.

Soulstorm, trans. Alexis Levitin. New York: New Directions, 1988.

Criticism

Earl E. Fitz. *Clarice Lispector.* New York: Twayne, 1985.

Vieira, Nelson H. "A Expressao Judaica na Obra de Clarice Lispector." *Remate de Males* 9 (1989):207–9.

Szklo, Gilda Salem. "'O Búfalo': Clarice Lispector e a herança da mistica judaica."
  Remate de Males 9 (1989):107–13.

ALCINA LUBITCH DOMECQ (b. 1953)
El espejo del espejo, o La noble sonrisa del perro. Mexico: Joaquín Mortiz, 1983.
Intoxicada. Mexico: Joaquín Mortiz, 1984.
"It Just Isn't Right [On Being a Freak]," trans. Ilan Stavans. *The Albany Review* IV
  (Summer 1990):54–61.

ANGELINA MUÑIZ-HUBERMAN (b. 1937)
La morada interior. Mexico: Joaquín Mortiz, 1972.
Tierra adentro. Mexico: Joaquín Mortiz, 1977.
La guerra del unicornio. Mexico: Artífice, 1983.
Huerto cerrado, huerto sellado, 1985. *Enclosed Garden*, trans. L. Parkinson Zamora.
  Pittsburgh: Latin American Literary Review, 1988.
De magias y prodigios. Mexico: Fondo de Cultura Económica, 1987.
De cuerpo entero [Autobiography]. Mexico: UNAM-Ediciones Corunda, 1991.
Dulcinea encantada. Mexico: Joaquín Mortiz, 1992.

Criticism
Poniatowska, Elena. "Afterword" to *Enclosed Garden*, trans. Lois Parkinson Zamora.
  Pittsburgh: Latin American Review, 1988, 97–103.

VICTOR PERERA (b. 1934)
The Conversion. New York: Little, Brown, 1970.
The Last Lords of Palenque (with Robert D. Bruce). Boston: Little, Brown, 1982.
Rites. A Guatemalan Boyhood. San Diego: Harcourt Brace Jovanovich, 1986.

SAMUEL RAWET (1929–1985)
Contos do imigrante. Rio de Janeiro: L&PM, 1956; 2d ed., 1972.
O terreno de uma polegada quadrada, 1969.
Os Sete Sonhos. Benfica, Bra.: Olivé Editor, 1967; 2d ed., 1971.
Viagens de Ahasverus. Benfica, Bra.: Olivé Editor, 1970.
Eu-tu-êle [Analise eidética]. Rio de Janeiro: José Olympio, 1972.

Criticism
Tolman, Jon M. "Brazil's New Prose." *The Literary Review* 27, 4 (Summer 1984):
  397–410.

GERMÁN ROZENMACHER (1936–1971)
Cabecita negra. Buenos Aires: José Alvarez, 1963.
Los ojos del tigre. Buenos Aires: Galerna, 1967.
Cuentos completos. Buenos Aires: Centro Editor de América Latina, 1971.
Réquiem para un viernes a la noche. Buenos Aires: Talia, 1971.
"Testamento de Rozenmacher." *Primera Plana* 446 (17 August 1971):46.

MOACYR SCLIAR (b. 1937)
O exército de um homem só, 1973. *The One-Man Army*, trans. Eloah F. Giacomelli.
  New York: Ballantine, 1986.

O carnaval dos animais, 1976. *The Carnival of the Animals,* trans. Eloah F. Giacomelli. New York: Ballantine, 1986.

A balada do falso messias, 1976. *The Ballad of the False Messiah,* trans. Eloah F. Giacomelli. New York: Ballantine, 1987.

Os deuses de Raquel, 1978. *The Gods of Raquel,* trans. Eloah F. Giacomelli. New York: Ballantine, 1986.

Os voluntários, 1980. *The Volunteers,* trans. Eloah F. Giacomelli. New York: Ballantine, 1988.

O centauro no jardim, 1980. *The Centaur in the Garden,* trans. Margaret A. Neves. New York: Ballantine, 1985.

A guerra no Bom Fim. Porto Alegre: L&PM, 1981.

Max e os felinos, 1982. *Max and the Cats,* trans. Eloah F. Giacomelli. New York: Ballantine, 1989.

A estranha nação de Rafael Mendes, 1983. *The Strange Nation of Rafael Mendes,* trans. Eloah F. Giacomelli. New York: Harmony Books, 1987.

Os melhores contos de Moacyr Scliar. Sel. Regina Zilberman. São Paulo: Global, 1984.

A condição judaica: das Tábuas da Lei à mesa da cozinha. Porto Alegre: L&PM, 1985.

O olho enigmatico, 1986. *The Enigmatic Eye,* trans. Eloah F. Giacomelli. New York: Ballantine, 1989.

Criticism

Brunn, Alberto von. *Die seltsame Nation des Moacyr Scliar. Jüdisches Epos in Brasilien.* Frankfurt-am-Main: Lusorama, 1992.

Glickman, Nora. "*Os Voluntarios:* A Jewish-Brazilian Pilgrimage." *Yiddish* 4, 4 (Winter 1982):58–64.

Igel, Regina. "Jewish Components in Brazilian Literature: An Interview with Moacyr Scliar." *Folio* 17 (1987):111–18.

Lindstrom, Naomi. "Oracular Jewish Tradition in Two Works by Moacyr Scliar." *Luso-Brazilian Review* 21, 2 (Winter 1984):23–33.

Silverman, Malcolm. "A ironia na obra de Moacyr Scliar." *Moderna Ficção Brasileira.* Rio de Janeiro: Civilição Brasileira, 1982, 170–89.

Szalo, Gilda Salem. *O bom fim do shtetl: Moacyr Scliar.* São Paulo: Editora Perspectiva, 1990.

Stavans, Ilan. "Mixed Traditions: An Interview with Moacyr Scliar." *The Albany Review* 111, 3 (1989):16, 37.

ESTHER SELIGSON (b. 1941)

Tras la ventana, el árbol. Mexico: Editorial Bogavante, 1969.

Otros son los sueños. Mexico: Editorial Novaro, 1973.

Tránsito del cuerpo. Mexico: La máquina de escribir, 1977 (expanded in *Diálogos con el cuerpo,* Artífice, 1981).

Lus de dos. Mexico: Joaquín Mortiz, 1978.

De sueños, presagios y otras voces. Mexico: UAM, 1978.

La morada en el tiempo. Mexico: Artífice, 1981.

Sed de mar. Mexico: Artífice, 1987.

La fugacidad como método de escritura. Mexico: Plaza y Valdés, 1988.

Indicios y quimeras. Mexico: UAM, 1988.

Teatro, festín efímero. Mexico: UAM, 1989.
Isomorfismos. Mexico: UNAM, 1991.

Criticism

Duncan, J. Ann. "Esther Seligson." *Ibero-Amerikanisches Archiv* 10 (1983):23–43.

Stavans, Ilan. "Sobre *La morada en el tiempo*." *Unomásuno* 472 (25 October 1986):6–7.

———. "¿Quién es Esther Seligson?" *El Universal* (17 to 26 January 1992):4.

ILAN STAVANS (b. 1961)

Manual del (im)perfecto reseñista. Mexico: UAM, 1989.

Talia y el cielo, o el libro de los ensueños (with Zuri Balkoff). Mexico: Plaza y Valdés, 1989.

"In the Margins of Time," *Present Tense* 15, 2 (1988):24–30.

"Letter to a German Friend," *Midstream* XXXVI, 3 (April 1990):30–32.

Prontuario. Mexico: Joaquín Mortiz, 1992.

La pianista manca. Caracas: Alfadil, 1992.

Imagining Columbus: The Literary Voyage. New York: Twayne-Macmillan, 1993.

La pluma y la máscara. Mexico: Fondo de Cultura Económica, 1993.

Growing Up Latino: Memoirs and Stories (coedited with Harold Augenbraum). Boston: Houghton Mifflin, 1993.

Criticism

Varderi, Alejandro. "Conversación con Ilan Stavans." *Brújula/Compass* (November-December 1991):17–18.

Guzmán, Patricia. "Escribir por culpa de Dios." *Imagen* (Venezuela) 100–89 (May 1992):4–6.

Gazarian Gautier, Marie-Lise. "Ilan Stavans: A Character among His Characters." *Brújula/Compass* 14 (July 1992):7.

Pakravan, Saïdeh. "The Writer in Exile: An Interview with Ilan Stavans." *Chanteh* (Winter 1993):29–34.

ALICIA STEIMBERG (b. 1933)

De músicos y relojeros. Buenos Aires: Centro Editor de América Latina, 1971.

La loca 101. Buenos Aires: Ediciones de la Flor, 1973.

El espíritu inocente. Buenos Aires: Pomaire, 1981.

El árbol del placer. Buenos Aires: Emecé, 1986.

Criticism

Flori, Mónica. "Alicia Steimberg y Cecilia Absatz: Dos narradoras argentinas." *Chasqui* 17,2 (November 1988):83–92.

MARIO SZICHMAN (b. 1945)

Los judíos del Mar Dulce. Buenos Aires and Caracas: Galerna/Síntesis 2000, 1971.

La verdadera Crónica Falsa. Buenos Aires: Centro Editor de América Latina, 1972.

Manuel Otero Silva. Mitología de una generación frustrada. Caracas: Universidad Central de Venezuela, 1975.

Uslar: Cultura y dependencia. Caracas: Vadell Hermanos, 1975.

A las 20:25 la señora entró en la inmortalidad, 1981. *At 8:25 Evita Became Immortal*, trans. Roberto S. Picciotto. Hanover, N.H.: Ediciones del Norte, 1983.

Criticism

Borinsky, Alicia. "Lost Homes: Two Jews in Argentina." *Folio* 17 (1987):40–48.

Flori, Mónica. "La identidad judía argentina en la ficción de Mario Szichman." *Selecta: Journal of the Pacific Northwest Council on Foreign Languages* 6 (1985):111–15.

Morello-Frosch, Marta. "Las caretas de la historia en Mario Szichman." *Folio* 17 (1987):49–56.

DAVID UNGER (b. 1950)

Neither Caterpillar nor Butterfly. New York: Es Que Somos Muy Pobres Press, 1986.

3

Absatz, Cecilia. *Los años pares.* Buenos Aires: Legasa, 1985.

———. *Té con canela.* Buenos Aires: Sudamericana, 1982.

Aguinis, Marcos. *Refugiados. Crónica de un palestino.* Buenos Aires: Planeta, 1976.

———. *La conspiración de los idiotas.* Buenos Aires: Emecé, 1980.

———. *Carta esperanzada a un general: Puente sobre el abismo.* Buenos Aires: Sudamericana/Planeta, 1983.

Aridjis, Homero. *1492. Vida y tiempos de Juan Cabezón de Castilla*, 1985. *1492. The Life and Times of Juan Cabezón of Castile*, trans. Betty Ferber. New York: Summit Books, 1991.

Barnatán, Marcos Ricardo. *Gor.* Barcelona: Barral, 1973.

———. *El laberinto de Sión.* Barcelona: Barral Hispanova, 1971.

———. *Los pasos perdidos.* Madrid: Rialp, 1968.

Calny, Eugenia. *Clara al amanecer.* Buenos Aires: Crisol, 1972.

Cony, Carlos Heitor. *Pessach: a travessia*, 1967. *Passover, the Crossing*, trans. Nelson H. Vieira, *Jewish Spectator* (Winter 1984):30–32.

Costantini, Humberto. *De dioses, hombrecitos y policías*, 1977. *The Gods, the Little Guys, and the Police*, trans. Toby Talbot. New York: Harper & Row, 1983.

Cozarinsky, Edgardo. *Vudú urbano.* Barcelona: Anagrama, 1985.

Darío, Rubén.*Canto a la Argentina.* Buenos Aires: Libro Amigo, 1935.

Dorfman, Ariel. *Viudas*, 1981. *Widows*, trans. Stephen Kessler. New York: Random House, 1983.

———. *La última canción de Manuel Sendero*, 1982. *The Last Song of Manuel Sendero*, trans. George R. Shrivers. New York: Viking, 1987.

Eichelbaum, Samuel. *El viajero inmóvil y otros relatos.* Buenos Aires: Paidós, 1969.

Feierstein, Ricardo. *Cuentos para hombres solos.* Buenos Aires: Instituto Amigos del Libro Argentino, 1957.

———. *El caramelo descompuesto.* Buenos Aires: Editorial Nueva Presencia, 1979.

———. *Cuentos de rabia y oficina.* Buenos Aires: Stilcograf, 1965.

Fihman, Ben Ami. *Mi nombre Rufo Galo.* Caracas: Monteávila, 1973.

———. *Los recursos del limbo.* Caracas: Monteávila, 1981.

Freilich, Alicia. *Cláper.* Caracas: Planeta, 1987.

Fuentes, Carlos. *Cambio de piel*, 1967. *A Change of Skin*, trans. Sam Hileman. New York: Farrar, Straus & Giroux, 1968.

———. *Terra Nostra,* 1975; trans. by Margaret Sayers Peden. New York: Farrar, Straus & Giroux, 1976.

———. *La cabeza de la hidra,* 1978. *The Hydra Head,* trans. Margaret Sayers Peden. New York: Farrar, Straus & Giroux, 1978.

Levinson, Luisa Mercedes. "El abra," 1967. "The Cove," trans. Sylvia Lipp, *Short Stories by Latin American Women: The Magic and the Real,* ed. Celia Correas de Zapata. Houston, Tex.: Arte Público Press, 1990.

Muchnik, Mario. *Mundo judío: Crónica personal.* Barcelona: Lumen, 1984.

Orgambide, Pedro. *Aventuras de Edmundo Ziller en tierras del Nuevo Mundo,* 1977. Mexico: Nueva Imagen, 1984.

Pacheco, José Emilio. *Morirás lejos,* 1967. *A Distant Death,* trans. Linda Sheer, introd. Ilan Stavans. Los Angeles: Sun & Moon, 1994.

———. *Las batallas en el desierto,* 1981. *Battles in the Desert and Other Stories,* trans. Katherine Silver. New York: New Directions, 1987.

Portnoy, Alicia. *La escuelita,* 1981. *The Little School,* trans. by the author. London: Virago, 1988.

Rozitchner, León. *Ser judío.* Buenos Aires: Ediciones de la Flor, 1967.

Satz, Mario. *Sol,* 1975. *Sol,* trans. Helen Lane. Garden City, N.Y.: Doubleday, 1979.

———. *Luna.* Barcelona: Noguer, 1976.

———. *Tierra.* Barcelona: Noguer, 1978.

———. *Marte.* Barcelona: Barral, 1980.

Timerman, Jacobo. *Preso sin nombre, celda sin número,* 1981. *Prisoner Without a Name, Cell Without a Number,* trans. Toby Talbot. New York: Alfred A. Knopf. 1981.

Tiempo, César [Israel Zeitlin]. *El becerro de oro.* Buenos Aires: Paidós, 1973.

———. *El último romance de Gardel.* Buenos Aires: Quetzal, 1975.

———. *Mi tío Sholem Aleijem y otros relatos.* Buenos Aires: Corregidor, 1978.

———. *Manos de obra.* Buenos Aires: Corregidor, 1980.

Vargas Llosa, Mario. *El hablador,* 1988. *The Storyteller,* trans. Helen R. Lane. New York: Farrar, Straus & Giroux, 1989.

Verbitsky, Bernardo. *Café de los angelitos.* Buenos Aires: Siglo XX, 1950.

———. *Una pequeña familia.* Buenos Aires: Losada, 1951.

———. *Villa miseria también es América.* Buenos Aires: Kraft, 1957.

———. *Un hombre de papel.* Buenos Aires: Jorge Alvarez, 1966.

———. *Etiquetas a los hombres.* Barcelona: Planeta, 1972.

Viñas, David. *Los dueños de la tierra.* Buenos Aires: Losada, 1958.

———. *Dar la cara,* 1962. Buenos Aires: Centro Editor de América Latina, 1967.

———. *En la Semana Trágica.* Buenos Aires: Jorge Alvarez, 1966.

———. *Jauría.* Mexico: Siglo XXI, 1979.

THE AUTHORS

Isidoro Blaisten, an Argentine born in 1933, is the author of *South of Dublin.*

Jorge Luis Borges, the celebrated creator of stories such as "Pierre Menard, Author of the Quixote" and "The Garden of Forking Paths," was born in 1899 and died in 1986. He is the author of the collections *Labyrinths, Selected Stories & Other Writings,* and *Other Inquisitions.*

Aída Bortnik, an Argentine, wrote the screenplay, together with Luis Puenzo, of *The Official Story,* which won the Oscar for Best Foreign Film in 1987.

Alberto Gerchunoff, the author of *The Jewish Gauchos of the Pampas,* who died in 1950, is the renowned Argentine man of letters who helped shape the tradition of Jewish-Latin American literature. He wrote some twenty books and regularly contributed to national newspapers.

Margo Glantz, a Mexican writer and critic, teaches at the Universidad Nacional Autónoma de México. She is the author of numerous books of criticism.

Nora Glickman, an Argentine, teaches at Queens College. She is the author of a scholarly study on the Yiddish playwright Leib Malach.

Isaac Goldemberg, a Peruvian born in 1945 and living in Manhattan, is the author of *The Fragmented Life of Don Jacobo Lerner* and *Play by Play.*

Gerardo Mario Goloboff, a lawyer by profession, is the Argentine essayist and short-story writer who wrote the trilogy *Pigeon Keeper, Moon Descending,* and *The Dreamer of Smith.* He lives in Luxemburg and France, where he teaches at the Université de Paris-Nanterre.

Elisa Lerner is a Venezuelan writer and diplomat.

Clarice Lispector, a Ukrainian-born Brazilian writer, is the author of *Family Ties, The Passion According to G.H.,* and *The Hour of the Star.* She died in 1977 at the age of 55.

Alcina Lubitch Domecq, born in Guatemala in 1953, is the author of *The Mirror's Mirror: or, The Noble Smile of the Dog.* The majority of her thirty or more stories were collected in 1988 in *Intoxicated.*

Angelina Muñiz-Huberman, a Mexican editor, poet, and novelist, was born in 1936 to Spanish parents in France. The author of *Enclosed Garden,* she teaches Comparative Literature at Universidad Nacional Autónoma de México.

Victor Perera, a Guatemala-born essayist who lives in the United States, is the author of *Rites: A Guatemalan Boyhood* and *The Last Lords of Palenque* (with Robert D. Bruce). A former editor of *The New Yorker,* he teaches at the University of California, Berkeley.

Samuel Rawet, a Polish-born Brazilian engineer and short-story writer, died in 1985 at the age of 56. He is the author of *Immigrant Stories* and *The Seven Dreams.*

Germán Rozenmacher was an Argentine playwright and short-story writer who died in 1971 at the age of 35. He is the author of *Saturday Night Requiem.*

Moacyr Scliar, a Brazilian fabulist, has been widely translated into English. He is best known as the author of *The Centaur in the Garden* and *The Strange Nation of Rafael Mendes.*

Esther Seligson, a Mexican born in 1941, writes on Kabbalah and Jewish mysticism. Her books include *Other Dreams.*

Ilan Stavans, a Mexican novelist and critic born in 1961, is associate professor of Latin American Literature at Amherst College. His books in Spanish include *Talia y el cielo,* written in collaboration with Zuri Balkoff, which won the 1992 Latino Literature Prize; *Prontuario* and *La pluma y la máscara,* two collections of essays; and *La pianista manca,* a volume of stories awarded the Gramma Literature Prize in Spain. In English, he has written *Imagining Columbus: The Literary Voyage,* and forthcoming, *The Hispanic Condition: Reflections on Culture and Identity in the Americas.* He has translated Felipe Alfau into English in a bilingual edition of *La poesia cursi/Sentimental Songs* and is coeditor, with Harold Augenbraum, of the anthology *Growing Up Latino: Memoirs and Stories.*

Alicia Steimberg, an Argentine, is the author of four novels and a collection of short stories.

Mario Szichman, an Argentine born in 1945, is a journalist and novelist living in New York. He is the author of *At 8:25 Evita Became Immortal.*

David Unger is a Guatemalan writer and translator living in New York City.

P E R M I S S I O N S